Asian Americans and the Media

Asian Americans and the Media

Kent A. Ono and Vincent N. Pham

polity

First published in 2009 by Polity Press
Reprinted 2010 (three times), 2011, 2012, 2013 (twice), 2014, 2015

Polity Press
65 Bridge Street
Cambridge CB2 1UR, UK

Polity Press
350 Main Street
Malden, MA 02148, USA

ISBN-13: 978-0-7456-4273-4
ISBN-13: 978-0-7456-4274-1(pb)

A catalogue record for this book is available from the British Library.

Typeset in 10.5 on 13 pt Swift
by Servis Filmsetting Ltd, Stockport, Cheshire
Printed and bound in the USA by Courier Digital Solutions

For further information on Polity, visit our website: www.polity.co.uk

Contents

Acknowledgements

We would thank the kind and talented staff at Polity Press, especially Andrea Drugan, who brought the idea of this book to us, who consulted closely with us all along the way, and who provided just the right mix of encouragement, flexibility, and sage advice. Neil de Cort, the production manager, brought the manuscript into production skillfully. Caroline Richmond, our copyeditor, was amazingly helpful and patient with us. We appreciate Polity's marketing team's work to promote our book.

The comments of the original anonymous reviewers of the book prospectus as well as the comments of the anonymous reviewers of the completed manuscript were very helpful; we attempted to address their many suggestions and think the book is stronger as a result. We greatly appreciate Quentin Lee taking the time to provide us with possible images for the cover, and Peter Feng, Kendall Phillips, and Lisa Nakamura helped us puzzle through which image was best for the book. We appreciate the hard work of Jon Stone, who put together our index and did fact checking throughout. Two research assistants, Michelle Bernardi and Paul Hartley, helped out at different stages. Also, thanks to the students of the Asian American Popular Culture course at UIUC (summer 2007), who previewed a lot of the ideas that made their way into print here.

We would also like to thank Sarah Projansky, who read multiple drafts of the book and gave much appreciated advice throughout the process. Thanks, too, to the shorter ones who give their big support (mostly hugs) everyday, Mina and Daniel.

Thanks go out to a number of colleagues who, without this acknowledgement, would not know that they inspired us to write this book, even though they had no direct involvement in the project: John Sloop, Bruce Gronbeck, Robert Weiss, Carole Blair, Darrell Hamamoto, Elena Tajima Creef, Peter Feng, Gina Marchetti, Tom Nakayama, Rona Halualani, Rosa Linda Fregoso, Herman Gray, Sarah Banet-Weiser, Wendy Ho, Carolyn de la Pena, Jay Mechling, Angie Chabram-Dernersesian, Keith Osajima, Elyce Helford, Karen Shimakawa, Ruth

Frankenberg, Ella Maria Ray, Judith Newton, Susan Kaiser, Christine Acham, Sergio de la Mora, Sophie Volpp, Kevin Johnson, Leah Vande Berg, Fernando Delgado, Ben Attias, Bernadette Calafell, Lisa Flores, Dreama Moon, Marouf Hasian, Derek Buescher, Nadine Naber, Laura Lindenfeld, Rachel Dubrofsky, Shoshana Magnet, Diem-My Bui, Ted Gournelos, Joann Wright, Mike Perry, and Susan George.

Finally, many thanks to the graduate students from the Asian Pacific American Graduate Student Organization at the University of Illinois at Urbana-Champaign who provided support and a needed nudge in times of stasis. Thanks also to everyone in the Asian American Artists Collective of Chicago, the Foundation of Asian American Independent Media, and the faculty and graduate students in the (Speech) Communication Department, the Institute of Communications Research, and the Asian American Studies Program at UIUC. Particular thanks go out to colleagues James Hay, John Nerone, Ivy Glennon, Angharad Valdivia, Cameron McCarthy, Norman Denzin, Cliff Christians, Sharon Lee, Martin Camargo, Sandy Camargo, Cara Finnegan, Debra Hawhee, Ned O'Gormann, Lisa Nakamura, Christian Sandvig, Leslie Reagan, Daniel Schneider, Julia Johnson, Viveka Kudilagama, Pia Sengsavanh, Mary Ellerbe, and Bill Berry.

Introduction

During the week of January 17, 2005, the *Miss Jones in the Morning Show* (New York City, WQHT, 97.1, "Hot 97") played a song for four days straight called "USA for Indonesia" (later simply known as "The Tsunami Song"). The song used humor to comment on the devastating December 2004 tsunami that ravaged Asia, killing hundreds of thousands. In the form of parody, and against the backdrop of "We are the World,"[1] the song referred to people who died in the tsunami as "chinks," made light of children rendered parentless by the disaster, and referenced Michael Jackson as a possible molester of children orphaned as a result of the tsunami. One segment of the song described what it might have been like to witness the tsunami: "And all at once you could hear the screaming chinks and no one was safe from the wave. There were Africans drowning, little Chinamen swept away. You could hear God laughing, 'Swim you bitches swim.'" The following segment is the song's chorus and comments on what the fate of those affected by the tsunami might be: "So now you're screwed. It's the tsunami. You better run or kiss your ass away. Go find your mommy. I just saw her float by, a tree went through her head, and now your children will be sold in child slavery."

On January 28, a multiracial coalition of activists, including politicians, assembled outside of the Hot 97 studio to protest the station's airing of the song. Later, figures such as iconic hip-hop artist Afrika Bambaataa participated in another rally challenging the station's misuse of hip-hop. As a result of the protests, Hot 97 apologized, and several employees lost their salaries; Emmis Communications, the parent organization for the station, gave $1 million for tsunami relief; and radio personality Miss Jones provided an on-air apology. The rest of the workers on the show, including Miss Jones, were suspended for two weeks. Additionally, one of the morning show hosts, Todd Lynn, and the producer of the show, Rick Delgado, were fired.

This example invites us to ask some serious questions about Asians and Asian Americans and the media, such as: If we are indeed in a "post-racist" society, how does one explain the presence of this kind of offensive communication targeting Asians and Asian Americans on the airwaves? If Asian Americans had more political power and presence in the media industry, would songs like this be made and aired? Is there something students and professors in universities and the broader public can do to change society so that these kinds of songs are unthinkable, and so that ones that portray Asians and Asian Americans in more respectful ways find their way on air?

Asian Americans and the Media seeks to provide a critical way to approach contemporary media, in part to help us answer such questions about Asian and Asian American representation and presence in the media. Part textbook and part monograph, it surveys work in Asian American studies, communication arts and sciences, and media and film studies, and it provides an overview of representations of Asians and Asian Americans in the media in order to find the various ways in which they are constrained by historical and contemporary dominant representations and also how they challenge the dominant media through protest, the production of creative, independent media, and the creation of independent Asian American organizations. The book surveys the broad media; thus, it examines film, TV, radio, music, the Internet, and the like in an attempt to draw attention to the collective effects of media on Asian Americans. By looking across media contexts, at what Douglas Kellner (1995) calls "media culture," we argue that a critical intervention into media is possible. The book addresses examples such as "The Tsunami Song," but does not devote entire chapters to individual case studies. Instead, by addressing multiple smaller examples in each chapter, it demonstrates that theoretical and critical tools can be used to analyze media and simultaneously to make evident the broad historical and contemporary field of representations in which Asian Americans find themselves.

We argue that historical representations of Asians and Asian Americans have residual effects that continue to this day. While the field of representation has changed, especially after the protest movements of the 1960s and 1970s, historical representations of Asians and Asian Americans have set the parameters. Until major shifts in the structure of production occur, the residual effects of these historical strategies will continue to shape and structure the representation of Asians and Asian Americans into the future. We also argue that, in order to understand Asian Americans and the media, and in order to understand how changes in the larger representational field occur now and may continue in the future, an examination of independent Asian American media is needed. A wide array of complex anti-racist Asian American media works already exist for analysis. But we also suggest that, in looking at such independent work, a critical perspective is needed.

This introduction does six things to help readers understand the topics of media and Asian Americans we study in the book: (1) introduce prefatory theoretical assumptions; (2) define terms; (3) state our intellectual and disciplinary perspective; (4) lay out the scope of the book; (5) review relevant literature; and (6) provide a synopsis of the chapters in the book.

Theoretical Assumptions

We make several assumptions right from the start that function to support the way we study Asian Americans and the media throughout the book.

It makes sense to begin by stating that significant transformations in media technology, in global economic conditions and forces, and in modern and neoliberal environments render it necessary to study media carefully. A fresh examination of media such as we provide in this book is needed, in part because the world has changed. Communication technologies have changed. And these changes may significantly affect the way members of communities interrelate with one another. We now live in a *hyper-information society*. Media play an increasingly significant educational and social networking role and are noteworthy because they help people make sense of themselves and their relationships with others.

Marshall McLuhan imagined media (radio and television for him) would bring us closer and closer together across geographical boundaries to create one, big "global village" (McLuhan and Fiore, 1967, 63). But, as Benedict Anderson (1983) has suggested, media create the *illusion* of proximity, the illusion of being one large "imagined community." Because we can send an e-mail message to someone in another country, and that person's response can be received as if it had just been sent, this gives us the sense that the world is not so big after all, that we are all close together.

While we might imagine we have become closer together because of our increasing ability to communicate quickly and across vast distances worldwide, when our differences in, among other things, belief, religion, and experience emerge, we may suddenly seem further apart rather than closer together. *The illusion of close proximity may mask our actual lack of contextual knowledge and understanding of our material relationships with others.* Communication can, in these cases, hyper-accentuate our differences rather than draw attention to our commonalities. After all, even as we may be able to communicate quickly in a way that may simulate face-to-face dialogue, we know that even access to "instant messaging" does not replace face-to-face bodily interaction, where we can see, touch, hear, feel, and even smell humans in our presence. Indeed, transnational films, global television, multilingual websites, and cross-cultural exchanges of information via e-mail have the potential to "exoticize" those outside the mainstream United States media, make them appear intriguing, but also curious, strange, and alien to us, and, thus, underscore differences *not* similarities.

Because media provide so much information, and do so quickly – perhaps creating the illusion that we have access to all of the information we could ever possibly want – we may be lured into believing we *know* other people, know what they feel, understand what matters to them, and therefore can imagine how they live. Additionally, because what we see is what we remember, *what we do not see*, the part that is edited out or simply not captured in media, does not become part of our memory. What does not appear on television or on the Internet is equally, if not more important than, what is seen/heard/read. That quirky movement, that unique facial expression, that perfectly phrased comment, that moment of care that is not represented, especially an accumulation of such moments, may make all of the difference in the world; it may be that one image or expression of humanity that would completely alter our evaluation and assessment of a person that is missing. What is made available to us in media may be either a distortion or a highly subjective snapshot of a broader life or experience. In this context, a book like this is needed, in part, to dispel the misconception that media represent Asian Americans accurately, to cut through the misinformation presented daily in mainstream media, and to gesture toward that part of Asian American lives, identities, and experiences that are not available, at least in mainstream media. This book does this by offering complex ways to view Asian and Asian American images, as well as by countering misinformation, and by drawing attention to independent media produced by Asian Americans.

Because media create the illusion of closeness, and because we know that media representations provide us with only a limited snapshot of people, and a subjective one at that, it is important to understand a significant context that influences the way in which media represent people of color. Many societies have experienced colonialism, and, while it is not as often overtly practiced today, institutional structures and remnants of colonial societies (and, as we suggest in this book, the way in which colonial relations continue to be taught regularly in media) as well as belittling media representations, continue to help to justify oppression – oppression that first materialized as a result of colonialism and colonial expansion. For instance, media representations of the colonizer and the colonized continue to play a significant role in the continuation of colonial rule and colonial relations. Ella Shohat and Robert Stam suggest that "The dominant media constantly devalorize the lives of people of color while regarding Euro-American life as sacrosanct. . . . The same regime that devalorizes life then projects this devalorization on to those whose lives it has devalorized" (1994, 24). Thus, derogatory representations signify a continuing psychological trauma and the perpetuation of past oppressions. The specters of earlier eras of US history continue to haunt our psyche and reside importantly, if not primarily, in our mass-mediated imagery. What does one do with such disparaging images and representations of Asian Americans today as the *Milwaukee Magazine*'s reference to a Filipino child in a restaurant as a "rambunctious little monkey?"[2] Such representations consolidate desires for continued racial, sexual, and gendered power, and perhaps, relatedly, for continued racial, sexual, and gendered oppression, including even violence.

Our overall theory about how media operate with regard to Asian Americans is that, because of a lack of systemic power within mainstream media production, they typically appear in ways that comport with colonial representations and thus do not represent a true lived experience. Within the media, Asian Americans are often at the sidelines, feeling the effects of dominant media representation but hardly ever appearing in the spotlight. The subjugation, invalidation, and persecution on screen of those without power should be taken seriously. Such images (e.g., the woeful representation of Mickey Rooney's character in *Breakfast at Tiffany's* (1961), and the equally problematic representation of character Tracey Tzu in *Year of the Dragon* (1985), both of which we discuss in more detail later in the book) are not only incendiary but also have a mass psychosocial effect within US society; more importantly, these images are part of a history of image-making and story-production linked to historical and continuing systems of oppression.

Because these images are remnants of colonial times and exist as part of earlier ideologies, remaining institutions, and continuing social and cultural relations, derogatory representations of Asians and Asian Americans are pervasive and exist both historically and contemporarily. The fact that such representations occur frequently, if unpredictably, and across wide-ranging and varied media contexts, suggests that there continues to exist a lack of information, perhaps a willful ignorance, about, and a (sometimes) unspoken hostility toward, Asians and Asian Americans.

The airing of "The Tsunami Song" on a popular big city radio station, and the response by protestors, is only one example, but it suggests a pattern of disturbing discourse about Asians and Asian Americans that is expressed publicly but then is also protested by Asian Americans and allied groups and organizations. Examples such as this do not generally make the national news, and news flashes do not alert people that similar incidents are commonplace – a normative condition in media; thus, it makes sense that many might not recognize just how common they actually are. Part of the goal of this book is to show that offensive and troubling representations of Asians and Asian Americans are replete throughout media contexts and that, through careful study and theoretical analysis, we can see that these sometimes haphazard but incessant media spectacles are part of a much larger social logic, one that should lead us to speak out in protest as caring and thoughtful people. Such a social logic manifests in habitual representations of Asian Americans throughout media history and across media formats.

One reason it is important to study Asian Americans and the media is because Asian American productions of images on TV, film, and other mainstream media have historically been, and continue today to be, extremely limited. Thus, the ability of Asian Americans to create and distribute self-representations to counter those produced early in US history as part of colonial relationships is limited.[3] The majority of images in the dominant media have been produced by those with little first-hand knowledge of the Asian American experience. And these images and representations can have a long-term psychosocial impact on both Asians and Asian Americans and non-Asians and non-Asian Americans. It is therefore important to analyze the images about Asian Americans created and distributed by those outside of the community. Seeing media products with a veneer of underlying racial resentment toward people of Asian heritage illustrates that Asian Americans are still not in control of their own image and therefore requires a scholarly approach (such as the one we provide here) to the study of Asian Americans and the media. In part, we need such a book to note recurring patterns in media representation as well as changes that have occurred. The fact that there is an archive of media projections of Asians and Asian Americans allows for sustained analysis and critique, moving us beyond simple critiques of "bad/good" and "racist/not racist" representations and into a broader understanding of the logics behind them and their rhetorical salience.

Representations of Asian Americans in the media also affect non-Asians and non-Asian Americans, as they sometimes play a pedagogical role in (mis)educating people about Asians and Asian Americans. For instance, it is possible to imagine that problematic media representations helped play a part in one legislator's use of a loaded racist term during his 2000 presidential bid. During that campaign season, Senator John McCain said, "I hated the gooks. I will hate them as long as I live"

– seemingly unaware that "gook" is a racist term often used indiscriminately to malign Asians and Asian Americans from all backgrounds. Despite McCain's caveat that he used the term to refer specifically only to his captors, who tortured him when he was a prisoner of war during the US war against Vietnam, the fact that he professed to be unaware that it is commonly used to refer to Asians and Asian Americans as a racial group suggests an ignorance of particularity. This insensitivity toward the differences among Asian American groups and lack of awareness of particularities is commonplace in dominant mainstream media. Thus, it is crucial to understand the larger racial structure, the logics of race, racism, and racial representation, and the media's relationship to the production and reproduction of race, racism, and racial discourses. As a result, one question we seek to answer, a question that structures the approach we take to the study of Asian Americans and the media in this book, is: Do TV, film, and other media systems play an important role in maintaining a racialized social order and, if so, how do we explain the particular role that media culture plays in the case of Asian Americans?

As one example of this racial social ordering, we briefly mention here our argument that the image of Asian Americans as model minorities (discussed in detail in chapter 5) is key to that ordering. Media representations of Asian Americans as model minorities function to draw distinctions between Asian Americans and other racialized communities. Such representations figure them as a "minority" (hence not on the same level as dominant white Americans) that is contrasted to, pitted against, or put in competition with, African Americans, Latinas/os, and Native Americans. This is not a contrast, a contest, or a competition that Asian Americans create, control, or seek themselves but rather one that is created, produced, and often amplified by the dominant media. Hence, with this example we can see that media play a significant role in establishing a racial order within a social hierarchy of power.

Definition of Terms

Having laid out several theoretical assumptions, we provide definitions of four key terms used throughout the book – representations, media constructions, Asian Americans, and media racial hegemony. Additional definitions of important terms we use appear in the glossary near the end of the book. We define these four concepts here in order to render unfamiliar terms more familiar from the outset but also in order to continue to frame the way we view the subject of this book.

When we say *representations* of Asians and Asian Americans, we mean the complex range of strategies used by the media, sometimes arbitrarily, to characterize Asians and Asian Americans. These representations have effects, both immediate and deferred. While they register on the senses and in the mind, the collective and often repeated images, narratives, and narrative structures become part of memory, both individual and social. We also mean to suggest that early representations of Asians and Asian Americans, through their repetition and power to educate audiences, may be reproduced across time unwittingly, since new templates may not be available.

For example, actors may be typecast in particular kinds of roles, such as the medical professional – for example, Sendhil Ramamurthy as Dr Mohinder Suresh on NBC's television show *Heroes*. Or, despite speaking English flawlessly, actors such as Daniel Dae Kim on *Lost* may be asked to play characters who do not speak English. Additionally, Japanese American actors Masi Oka and George Takei play Japanese characters on the contemporary television show *Heroes*. In their case, the characters speak Japanese, but we hear their Japanese in English, and sometimes they learn enough English to speak it to other characters. Thus, those who produce the media make particular kinds of choices about whom to hire as actors, what narratives it makes sense for those characters to appear in, how characters represent race and ethnicity, how audiences are invited to respond to characters, which audiences might watch their productions, and what particular meanings might be created through all these choices.

It is important to suggest that media representations are in fact *media constructions*, a concept which emphasizes that they are created, produced, and manufactured and hence are not forever set in stone. They are not there for all times and hence are changeable. The concept helps us understand that film, television, radio, music, the Internet, newspapers, magazines, and advertising representations are the effects of production choices, whose meanings, importance, and effects can, once recognized as constructions, be discussed, debated, and challenged. Specifically, as we discuss stereotypes and media activism, we align ourselves with Stuart Hall's[4] theoretical stance that representation cannot be simplistically "positive" or "negative," because there is always a cultural context in which representations are produced and audience evaluations and assessments are given. Just because they have no innate positivity or negativity, however, does not mean those images do not have powerful and/or problematic effects. Thus, in this book, we address both stereotypical and more complex representations of Asian Americans, fully aware that individual representations may be interpreted and acted upon quite differently and that audiences may in fact do something quite unexpected with them. It is important to say that, despite the potential and actual alternative readings and interpretations of media, there often exist dominant readings and interpretations that may have widespread effects. Thus, while stereotypes and dominant interpretations of representations are not determinative, they may still have a controlling social power.

By *Asian Americans*, we mean the loose concatenation of people who claim this moniker to represent themselves. "Asian American" signifies both the history and the present of Asians and Asian Americans in the Americas, their struggle against oppression, and the collective and collaborative organizing efforts to fight such oppression by people across racial, ethnic, gender, and sexual identities, and across other collectivities. Asian American studies, the field out of which research, teaching, and community service relating to Asian Americans emerges, is said to be by, for, and about Asian Americans.

Asian American is a term first said to have been coined by Yuji Ichioka at the San Francisco State University Third World Strike in 1968 (R. Kim, 2002). It is and continues to be a political term of identification that people choose as a self-descriptor – not a racial or biological term of identification, but rather a term descriptive of a particular epistemology that challenges racism and seeks empowerment and democratic power relations. Ichioka used the term to articulate the kinds of concerns Asian American students had about the political position of people of Asian heritage living in the United States. Out of this history, the term has become one of political and panethnic identification,[5] but it also connotes a desire for a different and better world where Asian American contributions are recognized; where solidarity among people across racialized communities is realized; and where racial, gender, class, and sexual oppression, among other forms of oppression such as language discrimination and discrimination against both documented and undocumented immigrants, is not tolerated and is actively discouraged, challenged, and resisted.

The book takes Asian Americans, including broader categories such as South Asian Americans, Filipino Americans, Southeast Asian Americans, Chinese Americans, Korean Americans, and Japanese Americans, seriously in terms of the way media represent them. While the book focuses on one racial group, diversity within that group is of fundamental importance. Within these broader categories are a tremendous diversity of smaller ethnic groups, such as Thai Americans, Hmong Americans, Mien Americans, Indonesian Americans, Sri Lankan Americans, Pakistani Americans, Okinawan Americans, Indonesian Americans, Malaysian Americans, Vietnamese Americans, and many, many, many other groups. Because of the sheer number that may identify themselves or be identified by others as Asian Americans, this book does not aim to represent all groups equally. What we do is highlight the diversity within the community and provide examples that cross a number of groups so as to suggest the larger ambit of Asian America.

We define *media racial hegemony* for the purposes of this study as the media's role in both continuing and contesting racial and colonial power relations. Media racial hegemony helps us demonstrate how the ways people think about race, the things people do that are racialized, and people's racial identities are represented through media and that media representations help guide and regulate beliefs and actions of those within society, primarily in unforeseen ways. It is not surprising that such images are highly intimate with regard to viewers' own sense of self. How is it that someone comes to identify with images of violence against people of color, women of color, and queers of color? Do we close our eyes, turn a cheek, overcome our fear of seeing, feel disgust, let our stomachs churn, fight back, feel resecured in who we are, feel a sense of excitement or exhilaration, or do emotions of violence surge within us? By studying the representations, it becomes clear that there is in existence a kind of racial hegemony – that is the existing power dynamic and forces that, through negotiation, regulate it – and that such a hegemony is communicated to us through media.

Intellectual and Disciplinary Perspective

Our goal in writing this book is to theorize, study, and, by doing so, center the Asian American media experience, as well as to understand what media do with and to Asian Americans. Our aim is to construct theoretical observations directly relevant to Asian Americans, which at times may be informed by and correspondingly may inform studies of media and African Americans, Latinas/os, Native Americans, Arab Americans, and whites. In addition to analyzing dominant representations, we also look at how Asian American activists, media makers, and artists, themselves, have addressed stereotypes, images, and representations. Alternative media frameworks such as independent media formats and new media offer spaces for the creative construction and active production of representations more in concert with Asian American experiences and concerns, even as they may sometimes borrow from and even replicate dominant representational patterns.

To address the Asian American experience in relation to media adequately requires a positioning of our work within the field of Asian American studies. We center Asian American experiences through our analysis and theorization; thus, our approach requires an understanding of Asian American studies, including an understanding of media representations within a system and history of Asian American media representation, theoretical context, and finally social, historical, economic, and political contextualization. Specifically, this book aims to construct a theoretical platform that addresses Asian American representation and media presence from several different angles. We do this by setting up a dialogue between scholarship produced about media and Asian American representation and scholarship in communication studies and cultural studies. While social scientific scholarship informs our analyses, this book takes primarily a critical and cultural studies approach to the study of Asian Americans and the media and thus centers Asian Americans within the analyses.[6] The critical framework, theory, and base assumptions regarding representation employed here have not, as yet, been fully developed when applied to Asian Americans. Our approach requires analysis of what representations of Asians and Asian Americans exist, who created them, for whom they were created, and their ultimate impact. We take this approach in order to develop theoretical grounding for our claims and to investigate ways in which media affect and influence culture.

Central to this approach is an interdisciplinary understanding of Asian American history, sociology, communication, politics, culture, and arts. The specific contribution we make in this book, however, has not been in any of these individual fields and thus must be taken on as an interdisciplinary project, one that cuts across fields in order to address its subject fully.[7] Thus, in addition to addressing cultural studies and the humanities, our work here has the potential to inform social scientific and empirical research and may help to produce useful questions and concerns that could be taken up in scientific experiments.

We do not intend to cast our net too far, however, attempting to understand and treat each discipline equally and fairly. For instance, although the political economy of media play a role in media production and media industries, our focus is not primarily upon the media industry, and it is also not from the production side. Thus, we will not conduct an industry analysis. Part of the purpose in uniting literature in communication and Asian American studies is not to let academic boundaries prevent us from addressing the challenges of analyzing and critiquing visual culture and narratives about Asian Americans. The methodology for each media event/discourse/text studied often requires us to cut across disciplinary boundaries, and we adapt our method to each case for explanatory power. In crossing interdisciplinary boundaries, we employ methods and theories that best equip us with the abilities and faculties to explore, analyze, and understand Asian American media representations, while gleaning new ideas from thinking through various perspectives from the concepts and research of other fields.

Scope of the Book

Asian Americans and the Media examines the way media, such as film, television, radio, music, the Internet (including *YouTube* videos, web logs, and other website productions), newspapers, and magazines represent Asians and Asian Americans historically and contemporarily. In addition, it explores various ways Asian Americans have resisted, responded to, and conceptualized the terrain of challenge and resistance to those representations. The book suggests media representations are profitably understood within historical, cultural, political, economic, and social contexts. In doing so, it reads across a variety of representations: from commonly reproduced and iconic images of Asian Americans to uncommon and everyday images; from ones meant for the mainstream consumption, pleasure, and service of dominant society to ones that perpetuate structural and institutional logics that produce a racially ambivalent discourse about Asian Americans. This book argues it is necessary to critique both dominant and vernacular media as part of a socio-historical relationship of power as well as to analyze how media alter power relations. In some ways, then, the book is exemplary of the argument made by Kent Ono and John Sloop (1995) that the critique of both dominant discourses and vernacular discourses is important to critical cultural communication studies. Thus, in our conception of Asian Americans and the media, ideological content exists in stereotypes, in more complex representations, and even in self-representations, all of which must be studied. The book also seeks to provide important critical and analytical tools with which to study Asian Americans and the media.

Moreover, because audiences of mainstream cinema might lack a complex notion of the diversity of Asian American experiences, conducting audience reception studies that address Asian Americans across the multiplicities of identities would be a highly complex endeavor. Hence, because our main interest is in examining the myriad media texts that have been produced, our book does not conduct such studies, although we note reception-related research when possible and often make arguments that relate to audiences. Additionally, in resistance to the generalizing practice of seeing all Asian Americans as the same – or even at times all minorities as of the same cloth – and not recognizing and honoring ethnic differences, we aim to address differences and specificities when possible.

While the book focuses primarily on US media, examples from Canada are sometimes included, particularly the work and experiences of Asian Canadians, such as in our discussions of film and TV actor Sandra Oh. Thus it benefits from information highlighting the transnational dimension of contemporary and historical racial and ethnic groups in relation to media narratives and practices. Comparisons across national/international, racial/interracial, and racial/gendered/sexual dialectics, for instance, are also important to the framework through which we examine and understand Asian American media. While the book is about Asian Americans, it touches upon and provides theoretical grounding for understanding the inter-relationship of media representations of other racialized communities, such as African American, Latina/o, Native American, and Arab American groups.[8]

While talk of living in a post-racist, non-racist, race-neutral, multi-cultural world saturates the media cultural environment, *Asian Americans and the Media* suggests the study of media representations of Asians and Asian Americans and their responses and media self-constructions continues to be necessary. We take exception to the argument that identity politics are somehow passé or are otherwise outdated and no longer necessary. We see them as very much needed. And, while we position our book in terms of representation and dis-course, we see the need to ground ways to engage society politically as well. Whether this is to help make sense of the emergence of *American Idol* phenom William Hung, who burst on to the scene in early 2004 with his off-key audition performance of Ricky Martin's song "She Bangs," or the airing of a prank telephone call to a Chinese restaurant on the radio show *Doghouse with JV and Elvis*, in which the good-spirited nature of the persons accepting an order at a Chinese restaurant leads to repeated acts of ridicule and humiliation by the person making the order, careful and effective analysis and critique of media construc-tions of Asian Americans continue to be quite necessary in the early twenty-first century.

The racism in the controversy of "The Tsunami Song" and William Hung is not new, but is, as this book demonstrates particularly in chap-ters 2 through 5, *historically embedded*. The reason some may imagine this phenomenon of explicit racism to be new is that race is often understood to mean individual acts of racial discrimination, not to evi-dence of continuing structural and institutional practices that are embedded in a social system or to ideology that repeats historically as part of the larger racial context relating to colonialism and imperial power in the United States. Today, people sometimes think the racial landscape has shifted, even improved, but examples such as these, when read in the context of what we know about race in social, cul-tural, historical, political, and economic life, indeed suggest that repeated incidents across time and space occur because of structural and institutional constraints that lie just below the surface. Thus, it is necessary to look at media persistently, to monitor them regularly, and to be vigilant in efforts to challenge them.

The second part of the book focusing on Asian American independent productions and activism is a counterweight to the first part of the book focusing on dominant and mainstream representations; hence, the second part centers texts that mainstream media often displace. It is important to note that there are many more analyses of mainstream media representations of Asian Americans than analyses of independent media. One of the central contributions of this book to scholarship is the emphasis it places in the second part on the role of Asian American media producers and media independence. It encourages research, study, critique, activism, and engagement with continuing forms of racism through study and critique of the media. Racism continues to appear in media, which is why a critical cultural analysis continues to be necessary.

Studies of Asian Americans and the Media to Date

Before concluding with a summary of chapters, we briefly review relevant scholarship that has been produced on Asian Americans and the media. We should be clear that, to date, not that much research has been conducted on this subject. What is available, however, should be discussed. Indeed, one of our goals in this book is to foreground the work on media that has been published by Asian Americanists, while simultaneously drawing attention to scholarship in communication, media, and cultural studies germane to the study of Asian American media representation. The approaches taken include appreciative or supportive studies that aim to highlight significant work that Asian Americans have done in producing media. Perhaps most work, however, criticizes stereotypes, drawing attention to resistant approaches to the study of Asian American media, Asian American independent media production and distribution, and Asian American groups collectively organizing to protest misrepresentations.

While existing research has focused on Asian Americans and the media, early works included Asian Americans as one of five (African American, Latina/o, Asian American, Native American, white) racial groups (e.g., Wilson and Gutierrez, 1985, 1995; Wilson, Gutierrez, and Chao, 2003). Important collections in the field of communication cutting across racialized communities, including Dines and Humez ([1994] 2003),[9] Valdivia (1995), Greco Larson (2006),[10] and Gonzalez, Houston, and Chen (1994), address multiple racial groups within one collection, but often spend relatively little space on Asian Americans.[11] Books on race and media more generally do discuss and have chapters on Asian Americans.[12] What we gain with an entire book on Asian Americans and media, however, is of pivotal importance. Across the media spectrum, we build a complex analysis of Asian Americans that informs and updates the work that has already been conducted, going deeper into the subject than previous work has been able to do and providing many more examples of Asian Americans and the media, as well as more complex theoretical grounding for the study of media than is possible when Asian Americans are only one of many groups covered.

Within Asian American media studies, Darrell Hamamoto's ground-breaking work *Monitored Peril* (1994) took a Marxist, historical materialist approach to the study of Asian Americans on US television. Hamamoto found a close relationship between the historical moment when images of Asian Americans on US television were created and the US wars abroad in Asian countries. Similarly, an article by Doobo Shim (1998) takes an historical approach to the study of Asian American media and argues, as does Hamamoto, that US international relations directly correlate with popular cultural depictions of Asian Americans.[13] Elsewhere, Asian American artists, activists, and scholars collaborated to compile an anthology of critiques of Asian American images (Galang, 2003).

Most work on Asian Americans and media thus far has concentrated on film.[14] Peter Feng (2002a, 2002b) has written books and edited collections on Asian American media, focusing primarily on film.[15] Similarly, Darrell Hamamoto and Sandra Liu (2000) edited a collection of essays on Asian American film. Thomas Nakayama (1994) has written an important essay about white/Asian American male sexualities in the film *Showdown in Little Tokyo*. The work of Gina Marchetti (1993) in this area, on Hollywood films depicting romantic relationships between whites and Asians and Asian Americans, has been highly influential.

More recent works, such as *Race in Cyberspace* (Kolko, Nakamura, and Rodman, 2000) and *Cybertypes* (Nakamura, 2002b), address race and new media; we refer to these in order to understand how Asian Americans figure within these studies of race and media. Throughout the book we draw on this (and other) work to provide historical examples, to initiate our own analyses, and to emphasize the important theoretical and critical work in this area that exists – and can be built upon.

Summary of Chapters

Largely, in part because of the history of racism in the United States and the media as a broad topic, *Asian Americans and the Media* historicizes the analysis and assessment of contemporary media representation, and encourages change. The book is divided into two parts: the first elucidates the historical construction of Asians and Asian Americans, focusing primarily on dominant imagery and representations in mainstream media sources; the second examines representations Asian Americans have created themselves and steps that have been taken to remedy and transform the media environment to be more inviting, accepting, and appreciative of Asian Americans. Although the two parts can be read separately, and although many readers may want to read the book as if it were not divided, we assert that it is difficult to understand contemporary representations of Asian Americans without knowledge of the historical development and durability of such images and representations.

In addition, the book is structured around a split between historical mainstream *dominant* media and contemporary *independent* alternative media. When we say *dominant media*, we refer to media that are most often circulated to and produced for general audiences. Producers of dominant media include Hollywood studios, network television, mainstream newspapers, and major record labels.

In his book *Watching Race* (1995), which focuses specifically on African American representations in the mainstream media context of US television, Herman Gray distinguishes among three discursive practices employed on TV, what he labels "assimilationist," "pluralist," and "multiculturalist" (1995, 84). Whereas assimilationist programming draws attention to the similarities among racialized and culturally different groups, and downplays the degree to which political, cultural, and ideological differences exist and matter (ibid., 85), pluralist programming maintains existing differential relations of power, even as it allows for "separate-but-equal" contexts – for example, all African American casts in traditional white Anglo-American situation comedy formats (ibid., 87). Multicultural programming represents classed and cultural complexity within African American communities and emphasizes the multiplicity of African American subject positions. Still, even multicultural programming on TV is not necessarily politically or culturally progressive, and the degree of resistance possible within the format of TV is limited (ibid., 91). Thus, the nature of the dominant media is to resist progressive and revolutionary change and to stay within the discursive practices categorized by Gray. That is why, in this book, we do not emphasize progressive changes in mainstream, dominant media; rather, we focus our attention on independent and activist media contexts, where the economic, political, and cultural strictures endemic in dominant and mainstream media contexts are less directly constraining on Asian American creative, artistic, and performative work.

When we refer to *independent media*, we refer to media that are not circulated in dominant, mainstream venues but most often appear in alternative or underground venues. Thus, the audience and producers of a general independent media often have different preferences for media products, and means of production are set apart and often differ from those of the dominant media. We will explicate what an Asian American independent media consists of in later chapters, but we want to elucidate the rationale for structuring the book into two parts. We also recognize that mainstream and independent media are not mutually exclusive; they are interrelated and draw upon each other. Nonetheless, it is fruitful to start by distinguishing the mainstream from the independent as a way to understand the role of Asian Americans and the media as a starting point for future dialogue.

To help understand the historical representations of Asian Americans and the media, we spend more time in part I of the book reviewing previous scholarship simply because there has been more research done on historical representations than on the current, ever-changing mediascape. We want to draw readers' attention to the important work on which we are building and to use that work to illustrate the historical persistence of many of these representations. For experts of Asian American media and film, what we say about the history of representations of Asian Americans in media is very likely unsurprising, although some of the arguments we make are new. This account is necessary, however, for those unfamiliar with the history of representations of Asians and Asian Americans and helps contextualize the particular position in which Asian American media producers find themselves today. In order to have a fuller picture of Asian Americans and the media, our approach necessitates putting contemporary and independent representations in the context of historical ones. Thus, part I of the book is the backdrop against which to understand part II. It is important to us to emphasize that the kinds of representations we find in independent media, which we discuss in part II of the book, do not exist in isolation from the historical and contemporary representations in more traditional media, such as film, television, and print.

Chapters 2 through 5 address the historical dominant representations of Asian Americans, setting the foundation of current understandings and stereotypes of Asian and Asian American imagery. These chapters trace the historical representation of yellow peril imagery (chapter 2), yellowface representations (chapter 3), gendered representations (chapter 4), and model minority representations (chapter 5).

In chapter 2, "The Persistence of Yellow Peril Discourse," we examine the particular representation of yellow peril and put our analysis in the broader context of US colonization and Orientalism. Drawing upon the work of Stuart Hall and Edward Said, we track the discourse of Asians and Asian Americans as a yellow peril that emerges across a variety of media throughout history and into the present. In doing so, we recall past scholarship about legislating Chinese migration and Chinese-exclusion era discourse at the time, before moving on to Asian and Asian American yellow peril representations in the early history of cinema, such as Fu Manchu. However, contemporary neocolonialism continues today, and we predict that yellow peril discourse will continue to emerge for a long time to come. Thus, we conclude with a summary of the 1980s Vincent Chin case and an analysis of *The Fast and the Furious* (2001) to witness the reconfiguration of yellow peril representation in the present.

Chapter 3, "Media Yellowface 'Logics,' " argues that, while yellowface is less prominent than it was in earlier periods of US history, the logics of the yellowface era are evident in contemporary media representations. In addressing yellowface, the practice of adorning white actors in Orientalist make up and costuming, we address explicit yellowface in films such as *Breakfast at Tiffany's* (1961) and *Norbit* (2007). The fundamental issue relating to yellowface was the effect on labor and the lack of inclusion of Asian American actors. Additionally, it created a peculiar power relation between whites and Asians and Asian Americans. However, practices of absenting Asian Americans and emphasizing their lack of power go beyond the practices of yellowface of the past and include new logics, such as the presence of implicit yellowface, as we will see in our discussion of the actor Philip Ahn and more contemporarily the television show *All-American Girl*. Yellowface logics continue to rely on what Homi Bhabha calls racial ambivalence, enacted through mimicry and mockery. Representations of Asian Americans oscillate between representations of fear and loathing and representations of idealization, desire, and praise. In looking at yellowface logics, we argue that racial ambivalence, mimicry, and mockery communicate conflicting messages about the place of Asian Americans within US society and media.

In chapter 4, "Problematic Representations of Asian American Gender and Sexuality," we focus on gender and sexuality to theorize the way representations are interlocking. That is, we cannot understand representations of women without looking at representations of men, and we cannot understand representations of Asian Americans without looking at representations of whites. First, we examine gendered and sexualized representations separately and historically, beginning with Anna May Wong and Suzie Wong and then Fu Manchu and Charlie Chan. After looking at examples of Asian American men and women represented in *Ally McBeal*, *The World of Suzie Wong* (1960), *Sixteen Candles* (1984), and *Showdown in Little Tokyo* (1991), we move to examples of Asian American gender and sexuality in the cases of *Details* magazine's offensive article "Gay or Asian" and Asian Americans in pornography. We conclude by reexamining the representation of Bruce Lee as asexualized and gendered icon.

The final chapter in the mainstream media section, chapter 5, "Threatening Model Minorities: The Asian American Horatio Alger Story," examines the model minority stereotype as applied to Asians and Asian Americans. Drawing on recent work by Yuko Kawai, this chapter argues that the model minority image is strongly interrelated with yellow peril, that images of Asian and Asian American educational success are constitutively related to the recurring, episodic, and perennial fears of Asians and Asian Americans taking over. First, we draw on work by Osajima to situate the model minority stereotype historically. Then we draw on Chan's argument that "Charlie Chan" is an early model minority figure. We also look at the "Connie Chung" figure and the current typecasting of Asian Americans as medical doctors, analyzing Ming-Na Wen and Sandra Oh's characters in *ER* and *Grey's Anatomy*, respectively. Next we look at the continuum between model minority and yellow peril, by drawing upon Mannur's scholarship about cooking show hosts Ming Tsai and Padma Lakshmi and Perez's scholarship about Tiger Woods and the stereotypical promise of mixed-race Asian Americans. We conclude by describing the way the model minority representation functions as yellow peril by analyzing an article about the "takeover" of Asian American students at the University of California, Berkeley, and in two Silicon Valley high schools.

In the second part of the book, we analyze many different types of media artifacts and areas of representations, although not exhaustive by any means, to see the complexity of Asian American media by itself and in relation to dominant media. This second part begins with a discussion of the way in which Asian Americans have mobilized to challenge mainstream imagery (chapter 6), then theorizes Asian American artistic movements for independence from the mainstream (chapter 7), explores a variety of Asian American independent media (chapter 8), examines possibilities for new media as a site for Asian American production (chapter 9), and concludes with a discussion of institutional change and various organizations that Asian Americans have built to facilitate transformation (chapter 10). We look at media protest movements, Asian American independent media, new media, and finally organizations and institutions. Although this organization might seem hierarchical in terms of resistant and activist work, we do not privilege one medium over another. In the end, the second part explores and analyzes the various ways Asian Americans have challenged, critiqued, and protested dominant media representations through protests, self-representation, organizational work, and media activism.

Chapter 6, "Asian American Public Criticisms and Community Protests," examines various ways Asian Americans have staged protests of problematic media representations. The chapter draws upon Espiritu's concept of "reactive solidarity" and distinguishes media activism from other instances of activism. This chapter also theorizes the concepts of mimicry and mockery and examines the way Asian Americans have mobilized against problematic representations in the case of *Miss Saigon*, Rosie O'Donnell's use of "ching chong" on *The View*, and the radio broadcast of a prank phone call to a Chinese restaurant on the *Doghouse with JV and Elvis*.

Chapter 7, "Asian American Media Independence," lays out a theoretical justification for Asian American independent media, separate from mainstream economics and institutions. It begins by defining independence, then discusses the history of Asian American independent arts, and concludes with a discussion of independent media as creating a unique Asian American vernacular.

In chapter 8, "The Interface of Asian American Independent Media and the Mainstream," we draw upon Ono and Sloop's critique of vernacular discourse to examine various kinds of independent work done by Asian Americans. We look at a variety of media artifacts, from Mike Park's work on the Asian Man Records label to Margaret Cho's stand-up comedy and Justin Lin's directorial work on *The Fast and the Furious: Tokyo Drift* (2006), to see how Asian American independent media resist, react to, comply with, and sometimes reinforce historical and current dominant representations. In the chapter, we explore the degree to which Asian American independent work sometimes reifies notions of individualism, even if sometimes in reaction to capitalism.

In chapter 9, "Asian American New Media Practices" we discuss new media as a site for Asian American media intervention. We are as interested in how Asian Americans enter into the world of new media and what kind of organization and creative work may emerge within that context. We attend to new media discourses, looking at *YouTube* and other Internet locales for Asian Americans. In particular, we discuss the webcomics of Lela Lee, the blogs of AngryAsianMan and KimChiMamas, and then, through a discussion of Asians' and Asian Americans' use of *YouTube* for the Jim Webb senatorial campaign in Virginia, consider the possibilities of the web as having an organizing potential.

The final chapter in this section, chapter 10, "Mobilizing Organizations," discusses organizational efforts to examine and challenge media representations of Asian Americans. First, we look at independent film festivals, such as the San Francisco International Asian American Film Festival, as recurring spaces of Asian American independent media distribution, exhibition, and convocation. Then we examine media activist organizations, such as the Center for Asian American Media (CAAM) – formerly known as the National Asian American Telecommunications Association (NAATA) – and the Media Action Network for Asian Americans (MANAA), as sustained and constant watchdogs of Asian American dominant media representations. In this way, we consider the possibilities of reactive, institutionalized, individual, and creative expressional activist media work.

In the book's conclusion we summarize the key points of the chapters, highlighting terms discussed and our overall approach, and imagine what lies ahead for Asian Americans and the media in the future. This conclusion ties the history of dominant media representations of Asian Americans together with Asian American independent and activist media production, remembering moments throughout history when media racism occurred while showing how activism and independent producers are actively reconfiguring the Asian American media landscape. The conclusion also considers the way the perpetual foreigner stereotype affects Asian American representation broadly. In addition, we point to other possible areas of scholarship that would be useful, including quantitative studies of Asian American stereotypes and linkages to issues of national security, emerging digital media of video games and the Internet, and the increasing presence of multiracial Asian Americans in the media. In the end, we conclude that Asian American critiques of the mainstream, production of independent arts, and collective efforts to institutionalize Asian American production are all key to the future of changing the ever shifting but continually problematic US media.

PART I

HISTORICAL AND MAINSTREAM MEDIA REPRESENTATIONS

CHAPTER 02

The Persistence of Yellow Peril Discourse

WHILE today some people might say that racism is over, that race no longer matters, or that Dr Martin Luther King's "dream" of a world where children from different racial groups hold each other's hands in friendship has been attained, research focusing on race suggests this is simply not the case. Academics label the mistaken idea that the problem of race has been solved and racism has been eliminated as "race neutrality" or "post-racism." As much as one might wish it no longer existed, racism is difficult to eradicate, and disturbing racial representations, which have deep institutional roots within complex systems of representation, show every sign of persisting well into the future.

For Asian Americans, perhaps the longest-standing stereotypical representation is that of "yellow peril." By yellow peril, we mean representations of Asians and Asian Americans as threatening to take over, invade, or otherwise negatively Asianize the US nation and its society and culture. Usually, yellow peril discourse constructs an Asian–white dialectic emphasizing the powerful, threatening potential of Asians and Asian Americans, while simultaneously constructing whites as vulnerable, threatened, or otherwise in danger. This chapter argues that, by understanding yellow power and by reviewing its history in the media, one can better understand the current condition of Asian Americans, have a position from which to examine critically that condition, and help make relevant social changes to improve it.

Contrary to the popular media story that we all live in a post-racist society, yellow peril has not faded away into the depths of history. Rather, as the title to this chapter highlights, yellow peril persisted throughout the twentieth century and continues in the twenty-first. As a discourse, it is so entrenched within the cultural fabric of the United States that media regularly represent Asians and Asian Americans today as yellow peril.

Scant scholarly attention has been paid to yellow peril as a *media discourse* specifically. Media discourse includes news articles, TV programs, films, and Internet sites. Discourse is produced and organized in particular ways and serves as the basis by which ideas are formed and knowledge is produced, and, ultimately, for how people relate to other people and how societies are formed and structured. There is, of course, abundant historical work that discusses yellow peril racism and ideology, but rarely does that research understand yellow peril as a phenomenon created and fanned by the flames of screen media or the press. It is true that yellow peril is a way of thinking, an ideology, and has a psychological component. But, how does an idea gain social acceptance? How does the idea of Asians and Asian Americans as yellow peril circulate? In order to answer these questions, it is necessary to study yellow peril media discourse. Thus, in this book, we conceive of yellow peril as something print, film, TV, the Internet, and other media produce, so that media can be critiqued and, ultimately, changed. Additionally, understanding that yellow peril is a media discourse suggests that, like historical, legal, and public policy analysis, media analysis is important to the study of Asian Americans. By recognizing how this media discourse has been constructed historically and continues to exist today, future producers of media armed with knowledge may be able to avoid the trappings of yellow peril themes and to create new representational strategies in order to tell more nuanced, complex, and intelligent stories about Asians and Asian Americans.

Conceptual Maps and Dominant Views of the World

There is no one-to-one correlation between what the media construct and what people think,[1] of course, or even between what media producers "intend" and what ends up on screen. Thus, in order to make sense of media, we must look at cartoons, news articles, TV programs, films, and Internet sites ourselves. Even if we examine contemporary representations of yellow peril in media today, however, in order to understand their significance we must also study the history of yellow peril discourse. We will begin to understand how Asians and Asian Americans are currently located within and identified by a conceptual map of characteristics and are associated with certain stories produced within dominant culture.

In Sut Jhally's video about Stuart Hall, *Representation and the Media*, Hall defines an important concept, *representation*, in terms of what he calls "conceptual maps," what he also refers to as "maps of meaning" or "frameworks of intelligibility." These are those concepts and memories of experiences unique to individuals that help dictate how dominant ideas of the world come into being. As Hall writes:

> Now it could be the case that the conceptual map which I carry around my head is totally different from yours, in which case you and

> I would interpret or make sense of the world in totally different ways. We would be incapable of sharing our thoughts or expressing ideas about the world to each other. In fact, each of us probably does understand and interpret the world in a unique and individual way. (1997, 19)

Because most dominant, mainstream media makers form their own ideas based on their subjective knowledge of and experiences with Asians and Asian Americans, powerful representations such as yellow peril may come into existence and, then, may help to define for the broader society who Asians and Asian Americans are.

Language, images, and communication more broadly offer people the ability to compare conceptual maps to determine the degree of overlap and agreement, the degree to which one person's experiences approximate those of another. In a sense, language, signs, body language, images, and communication are, as Hall puts it, *externalizations* of our meanings and conceptual maps. Once a word has been uttered, assuming another person is within earshot, that externalization becomes public communication with a public value. Unlike memories in our heads that remain private to us, externalizations through symbols are sharable and available for consideration, discussion, and engagement. We can compare our experiences to those externalized by others and, likewise, how others view reality to the way we view it, often through, as Hall suggests, conversations and dialogues. However, beyond conversations, certain privileged externalizations are disseminated widely – in large part by the media – and may ultimately become part of public memory.

Origin and Proliferation of Yellow Peril Discourse

In this chapter, we trace a selective history of yellow peril media discourse, illustrating its historical persistence and, thus, its *structural embeddedness* in the media. By structural embeddedness, we mean that some discourse exists across different sectors of society, is reproduced across time, space, and media, and is not easily changed or eliminated. First, we recount a history using scholarship that has described different episodes of yellow peril discourse. We focus on its origins and effects before investigating twentieth-century examples of yellow peril in the United States, paying particular attention to discourse in early cinema and in World War II newsprint and to the complex relationship between media representations and historical and social events and contexts. We end the chapter by examining the current situation, moving from anti-Japanese news discourse of the 1980s and anti-Chinese discourse in the 1990s to representations of Asian and Asian American gangsters in film.

While fears of yellow peril began to be spread broadly in the late nineteenth century, the conceptual framework for the term had much earlier origins. Gary Okihiro suggests the idea may date back to the fifth century BCE, as a way of thinking about the Persians by the Greeks (1994, 119).[2] In her book on "yellow peril" themes in Hollywood films, Gina Marchetti suggests the concept was rooted in medieval fears of Genghis Khan and Mongolian invasions of Europe.[3] She writes, "Yellow peril combines racist terror of alien cultures, sexual anxieties, and the belief that the West will be overpowered and enveloped by the irresistible, dark, occult forces of the East" (1993, 2). Thus, yellow peril discourse and imagery racializes xenophobia; those in the West can then widely distribute this representation of the East.

At its height in the late nineteenth century, yellow peril discourse constructed an image of Chinese people in which "nonwhite people are by nature physically and intellectually inferior, morally suspect, heathen, licentious, disease-ridden, feral, violent, uncivilized, infantile, and in need of the guidance of white, Anglo-Saxon Protestants" (Marchetti, 1993, 3). In his discussion of depictions of Asian Americans in juvenile literature, J. Frederick MacDonald provides a thorough summary of the yellow peril representation of Chinese and Chinese Americans at the turn of the twentieth century. He suggests there was a general fear of Chinese inundating America. The images ranged from Chinese running opium dens, to emphasizing the "strange" dress of Chinese men who wore their hair in queues,[4] to the mythology constructed around white slavery by Chinese who sought white women for physical and sexual labor,[5] to a profusion of ideas concerning Chinese moral depravity and depredations. According to MacDonald, Chinese were depicted as wearing pigtails, speaking with exaggerated dialects, and then portrayed as "stupid because American heroes cannot understand their speech" (1978, 162). They were compared with animals such as horses, were not trustworthy, inspired fear, were said to smell vilely and to smoke opium. In the book *Coming Man* (Choy, Dong, and Hom, 1995),[6] cartoons published in high profile magazines such as *Puck, Harper's Weekly*, and *The Wasp* depict Chinese Americans as heathens, frequenters of opium dens and gambling houses, managers of white slavery, and as animal-like. A striking feature of the cartoons in magazines and other visual materials in the book is that, regardless of the degree of sympathy depicted in the images, the exaggerated physical features of Chinese people mock them as inhuman and as other.

Importantly, the depictions of Chinese people in media were not operating within a vacuum but were connected to and concurrent with US policies concerning the perceived yellow peril. For example, yellow peril discourse preceded and continued to play a role in the passage of new legislation that restricted Chinese migration. As Eugene Franklin Wong writes, during the Chinese exclusion era, Chinese were perceived as being "non-Western in dress, language, religion, customs, and eating habits," as "human oddities," mysterious, unassimilable, and "completely immoral" (1978, vi–vii). Chinese women were "strumpets," with an "exotic strain of venereal disease," and a "danger to both the health and morals of America" (ibid., vii). Chinese were an "opium smoking" and "gambling" lot – hence prone to vice, which could become infectious – and were both cowardly and passive (ibid., viii–ix). Popular figures of the day, such as Mark Twain (Samuel Clemens), portrayed China in degrading ways as a matter of course. Twain commented: "The Yellow Terror is threatening this world to-day. It is looming vast and ominous on that distant horizon. I do not know what is going to be the result of that Yellow Terror, but our government has had no hand in evoking it, and let's be happy in that and proud of it" (1923, 200). Indeed, the US government induced measures to stop Chinese migration. The Angell Treaty of 1880 specified that China would self-limit emigration of Chinese workers planning migration to the United States. Additional legislation included the Chinese Exclusion Act of 1882, which "was the first federal law to bar immigration on the basis of race and class." Subsequent legislation in 1884, 1888, 1892, 1893, 1898, 1901, 1902, and 1904 further limited Chinese migration to the United States (Choy, Dong, and Hom, 1995, 19–20). To all intents and purposes, because of these exclusion acts – fueled by yellow peril media discourse and legal and policy debates – after 1882, large-scale legal migration of Chinese to the United States was curtailed until the late 1960s.[7] During the exclusion era, many images such as that shown in figure 2.1 appeared.

As this apocalyptic image graphically illustrates, yellow peril, or "yellow terror," as the cartoon has it, is both a gendered and a racialized discourse. Here, yellow peril, embodied in the figure of the Chinese man, who phallically wields a smoking gun and simultaneously sports a lengthy, curvy, fraying queue (which along with his apparel and distorted facial features demonstrates his absolute alterity), represents a mortal threat to white women, and thus to all she represents for the nation. Absent in the image is a figure of a white male, ostensibly the reader to whom the image is directed and from whom compensatory action is sought, and the Asian or Asian American woman, a character apparently not relevant to a narrative of an alien, masculine threat to the nation. To complete the reasoning of the image, in order to protect white women and the nation from further trespass and violation from animalistic and violent Chinese

Figure 2.1   "The Yellow Terror in all his Glory," editorial cartoon, 1899

aggression, white men must act and potentially eliminate the lawless Chinese aggressor.

Yellow peril found its way into twentieth-century discourse as well. Robert Lee suggests early twentieth-century yellow peril may have emerged out of fears of Anglo–Saxon race suicide.[8] He writes, "The American transformation from republic to (comparatively small) empire created anxieties about new immigration and 'racial suicide.' These anxieties were voiced in debates over nationality, naturalization, and family in which the Oriental was consolidated as the Yellow Peril" (1999, 106). Thus, yellow peril discourse, first used broadly to rationalize the expulsion of Chinese people, became entrenched and later seemed to threaten the very future of the white race. As the twentieth century progressed, yellow peril discourse continued to circulate, marking both Chinese and Chinese Americans and Asians and Asian American communities as threats.

Silent Threat on the Silver Screen: Yellow Peril in Early Cinema

Whereas writing and imagery of yellow peril in the late nineteenth century appeared in print in newspapers and mainstream magazines, similar representations emerged in turn of the twentieth-century cinema, even after Chinese migration to the United States had largely been curtailed. Eugene Wong (1978) mentions films that draw on yellow peril imagery in the silent film era, such as *The Heathen Chinese and the Sunday School Teachers* (1904) and *The Chinese Rubbernecks* (1903), in which a Chinese laundryman with a queue is chased.

Particularly well-known silent films such as *The Cheat* (1915) and *Broken Blossoms* (1919)[9] construct yellow peril specifically by problematizing Asian–white interracial sexual relationships, representing the Asian and Asian American man as a threat not only to the white woman or girl but also to the structure of the white patriarchal family and to white civilization writ large.[10] To illustrate this idea, it is helpful to read *Broken Blossoms* in more detail, taking account of the social and political context of the time. To start, we think it is instructive to examine the film in relation to the cartoon "The Yellow Terror in all his Glory" (figure 2.1). The main difference between the two is that, in the film, "Yellow Man" (as the film names him) has a romantic rather than a violent sexual desire for, and encounter with, a white girl, "Lucy" (whom he calls "White Blossom"). However, as in the cartoon, Yellow Man figures as a threat to white society: after Lucy's father, "Battling," has beaten her severely, he finds out she is living above Yellow Man's shop, where she has taken refuge to recover from her father's beating. Battling goes to the shop, destroys Yellow Man's room, takes Lucy back home, drags her through a hole in the wooden door he has made with an axe in the closet where she has run to hide, and beats her to death with a whip. When Yellow Man finds Lucy missing from his room, he grabs a gun and goes to Battling's home to look for her. There, he finds her lifeless body. Battling then enters from an adjoining room, but, before he can initiate an attack on Yellow Man with an axe, Yellow Man shoots and kills him. Yellow Man carries Lucy's corpse away from Battling's home and lays her on his own bed, as if on an altar, before plunging a dagger into his own heart, falling down in a crumpled pile next to her body to die.

Figure 2.2   Lucy convalescing in Yellow Man's room above his store

Peter Feng has submitted it is a misreading of *Broken Blossoms* to suggest, as at least one critic has done, that the East is portrayed favorably in the film (2002b, 4–5), despite the fact that the white man, Battling, is depicted as horrifyingly aggressive and mean and that the film does not shy away from representing interracial erotics as a possibility (if not a reality) in lower-class parts of cities, where the races live together. It is true that pugilism, alcoholism, domestic abuse, and in general what is problematically constructed as lower-class white masculinity are foregrounded in the character of Battling. For instance, we find out that he regularly beats his daughter Lucy, holds the fifteen-year-old hostage in his home, and forces her to cook for him. However, Yellow Man is no hero either. Like Battling, he lives in the same poor part of town. Where Battling drinks alcohol, Yellow Man smokes opium. And, like Battling, Yellow Man comes to the end of his life. But Battling is murdered, whereas Yellow Man meets his fate by his own dagger, enacting a Madame Butterfly-like suicide.

Broken Blossoms does deviate from the editorial cartoon in important ways. Yellow Man does not rape and murder the white woman in the film as Yellow Terror implicitly does in the cartoon, although everyone but Lucy and Yellow Man imagine a forbidden sexual encounter, if not relationship, having been consummated between them. A white man figures prominently in the film but is absent in, though implicitly addressed by, the cartoon. And while the film constructs Yellow Man as more feminine, his counterpart in the cartoon is more aggressive.

Yet, in both, the white woman dies in the end. And, like the Yellow Terror, Yellow Man is an irreconcilable sexual threat to women, and thus to what is good, wholesome, and pure (and what needs to be protected) about society, and an alien other that requires elimination. Despite being figured as more of an aggressor in the cartoon, Yellow Man nevertheless uses a gun, one that smokes, too, as he kills Battling. Like the Yellow Terror, Yellow Man is feminized and desexualized, often pictured stroking his face with his hand, and repeatedly retreating from kissing Lucy to consummate their relationship, not only as the film indicates because of the purity of their relationship, but also implicitly because of a consciousness of the social strictures against miscegenation.

The film goes beyond the cartoon in important ways, in part because of the technology of film, because it tells a narrative, but also because it more literally renders Yellow Man animal-like. Yellow Man is constructed as alien through the use of yellowface make-up that both renders the white actor's body not white and simultaneously draws attention to features that render Chinese different from whites. The film treats Yellow Man's Buddhist non-violence as not serious through shots of his addictive use of opium, his fawning and obsequious ineffectual sexuality in Lucy's presence, and particularly when the narrative culminates in his, at least in part, vengeful murder of Battling. He is also constructed throughout the film as primitive, his eyes almost nearly shut and his body pictured in a stooped position, his head as if in a perpetual bow. This representation of Yellow Man's otherness, primitivity, and asexuality (despite his longing for a white woman), renders him an indisputable threat to masculinity, if not a threat of impurity in the Anglo-Saxon genetic stock. If the film figures Battling's hyper-masculinity as excessive, and therefore as not acceptable within bourgeois, heterosexual normalcy, Yellow Man's hyperemasculation, his alienness, and his lack of humanity, while perhaps more agreeable to heterosexual white girlhood, pose a much greater and profound threat of dilution to Anglo-Saxon masculinity and a white racial project. In a sense, the film suggests Yellow Man is poor mating material; if Lucy and he were to have children, the logic of the film goes, future Anglo-Saxons would be less than masculine, normal, and human.

While the film, through intertitles, does construct Yellow Man's Eastern philosophical and religious non-violence somewhat sympathetically, as Gina Marchetti suggests (1993, 34–45), and constructs Battling as a brute whose fatal end is expected, if not deserved, it also shows no sympathy for Yellow Man in the eyes of the law, despite the fact that his encounter with Lucy was not of his making, but was in fact a result of Battling's physical abuse of her, and despite the fact that he kills Battling in self-defense. The film gives Yellow Man no way out; his existence within white society is simply irreconcilable, given the need for white racial survival. The speed with which the Spy, the police, and other men are assembled to hunt down Yellow Man suggests that, if he does not kill himself, they will do it for him. Thus, the film does not question the larger moral viewpoint that miscegenation between white and Asian is not tolerable and that, if it occurs, the death of the Asian man who trespasses the moral and sexual boundary is to be assumed, regardless of whether or not he would otherwise be a sympathetic character. Indeed, the film suggests that the Asian man knows as well as the rest of society that romance and sexuality across racial lines is forbidden and must be met with death, which is why he seeks the more respectable end of killing himself.[11]

Archetypes of Yellow Peril

While *Broken Blossoms* allows for a detailed study of the yellow peril representation of Asians and Asian Americans in film, the quintessential representation of yellow peril emerged in the iconic figure of Dr Fu Manchu. From 1923, when the English film *The Mystery of Dr Fu Manchu* was made, to 1940, when *The Drums of Fu Manchu* was released, a series of films constructed this character.[12]

The first US version of Fu Manchu was *The Mysterious Dr Fu Manchu* (1929).[13] Originally created in England, Sax Rohmer's character Dr Fu Manchu was imported into the United States. Wong suggests Rohmer had little contact or knowledge about Chinese people but viewed Chinatown fantastically: "With his limited contact with real Chinese and his generous imaginal conception of Chinatown, Rohmer, the man who created the single outstanding personification of anti-Sinicism, confessed his ignorance of the Chinese people, stating: 'I made my name on Fu Manchu because I know nothing about the Chinese'" (1978, 97–8). Dr Fu Manchu was diabolical, sinister, and evil, a particular, masculine representation of yellow peril – an image that continued into television in the 1940s and 1950s (ibid., 101–2). Thus this villainous character functioned across time to maintain a discourse of yellow peril and intersected with many other film and media representations, such as "Emperor Ming, the Merciless" (Charles Middleton) in the *Flash Gordon* films, which began in 1936.

Jachinson Chan suggests that Fu Manchu is a projection of Western desires for manifest destiny; hence, Fu Manchu, while being

Figure 2.3   Warner Oland in *The Mysterious Dr Fu Manchu*

de-sensualized, is projected as being aggressive, domineering, and hypervirile (2001, 16). As the incarnation of yellow peril, he "perpetuates the myth that the Chinese, and by extension, Asians, are trying to take over the Western world" (ibid., 27). Chan adds that, "at the end of each novel, the yellow peril is contained in spite of the exaggerated threat posed by the scheming Chinese man. White male supremacy, as an ideological construct, is reestablished as Asian men are ritualistically vilified in order to maintain a sense of superiority among White men" (ibid., 28).

Fu Manchu exhibits the ambivalence that we describe early on in the book. On the one hand he is fascinating, on the other he inspires fear. As Chan writes, "Dr. Fu Manchu is a Chinese Satan who, on the surface, is cat-like, calm and implacable but will strike you at any moment for no apparent reason" (2001, 33). Importantly, Fu Manchu represents the diametrical opposition of East and West. Chan continues, "the image of Dr. Fu Manchu encompasses both Eastern and Western characteristics (the brows, face, and cat-green eyes), reducing the character to a brilliant mutant. The ideological implication here is the perpetuation or confirmation of the cultural incommensurability between East and West" (ibid., 34). He is a representation of the threat of invasion and of a person addicted to vice. Important to his image is his totalitarian desire, which manifests itself in his sexual lust for and ultimate domination over white Western women. What makes him particularly frightening is his scientific experiments with hybrids, hence his "fascination with miscegenation and genetic hybridity" (ibid., 41). Ultimately, he is constructed as lacking sensuality; his sexuality can be best described as that of "an asexual rapist who uses force to capture his women in order to breed superior offspring" (ibid., 44).

Up to this time, the majority of yellow peril discourse focused on Chinese and Chinese Americans. As Darrell Hamamoto argues, much of Asian American media representation is directly linked to US foreign policy,[14] as we have seen with the link between yellow peril discourse and the exclusion of Chinese migration. Thus, following Japan's bombing of Pearl Harbor on December 7, 1941, a spate of anti-Japanese imagery appeared, reconstructing the yellow peril, this time in relation to Japanese and Japanese Americans. While there had been significant anti-Japanese movements throughout the century preceding World War II,[15] yellow peril media discourse peaked after the Pearl Harbor bombing. Caricatures of Japanese depicted them as rat-like, as uncaring animals, and as inscrutable, villainous, and treacherous.[16] The post-Pearl Harbor imagery of Japanese shared much in common with the exclusion-era imagery of Chinese and Chinese Americans, albeit with some added features. As Michael Shull and David Wilt suggest about the portrayal of the Japanese as the enemy in World War II films, "As for the Japanese, a generalized prewar Asian stereotype was crudely supplemented by glasses, buckteeth and the mordantly delivered 'so sorry' " (1996, 143).

World War II Hollywood propaganda depicted the Japanese as barbarians, "fanatical near-savages, sneaky, dirty fighters" (Wong, 1978, 156).[17] As Wong suggests, "The otherwise inhuman characteristics of early Asians in America were integrated into the Asian *enemy*, the competitor, the unfair and degrading threat to white labor, the culturally peculiar aliens whose low standard of living paralleled their own low value on human life, and the secretive Japanese farmer who was under his coveralls a barbaric samurai ready at a moment's notice to spearhead an invasion of white, Christian America" (ibid., 150). Through images created by Hollywood in particular, Wong notes that "Hollywood was able to manipulate the image of Japanese so as to create in the process intense and highly racialist attitudes among non-Asian Americans for the Japanese, and ultimately for all Asians" (ibid., 146). Not surprisingly, then, the first World War II film, the Academy Award-winning and box-office hit *Wake Island* (1942), highlighted the deviousness of the Japanese and emphasized that Pearl Harbor was a sneak attack. Like *Wake Island*, *The Purple Heart* (1944) participated in the propagandistic representations of racist yellow peril. Japanese were portrayed as savage and sadistic, but also as subhuman (ibid., 157).[18]

Figure 2.4   Arthur Szyk's image after Japan's bombing of Pearl Harbor appeared in *Collier's* on December 12, 1941. Reproduced with kind permission from the collection of Wm. Hallam Webber.

At the end of World War II, representations shifted from the Japanese, Germans, and Italians as threats to the danger of communism. In this context, once again, fear of Chinese made its way into cinema. As Wong writes, "The United States Government and the American motion picture industry, contrariwise, had not only succeeded in firmly establishing anti-Asianism in the public mind, but had also in the process set a backlog of anti-Asiatic imagery that would prove movable from one Asian group to another as international conditions changed" (1978, 168).

Wong suggests through his discussion of films that, although World War II had ended, themes developed during the war years continued. While historically, as we have shown, yellow peril discourses often have been tied to questions of war, politics, and immigration, the fact that the discourses are so well established (and naturalized in these contexts) makes them easily available for other uses. In the next section, we look at more recent examples of yellow peril to illustrate the similarities of representations over time and their cross-applicability to multiple Asian ethnic groups. Without providing an exhaustive review, here we present a few illustrations of more contemporary yellow peril imagery. We start with a discussion of a series of anti-Asian events and of the news media representations of those events, and then move to a discussion of the film *The Fast and the Furious* (2001) in order to emphasize the way in which the discourses in fictional media intersect with and support news media as yellow peril discourse continues on into the present.

Yellow Peril Persists

Since yellow peril media discourse is historically entrenched, its themes of Asians as savage, merciless, immoral, subhuman, and a threat to white women and whites in general have been reproduced in more contemporary media representations of Asians and Asian Americans. More recent instances of yellow peril discourse have been linked to questions about the labor force (e.g., exporting "US jobs" and the loss of state secrets [e.g., Wen Ho Lee]) and commodity globalization (e.g., danger of Chinese-made toys with lead paint). In light of the historical representations of yellow peril, of anti-Chinese and anti-Japanese sentiment, we see the tropes of yellow peril arising in the Vincent Chin case in the 1980s, fear of Japanese economic power in the 1980s and 1990s, the scapegoating of John Huang and Wen Ho Lee in the 1990s, and the post-9/11 actions as they ultimately affected South Asians and South Asian Americans.[19]

In the 1980s, as gas prices were on the rise, the US auto industry went into a serious slump, just as the sale of inexpensive, fuel-efficient Japanese cars escalated. The area quite possibly hardest hit was Detroit – the home of the US auto industry and known worldwide for making large eight-cylinder cars – which suffered from mass layoffs at automobile plants. In 1982, Vincent Chin, a 27-year-old Chinese American autoworker, was bludgeoned to death in Detroit by two white autoworkers (Ronald Ebens and his stepson Michael Nitz); Nitz had recently been laid off. The film *Who Killed Vincent Chin?* (1987) suggests this violence was an outgrowth of racial tensions in Detroit at the time and documents the local media's representations of those tensions. Helen Zia, one of the main activists and journalists investigating the Vincent Chin case, writes that friends of Chin's at the bar where he was on the night he was attacked "overheard Ebens say 'Chink,' 'Nip,' and 'fucker.' One of the dancers heard Ebens shout at Vincent Chin, 'It's because of motherfuckers like you that we're out of work' " (2000, 59). Ebens misrecognized Chinese American Vincent Chin as a Japanese foreigner and economic threat, thus reproducing the anti-Japanese sentiment, and resulting anti-Asian sentiment, in Detroit and in the rest of the United States at the time.

The swell of anti-Japan discourse rose to a fever pitch throughout the 1980s, perhaps culminating in the early 1990s. In December, 1991, fifty years after the bombing of Pearl Harbor, the owner of the Seattle Mariners put the team up for sale. A national furor arose over the prospective and eventual buyers of the team, an investment group consisting of four white investors and one Japanese American. However, because the majority investor, the Japanese American's father-in-law, was Hiroshi Yamauchi, owner of Nintendo, news media across the country suggested this was akin to another "Pearl Harbor." The pending purchase of the team was likened to a takeover of the nation, what many feared was the mixing of Japanese money with US money, or what Ono (1997) calls *economic miscegenation*. The fear was that, whereas at Pearl Harbor Japan threatened to take over the US militarily, Japan's threat today is an economic one, and the United States, unawares, would be taken over by Japanese money.

Following the disaggregation of the Soviet Union as a communist bloc and the martial put-down of political unrest at Tiananmen Square, there was some of the most virulent anti-Chinese yellow peril discourse since the exclusion era (Ling-chi Wang, 1998). During the mid-1990s, media discourse emerged surrounding John Huang, a Democratic fundraiser for President Clinton who was accused of taking donations from wealthy Chinese contributors. In what is referred to as "Donorgate," naturalized Asian American citizens used foreign or transnational ties to elicit donations from overseas business for the Democratic National Committee. Despite the fact that such campaign gifts were common in US politics, a hunt, led by Fred Thompson, ensued to ferret out evidence of campaign gifts from China in particular. News media discourse then characterized John Huang based on well-worn yellow peril imagery, constructing him as mysterious and inscrutable (Ono, 2005, 3). News media used the affair to offer a general characterization of President Bill Clinton's relationship with China. A March 24, 1997, cover of the conservative news magazine the *National Review* racialized the larger issue of campaign donations, relying on early yellow peril imagery. The cover contained caricatures of Bill Clinton, Hillary Clinton, and Al Gore in yellowface, buck-toothed and wearing clothing associated with China and implying some sort of nefarious or improper relationship between the US administration and China. John Huang, one of the most powerful Asian Americans in US politics at the time, became the primary scape-goat, but additional Asian Americans, primarily Chinese Americans, then came under a new redbaiting era of surveillance.

A similar kind of persecution followed: In 1999, Los Alamos nuclear scientist Wen Ho Lee was accused of being a spy.[20] As a nuclear scien-tist, he was alleged to have given key nuclear information to China. Despite having lived in the United States for thirty-five years, having been naturalized for twenty-five years, and having been a Los Alamos scientist whose work strengthened US national defense and security, Lee was accused of handing over top-secret information that would augment China's nuclear profile. News media in the United States took the opportunity to invoke themes of yellow peril. Lee was described as "sly," "uncooperative," "quiet," "mysterious," and "deceptive" (Ono, 2002, 79). As Ono argues, news media rhetoric about Wen Ho Lee drew "on paranoia, dramatically construct[ed] the nation as vulnerable masculine body fearful of masculine penetration, [was] prone to con-structing the other as primitive and the self as technologically supe-rior, and construct[ed] the other as a potential threat to the body of the nation" (ibid., 82). In other words, news media rhetoric invoked yellow peril themes and fears to construct Wen Ho Lee as a deceptive and sneaky person, infiltrating the US from within, stealing nuclear secrets, and compromising US safety.[21]

Yellow peril themes permeated media representations to construct Huang and Lee as threats to American democracy and safety. As a result, the media imply, US Americans must act accordingly – whether the evidence is there or not – to protect US interests. This yellow peril discourse about China continued building until September 11, 2001, when discourse about Arab and Arab American demonization took over as a response to the collapse of the World Trade Center twin towers and as a prelude to war. As we have seen, yellow peril themes are ready templates and frames that can be drawn upon by media produc-ers and politicians to characterize events, in this case 9/11.

Given the pervasiveness of the news media's production of yellow peril discourse, and given the history of the relationship between such discourse and social events (such as Pearl Harbor) and its depictions in fictional films, it should be no surprise that a number of films and television shows at the turn of the twenty-first century continue to thematize yellow peril. Here, we offer a more extended analysis of *The Fast and the Furious* in order to illustrate the persistence and com-plexity of yellow peril discourse in contemporary media. In the first movie in the series, Asian American characters represent yellow peril in the form of gangsters who are the lead suspects in an electronics hijacking ring. The character of Johnny Tran, played by actor Rick Yune, is a villain, the leader of the Asian American gang involved in the sports compact scene. Tran is a character to be feared, so much so that even Dominic Toretto, played by the hypermasculine Vin Diesel, fears being the subject of his wrath. In an early scene titled "Big Trouble in Little Saigon," Toretto and O'Conner, played by Paul Walker, flee the police, only to be surrounded by a gang of Asian Americans riding motorcycles and brandishing Uzis. The gang escorts Toretto and O'Conner to a stop and they exit the car, surrounded by Tran's gang. Speaking to Toretto, Tran states, "I thought we had an agreement. You stay away, I stay away. Everybody stays happy." Toretto replies, "We got lost Johnny. What do you want me to tell you?" A tension-filled conversation ensues and culminates with Tran letting them go, only to come back and shoot at Toretto and O'Conner's prized car until it erupts into a fiery blaze. In a later scene, Tran preys upon an old white man's garage shop and threatens him when he discovers that their cars have no engines. Tran eventually tortures the old man by pumping motor oil into his mouth until he volunteers the information about the missing engines. Tran concludes the scene by saying "Ted [the old white man], kiss my shoes." Coughing, Ted crawls over to kiss Tran's shoes, only to have Tran kick him away.

These scenes illustrate the tired trope of the Asian American gangster, a rehash of yellow peril. Asian Americans are merciless and deceptive. Tran misleads Toretto and O'Conner into believing that they have been spared and then comes back to destroy their car. Ted crawls over to kiss Tran's shoes only to be kicked while down. In this film, Asian Americans are evil and dubious, cold and unrelenting, and a danger to US business via hijackings and torture.

Whereas each yellow peril representation figured Asians and Asian Americans as threats to white women, US American jobs, and the moral fabric of the United States, yellow peril continues into the 1980s and 1990s as threats to US economic prosperity and opportunity, national security, and democracy. The imminent takeover by Asia, now reimagined to include the Middle East, remains strong in the psyche of Americans as both an international and a domestic threat (Kawai, 2005). From its earliest representations in the form of Persians and Mongol hordes, through the world wars and Cold War anxiety about Chinese and Japanese, to late twentieth-century anxiety about the globalized marketplace, to the post-9/11 distrust of anything that seems connected to the Middle East, to the most recent example (as of this writing) of anxiety over the dangers of globalization represented by lead found in the paint of inexpensive toys (blamed primarily on

Chinese subcontractors versus the companies hiring subcontractors and versus those responsible for inspecting imported toys), today's media culture remains rife with yellow peril discourse.

Controlling the Yellow Peril

Despite much vaunted talk of the United States being a "post-racist" society, this chapter suggests that yellow peril discourse has not ended and continues in contemporary media. By using Hall's understanding of representation and externalization, we can see how this discourse plays a role in the development of a dominant conceptual map of Asians and Asian Americans. As we can see through this relatively brief overview of different moments in US history, the demonization of Asians and Asian Americans as threats to the nation and to whiteness is persistent and continual. Part of the reason yellow peril remains a theme within media discourse is because of the historical and continuing unequal relations of media power, with dominant white society controlling the means of representation. Quite simply, Asians and Asian Americans have been unable to depict and represent themselves in the dominant mainstream US media, and therefore they have been depicted without much information, knowledge, or education about who they are. Once it is acknowledged that these images have had little informed content, then it becomes much easier to begin to talk about such issues as: Why would non-Asian Americans want to represent Asians and Asian Americans in the first place? Why do non-Asian Americans represent Asians and Asian Americans in a particular way? And, what struggles do those who want to try to produce images of Asian Americans with strong consciousness about Asian Americans and Asian American experiences face?

To help answer these questions, and to structure our discussion of Asian Americans in the media and of yellow peril media discourse, we recall Hall's conception and understanding of representation. Because so few Asian Americans were historically involved in externalizing images of themselves and other Asians and Asian Americans, the primary externalizations – public images, discourse, language, and signs – were created by non-Asian Americans, few of whom had any useful knowledge of Asians and Asian Americans and Asian and Asian American communities. Thus, yellow peril imagery was not a result of how Asian Americans understood their own presence in the Americas but, rather, an externalization of the dominant society's values of and attitudes and beliefs about them. Were Asians and Asian Americans to have more control over media institutions and media production, perhaps yellow peril themes would not be accessed so easily as ways to make sense of immigration, international relations, economic downturns, the auto industry, political campaigns, the sale of baseball teams, and the like.

Based on this theory of representation, we argue that yellow peril was a manufactured, not an "actual," threat to the power and stability of the United States as a nation-state. One might counter that, for example, Japan posed a "real" threat to the United States after Pearl Harbor, but the construction of yellow peril *as a discourse* did not match any real threat Japan posed. Thus, yellow peril *as a discourse* is primarily rhetorical; it shifts the public understanding and discussion of Asians and Asian Americans as a yellow peril whether or not it, or indeed any peril, exists. For instance, while no Japanese American was ever found guilty of treason, espionage, or spying, rumors and even official records at the time "imagined" Japanese Americans were Japan's "fifth column" and were attempting to help the enemy Japanese plan a mainland attack. Moreover, during World War II yellow peril was a racial construction; Japan did not characterize the United States in racial terms, but the United States constructed the Japanese not only as enemies, but also as *racial* enemies (Wong, 1978, 167–8). These racialized representations of yellow peril, then, helped rationalize the imprisonment of 120,000 Japanese Americans in concentration camps from 1942 to 1945.

As is evident in the case of Vincent Chin, as well as in many other cases we describe, international relations with Asian countries have a direct relationship with how Asians and Asian Americans are understood domestically. Furthermore, a reservoir of imagery, a conceptual map described by Edward Said as *Orientalism*, already exists about Asians that relates to media representation globally. In his book *Orientalism* (1978), Said describes the historical significance of the power and control of Western intellectuals, as well as Western culture more broadly, to conceive of the East as different from the West. Said suggests that Asian people did not create Orientalism, and that Orientalism does not describe Asian people. Oriental studies sought to characterize the East as a conception by the West, without input by the East. Thus, Orientalism was a European invention of what white Europeans believed about Asians, a European externalization, hence a fictionalized view of the world. Orientalism helped explain how Asian people and civilization related to European people and civilization. In a sense, from within the Western framework, it helped put the East in its place and defined more clearly what was East and what was West. Once the place for people in the East was defined, an investment in a relationship of power between East and West was reproduced.

To clarify the relationship between East and West, the West was constructed as in power and the East was constructed as needing the power of the West, because people in the East are unable to govern themselves. Thus, "A line is drawn between two continents. Europe is powerful and articulate; Asia is defeated and distant" (Said, 1978, 57). Additionally, Said suggests that Oriental studies then characterized their own projections of what the East was as having been arrived at objectively, thus positioning Western knowledge of the East as objective and any other understandings, such as non-academic, or non-Western, and certainly non-rational, understandings as illegitimate. Said's concept of Orientalism, then, helps us not only to understand the existence and logic of yellow peril discourse, but also to see how it is transnational, reproducing a relationship between the West and East and therefore defining Asians and Asian Americans as perpetual foreigners and as ever-present threats to the nation.

Furthermore, these examples illustrate that yellow peril is a media discourse that refers abstractly to the threat of Asian takeover and therefore does not allow for distinctions among groups. Yellow peril discourse gives little attention or meaning to ethnic, cultural, political, historical, and social differences. In other words, yellow peril imagery ends up subscribing to the notion that "all Asians look alike," thus diminishing ethnic, cultural, religious, and other differences.[22] As we have seen, while yellow peril imagery was perhaps most strongly used early on in relation to Chinese and Chinese Americans, it has throughout US history repeatedly appeared as a way to make all Asians and Asian Americans the "other" and the enemy/foe – as in the case of Vincent Chin, for example.

Our approach to studying yellow peril discourse in this chapter has been to take an Asian American studies perspective on the subject; to draw attention to the historical, social, political, and legal conditions that relate to its existence; to emphasize the multimedia dimension of the emergence of yellow peril; and to suggest the ability ultimately to change media representations through knowledge, study, and critical examination of such representations. As Ella Shohat and Robert Stam argue in *Unthinking Eurocentrism* (1994), the act of criticism itself is part of the process of dismantling systems of domination. Through critique, the possibilities for change become imaginable.

CHAPTER 03

Media Yellowface "Logics"

Tʜᴇ use of yellowface, the topic of this chapter, is, like the use of yellow peril discourse, heavily dependent on the historical treatment of Asians and Asian Americans.[1] The practice of white actors playing Asian and Asian American characters, especially in early twentieth-century Hollywood, has received at least some scholarly attention.[2] In part because of racism and specific racist and xenophobic policies against miscegenation, Asian and Asian American actors could not even play genuine character parts in early media culture.[3] Asians and Asian Americans were not ordinarily given jobs in Hollywood, and Asian and Asian American characters were scarce. When such characters did exist, a convention of yellowface ensured that they were played primarily by whites. In the 1960s, when codes and laws against miscegenation were relaxed, and when the Hollywood production code prohibiting depictions of miscegenation weakened and was ultimately replaced by a ratings system, one might assume that yellowface practices would die a natural and logical death. And it is true that at least some more Asian and Asian American actors did find work in Hollywood in the 1960s. However, as we argue in this chapter, explicit yellowface continued, as when David Carradine landed the lead role of Kwai Chang Caine in the television show *Kung Fu*, and techniques went beyond the explicit to include *implicit* yellowface strategies that, while retreating from more explicit representations, preserved *yellowface logics*.

Thus, explicit yellowface impersonation is part of a much broader field of media representational practice that controls and often excludes Asian and Asian American self-representation. This raises a very important question: Why would Hollywood and those regulating the movie industry not want Asians and Asian Americans writing stories about or playing roles of Asians and Asian Americans? Yellowface logics, which buttress the production of both explicit and implicit yellowface strategies, help support and maintain a condition of unequal power relations between whites and Asians and Asian Americans. Whereas whites, blacks, and others have played Asian characters, Asian Americans, for the most part, have not been accorded such masquerading "privileges."[4] White media producers have created imaginary and derogatory fictional representations of Asians and Asian Americans, while Asian and Asian American actors simultaneously are virtually excluded from writing or playing such roles. Additionally, yellowface is a practice of cultural appropriation; taking what is thought to be Asian or Asian American and making it into something that sells to audiences is a self-serving practice.[5] The production and distribution of imaginary Orientalist externalizations of Asianness helps reinforce the mainstream dominant control of cultural performance generally.

This chapter provides historical examples of the use of yellowface across media contexts, but particularly in film, and then argues that, after its widespread explicit use went out of vogue (even though it is still employed occasionally today), other practices, what we call *implicit yellowface*, continued, maintaining dominant media power and blurring the ethnic and cultural differences among Asian and Asian American groups. Together, both explicit and implicit yellowface strategies are part of *yellowface logics* in media culture.

To begin this chapter, we first define explicit yellowface and provide key examples of it throughout the history of cinema, in particular, but also in TV and theatre. Then we define implicit yellowface and provide both historical and contemporary examples. To explain the way yellowface affects Asian American media representation, we theorize the concept of ambivalence, of both the desire for and fear/hatred of the racialized "Other." Before concluding the chapter, we discuss the broader implications these ambivalent "yellowface logics" have for Asian Americans and the media.

Explicit Yellowface

We define explicit yellowface racially as when a non-Asian or non-Asian American plays the role of an Asian or Asian American. *Playing Asian* means wearing heavy white make-up as a base and exaggerated black make-up around the eyes, sometimes actually taping the eyes back to change their shape, using an accent imagined to "sound Asian," speaking words from a script that either sound vaguely like someone speaking an Asian language or that are distorted English or simply gibberish, wearing wigs, and performing in an obsequious manner, meaning acting in a subordinate, often docile, and sometimes basically stupid way. Wong refers to yellowface make-up – sculpting the white human face to appear Asian – as "racial cosmetology" (1978, 40). There is, of course, nothing wrong with make-up and costuming; both are intrinsic to theatrical performance, if not performances of everyday life. However, in the context of the history of Asian and Asian American representations we address in this book, it becomes clear that yellowface is not simply a costume but is also a racial joke addressed to white audiences, with Asians and Asian Americans serving as the butt of that joke.

Yellowface also serves a psychosocial function, mediating both the psychological perception of Asians and Asian Americans and the social interaction with them. It allows audiences to think the masquerading actor is both like and not like an Asian or Asian American. Like blackface, yellowface is a form of racial masquerade, a masquerade in which the audience knows the actor is masquerading, that they are not *actually* Asian. This masquerade allows the audience to play around with race – to imagine what aspects of performance align with an imagined Asianness, while simultaneously attempting to note aspects of the actors' whiteness, thus practicing the skills of discriminating between what is Asian and what is white.

Yellowface has a social dimension as well, for it was originally created for the pleasure of white audiences. Hence, it has more to do with the way white people relate to each other than it does with a genuine, humane relationship with Asians and Asian Americans. As Tchen suggests, "The visual language of yellowface came to signify a universe of meanings having far more to do with the host culture than with who and what were originally being represented" (1999, 129). While it is clear that Asian and Asian Americans were done a disservice by such representations – being inaccurately depicted as objects of the Orientalist gaze – consumers of yellowface culture were also negatively impacted. Tchen says, "Viewers who believed these representations became imprisoned in a world of racial caricatures and power relations" (ibid.). Additionally, by objectifying Asians and Asian Americans using bio-essentializing features, yellowface produces a dividing line between them and white audiences, limiting the potential for meaningful contact and confrontation, while creating possible alliances between white actors and audiences through the self-consciousness of knowing yellowface is merely a masquerade.

Yellowface is therefore a ruse – a scrupulously manufactured image dependent on the viewer and consumer's *suspension of disbelief* (their willingness for sake of play and performance to privilege the fake over the real) for long enough to experience the pleasure of a mocking humor that does a disservice to Asians and Asian Americans and to non-Asians and Asian Americans alike. It replaces a potentially genuine humane social encounter between Asians and Asian Americans and audiences with a shallow one that supports relations of whiteness.

Figure 3.1   Mickey Rooney as Mr Yunioshi in *Breakfast at Tiffany's*

More importantly, yellowface is a systematically manufactured way to maintain white dominance and Asian and Asian American subordination. Similar to blackface, yellowface for Asians and Asian Americans takes place on, and reproduces, an unequal playing field where Asian and Asian American actors are not allowed to play and engage in practices of white identity play.

The character of "Mr Yunioshi" in *Breakfast at Tiffany's* (1961), played by Mickey Rooney, is a clear example of how yellowface is performed for the pleasure of the non-Asian viewer.[6] The film makes clear that Mr Yunioshi is played in yellowface early on, as the text "Mickey Rooney as 'Mr Yunioshi' " appears in the opening credits. The character of Mr Yunioshi is inept, buck-toothed, puffy cheeked, and sexually depraved. In the opening scene he wakes up to the sound of Holly Golightly, played by Audrey Hepburn, ringing the doorbell: he hits his head on a Chinese lantern, stumbles out of bed, then runs into a counter, picks up a plant and accidentally triggers a flash from a camera that blinds him. He goes outside his apartment, peers down the staircase, and yells in mangled English, "Ms GoRightly, I protest!" Golightly replies, "Oh darling, I am sorry but I lost my key." Mr Yunioshi retorts, "That was two weeks ago. You cannot go on and ringing my bell. You disturba me." Holly Golightly, in an attempt appease Mr Yunioshi, says, "Don't be angry, you dear little man, I won't do it again. If you promise not to be angry I might let you take those pictures we mentioned." Mr Yunioshi's expression instantly changes from angry bumbling Asian man to eager infantile. He asks, "When?" Golightly replies ambiguously, "Sometime." Mr Yunioshi, in wonderment and humble eagerness, begs "Anytime." In this scene, Mr Yunioshi functions as comic relief, especially through his unrealistic desire for Ms Golightly. His broken English, excessive clumsiness, and implausible sexual fantasy are there for the comedic pleasure of the non-Asian audience. This representation both defines and degrades what is Asian, while aligning white audiences with Mickey Rooney, whom they are to know is not Asian and hence not being degraded, but who in fact is to be revered for playing such a degraded role in a superior way.

The absence of Asians and Asian Americans is key to the pleasure and performative effect of yellowface impersonation. Having Asian or Asian American actors play these characters would interrupt the mocking effect and alliances of whiteness and might suggest that those in power cannot exclusively play the masquerade. This would render the masquerade decidely impostural, hence inauthentic, potentially exposing the mechanics of power and pleasure that work together to control the representation of others.

Were Asians and Asian Americans allowed to play yellowface roles, an immediate conflict would arise. If the only roles available for Asians and Asian American actors were those that mock, degrade, and insult them while simultaneously providing pleasure for non-Asian audiences, would they take them on? If they played them, would they enjoy them? Would they be doing a disservice to Asians and Asian Americans, since accepting such roles might reproduce the need for them? And, if one has no money, might one feel forced to play degrading roles anyway?

The practice of yellowface is a form of mimicry and mockery; it is a substitution of an object for a subject, a substitution of a mocking mask for a human being. According to Bhabha (1994), mimicry is a strategy that appropriates the Other while simultaneously functioning to emphasize visually who has power in a relationship. Mimicry signals what is inappropriate in the Other through acts of mockery, which communicates the disavowal of the Other. Examples of this include "The Tsunami Song," William Hung on *American Idol*, and the Abercrombie and Fitch Asian-themed T-shirts.[7] Pham and Ono (forthcoming) argue that Abercrombie and Fitch's T-shirts circulated a yellow peril and yellowface representation of Asians and Asian

Americans as an act of mimicry and mockery. Asian Americans were not involved in the production of images. They were not *self-representations* but caricatured representations made by those unfamiliar with Asian Americans, lacking access to Asian American self-awareness, and perhaps dismissive and degrading of Asian American people and their views on the world.

In the process of disavowal and appropriation via yellowface, the mimic is often seen as more reliable, more valuable, and more acceptable than the original. For example, Asian-inspired goods are often more acceptable and valuable than real Asian goods. As John Tchen suggests, "Just as porcelains and goods manufactured in China prompted European pottery makers and designers to copy and make their own versions, so real Chinese performers and Chinese living in lower Manhattan prompted New York's cultural producers to mimicry. Much like chinoiserie or Murphy's *Orphan*, these copiers were often viewed as being superior to the Chinese originals" (1999, 123).[8]

The wariness about real Asians and Asian Americans performing, coupled with the comfort in seeing white European Americans in yellowface suggests that audiences were more familiar and comfortable with stereotypes than with the actual people being portrayed. White European audiences wanted to see Orientalism without seeing Asian and Asian American people and their bodies. Furthermore, it reminds us that, despite systematically excluding Asians and Asian Americans – from the screen, the stage, and even migration and citizenship – US Americans demonstrated enough interest, curiosity, and intrigue about them to construct a complex representational edifice to include them visually and narratively but to exclude them physically. These representations are thus very important to the way real Asians and Asian Amerians were treated and regulated in US society.

Non-Asian and non-Asian American actors played roles of Asian and Asian American characters in Hollywood movies and on television for the entire twentieth century.[9] In fact, just as we were writing this book, *AsianWeek* came out with an article listing their top twenty-five yellowface performances of all time (P. W. Chung, 2007). Many famous white actors have performed in yellowface, notably Mary Pickford, Katharine Hepburn, Shirley MacLaine, Yul Brynner, Fred Astaire, Myrna Loy, Jerry Lewis, Ricardo Montalban, Ingrid Bergman, John Wayne, Marlon Brando, Mickey Rooney, Peter Sellers, Helen Hayes, Peter Lorre, Lon Chaney, and Anthony Quinn.[10] These actors have donned yellowface in such famous films as *The Good Earth* (1937), *Love is a Many Splendored Thing* (1955),[11] and, as we have seen, *Breakfast at Tiffany's* (1961).

When trying out for the lead role of O-Lan in the *The Good Earth* (1937), derived from Pearl Buck's novel of the same title, which was ultimately played by Luise Rainer, Anna May Wong was offered the role of "second wife" (Hye Seung Chung, 2005, 162). Chung suggests this upstaging by Rainer ultimately led Anna May Wong to leave Hollywood and to make a pilgrimage to China. Her displacement exemplifies a moment that perhaps can best be described as an instance of racial disintegration into yellowface-dominant contexts for Asian American actors.

Despite the fact that yellowface most prominently affected Asian and Asian American and white relationships, it also had an impact on Latinas/os. In *The King and I* (1956), Yul Brynner is cast as King Mongkut of Siam (now Thailand), and Deborah Kerr as Anna Leonowens, the school teacher the King sends for to be a teacher for the many children living with him in the palace.[12] Apart from Brynner as the King, several of the other main roles are played in yellowface, such as Martin Benson as Kralahome and Terry Saunders as Lady Thiang. However, most interesting is famed Latina Rita Moreno as the Burmese Tuptim and Latino Carlos Rivas as Lun Tha, for while the casting of Asians or Asian Americans in the main adult roles is scrupulously avoided in this film, Latinos play beside whites in yellowface roles.[13] The one main exception to this among the principals is Patrick Adiarte's role as Prince Chulalongkom, the future king of Siam. Indeed, Asians and Asian Americans did play roles in the background of the film, roles that one might argue add to its *setting*, and roles that produce a kind of narrative and scenic ghetto within the film. For instance, they play some of the secondary wives of the King and the King's children – often off screen or in the background – casting that suggests both the gendered and the infantilizing ways in which Asians and Asian Americans take a back seat to whites and Latinos.[14]

Moving forward in time, an important example of yellowface on television was the 1970s show *Kung Fu*. Even though Bruce Lee was responsible for the concept of the show, he did not land the lead. Instead, David Carradine played the part in yellowface. As Greco Larson explains it:

> Actors of Asian descent are excluded from lead roles on television, too. Despite working with creators of *Kung Fu* (1972–1975), Bruce Lee did not get the role of Kwai Chang Caine in the television show because he looked "too Asian." Instead, the role went to white actor David Carradine, and the character was said to be half American and half Chinese. This casting decision influenced the story lines, making it easier for the writers to portray him as heroic. (2006, 68)

Thus, in terms of labor, yellowface plays a role in typecasting: Asian Americans are not allowed to play roles that *have* to be given to whites or other marginalized groups. The number of jobs Asian Americans missed out on because of yellowface, the lost equity, is amazing when one thinks about it historically *and into the present.* This yellowface logic might also mean that an Asian or Asian American character is transformed into a non-Asian or non-Asian American character, thus erasing these roles for actors. Indeed, this kind of yellowface may lead to the assumption that there are no Asian or Asian American actors to play such roles or that the audience cannot tolerate or envision Asian or Asian American actors.[15]

While it was perhaps more common in earlier historical periods, yellowface is also in practice in more contemporary films and performances. One of the more recognizable moments of contemporary yellowface occurred as recently as 1990, in the musical *Miss Saigon.* Robert B. Ito (1997) describes how Jonathan Pryce, a Caucasian actor, was cast in the lead role of the Eurasian pimp. As we will show in chapter 6, Asian Americans protested, arguing that they were excluded from trying out for the part. The play was pulled as a response, but Pryce was later reinstated based on arguments about the right to artistic license. Because of the lack of roles for Asian Americans in mainstream media, different forms of yellowface persist. White actors playing Asian and Asian American characters continue, such as Alex Borstein's "Ms Swan" from *Mad TV.* Even more recently, in 2007, Eddy Murphy played an Asian American man in *Norbit* (2007)[16] and Christopher Walken played Feng in *Balls of Fury* (2007).

In *Norbit,* Eddie Murphy plays both the title role and that character's adoptive father, "Mr Wong." Through the transformation of Murphy into Mr Wong, an African American man into an elderly Chinese man, black into yellow, the film highlights his comedic and acting talents and the special effects and make-up artistry, while the offensiveness of the racial masquerade and racial humor and the absence of Asian and Asian American actors are all downplayed. Ironically, Mr Wong is a racist with a heart of gold. With copious amounts of silicone, make-up artist Rick Baker sculpted Mr Wong to look "Asian," facilitating Murphy's acting job of playing Asian.

Mr Wong's racism serves as comic relief in the narrative. Having saved the orphan Norbit from curious coyotes outside his orphanage/Chinese restaurant, Mr Wong picks him up, looks at him, and says, "Oh crap. Another black one. Can't give these away. Ooh, you an ugly black one too. You be here long time." Later on in the film, during his philosophical motivational speech to Norbit, he says, "You can't run from your problems, Norbit. Black people run fast, but problem even faster." Norbit replies, "That's kind of racist." Mr Wong answers, "Yes, Wong very racist. I no like black. I no like Jew, either. But black and Jew love Chinese food. Go figure."

An even more recent example of contemporary yellowface appears in television advertising. David Carradine reprises his role in *Kung Fu,* or something akin to that role, when he appears as the "ad guru" in a commercial for Yellow Book, a telephone book marketed nationally within the United States. In the commercial,[17] Carradine wears a black robe and beads and sits atop a long rectangular office table, where three men, advertisers for an unnamed company, say they are searching for a way to market their product to consumers. Carradine offers three "paths" to successful marketing for them: yellow book, yellow book dot com, and allowing yellowbook to advertise on the Internet. The setting is sparse, but Orientalist props (e.g., two lamps on the table in front of Carradine, a mat, possibly bamboo, on which he sits with his legs crossed) along with Orientalist music (possibly a bamboo flute) and Carradine's dialogue, which contains few verbs, code the scene as spiritual or mystical and unmistakably Asian. The ad codes the scene as Oriental in these ways, not to mention the awkward analogy between Carradine's *yellowface* appearance in an advertisement for *Yellow* Book, which further links his star persona to the company. While he is not actually in yellowface make-up, his cameo appearance in yellowface garb and language directly references his earlier yellowface role in *Kung Fu*.

Some might argue that having white or black actors play Asian or Asian Americans at least provides some level of inclusion in the narrative of a film.[18] However, as is apparent in the case of Anna May Wong, in fact, such "inclusion" became part of the wholesale exclusion of Asian and Asian American actors from acting jobs and marginalization within the Hollywood industry.[19] In the case of *Norbit*, not having an Asian or Asian American play Mr Wong allows for his character to be constructed stereotypically as someone who is unapologetically racist. And, as is apparent in the cases of both *Norbit* and *Breakfast at Tiffany's*, yellowface exclusion authorizes racist and degrading representations to be played for comedic effect.

Implicit Yellowface

Explicit yellowface seems straightforward enough, but we want to stress that the general use of yellowface logics goes beyond the explicit; it is much more than the substitution of one (non-Asian) body for another (Asian) one. Yellowface logics, whether explicit or, as this section suggests, implicit, entail employment discrimination, anxiety about miscegenation, the necessity of misrecognition, mocking humor, visual technologies, and Orientalist cultural imaginings. Implicit yellowface works in three primary ways. First, it suggests that there is an "authentic" Asian look and character that can be played. Much as African Americans are sometimes held to standards of racial authenticity, so are Asians and Asian Americans held to such a standard. Confronted with this standard, Asian or Asian American actors often play roles in which they must perform Asianness, hence implicitly playing yellowface. Second, it assumes the similarity of Asians and Asian Americans across the board. Thus, Asians and Asian Americans are understood in the US media to be interchangeable, having no unique qualities worth mentioning, and so they often find themselves having no choice but to play roles of Asian ethnic groups other than ones most aligned with their own ethnic and cultural experiences. According to the same logic, mixed-race Asians and Asian Americans play monoracial Asian and Asian American roles. Finally, as we show through an example of video games, video game players are asked to take on Asian and Asian American racial identities that may or may not align with their own; such identities, however, are highly stereotypical and limited and invite players to participate in an essentializing, typecast Asian and Asian American performance.

Like explicit yellowface, implicit yellowface involves both stage and social actors looking, sounding, and acting according to some notion of normativized, authentic standard of Asianness. The situation is analogous to that of African Americans. For instance, while the white Al Jolson played the most famous blackface role in the 1927 film *The Jazz Singer*, African Americans, such as Bert Williams, also performed in blackface in the Ziegfeld Follies theater revises in the early twentieth century. Blackface during that era was required of performances of blackness, regardless of the racial and ethnic identity and experience of the actor. Asians and Asian Americans, too, have been made up to look more *authentically Oriental*. For instance, as Wong notes, "those roles which Asians do secure often call for stylized and patterned displays, requiring less in the way of acting than a series of directed Oriental affectations, which satisfy the institutional demands of the industry" (1978, 15). Philip Ahn's make-up, costuming, and an accent "played a pivotal role in orientalizing" him (H. S. Chung, 2005, 45). Thus, implicit yellowface requires that actors meet a predefined and arbitrary notion of authenticity and downplay their own existential identities and experiences.

In addition to their being made up to look Oriental, implicit yellowface includes Asian and Asian American actors playing ethnic groups other than those they themselves know most intimately. One might argue that this is not a problem; whites often play non-white ethnic roles. However, implicit yellowface results from the racial expectation that Asians and Asian Americans, regardless of nationality or ethnicity, are all the same and have no unique, cultural differences.

In order to highlight just how often the media treat Asians and Asian Americans as one homogeneous group, we offer the acronym **ASIAN** as

a shorthand way to emphasize this troubling and generalizing practice. While ASIAN might strike readers as a jarring neologism, we
think it important to suggest that current practices of yellowface,
which are part of the structure of the institution and industry of
media production, blur Asian American identity and deploy cultural
essentialism to view "Asian" and "Asian American" people as *All Seem
Identical, Alike, No different.*" ASIAN signals the tremendous violence
done in treating all groups the same and in writing narratives, assigning character roles to actors, in a way that assumes biological and phe-
notypical commonalities. ASIAN, then, is a strong part of explicit and
implicit yellowface and makes up a determining part of yellowface
logics. The use of ASIAN strategies encourages audiences to view Asians
and Asian Americans as inhuman, trivializes their lives and experiences, and facilitates the reproduction of institutional and structural
processes of disempowerment and disenfranchisement, which include
the continuation of Orientalization and the foreignization of Asians
and Asian Americans.

For example, in the film *Daughter of Shanghai* (1937), because of rules
prohibiting on-stage romantic acting between Asian American actors
and white actors, there occurred the unusual circumstance of two
Asian American romantic leads (H. S. Chung, 2005, 164). Nevertheless,
the relationship between Anna May Wong's character and that of
Philip Ahn remains a form of yellowface, since Ahn, who is Korean
American and son of a key Korean anti-Japanese colonial figure, plays
a Chinese American in the film.[20] According to Hye Seung Chung, Ahn
often played both Chinese and Japanese characters.[21] Chung suggests
that, to support Korean nationalism and Korean resistance to Japanese
violence and domination, when Ahn took on the role of evil Japanese
characters he played them as powerfully as he could.[22] In other films,
according to Chung, Ahn took the opportunity, provided to him by the
assumption that all Asian languages are the same, to speak Korean,
while people assumed he was speaking Chinese (see Chung, 2005, 172).

Contemporarily, mixed-race Asian Americans play a significant role
in ASIAN implicit yellowface representations. As the 2006 Asian
American Justice Center's study about Asian Americans on prime-time
television suggests, not only are Asian American roles on TV extremely
limited and not in synch demographically with the size of the Asian
American population, but mixed-race Asian Americans often play
monoracial Asian American roles or monoracial white roles. Examples
are Rob Schneider, best known for being the first Asian American cast
member on *Saturday Night Live*; Mark Paul Gosseler, best known for his
role in *Saved by the Bell*; and Kristen Kreuk, known for her parts in
Smallville and *Edgemont*, and for playing *Snow White: The Fairest of Them
All* (a made-for-TV movie) and without having access to mixed-race

roles. Lou Diamond Phillips, who is of Scottish, Irish, Hawaiian, Cherokee, Filipino, Chinese, and Japanese descent, has played primarily Latino characters, as in the films *La Bamba* (1987) and *Stand and Deliver* (1988), which suggests another way Asian Americans have been typecast.

It is extremely rare for dominant film or television, or dominant media generally, to create a role for a mixed-race Asian American character.[23] While one might read this as a positive sign of the flexibility of mixed-race Asian Americans, it is also clearly a problematic limitation, an extreme one, for mixed-race Asian Americans are confined to playing monoracial roles (only).

The first television sitcom show with an all-Asian American cast, *All-American Girl*, which ran from 1994 to 1995, illustrates the way Asian and Asian American actors are expected to play stereotypical roles; the way they are put in the position of having to play cross-Asian and Asian American ethnic roles; and the way mixed-race actors play monoracial Asian and Asian American roles.[24] The show came under critique for having more actors who were not Korean American than those who were.[25] Amy Hill, who is of Japanese and Finnish descent, Clyde Kusatsu, who is Japanese American, Jodi Long, whose background is Japanese, Chinese, and Scottish, and B. D. Wong, who is Chinese American and famous for his portrayal of Song in David Henry Hwang's *M. Butterfly*, play members of the all-American girl's Korean American family. Only Margaret (Margaret Cho) and her far less central little brother (J. B. Quon) are played by Korean American actors. And, while the show was based loosely on Cho's life, apparently that was not enough. Producers hired an acting coach to help her act more authentically Asian. To mention just a few more examples, Keiko Agena, a Japanese American, plays a Korean American in *Gilmore Girls*. As mentioned earlier, George Takei and Masi Oka (Japanese Americans) and James Kyson Lee (a Korean American) play Asian characters in *Heroes*. Thus, implicit yellowface can mean when Asians or Asian Americans play any Asian or Asian American ethnic role other than the one with which they identify.

What *All-American Girl* (and these other examples) suggests is that Asian American characters are regarded within the mainstream as "the same" and that, within US culture, Asians and Asian Americans are "ambiguous" categories. In US media it is common for Asians and Asian Americans to be lumped together rather than being depicted as members of individual ethnic groups. As Angharad Valdivia (1995) suggests, racial and ethnic ambiguity is economically and politically efficient. In this case it allows for a given ambiguous character to appeal to a broad spectrum of Asian American audiences. Additionally, rather than producers and financiers (studios, advertisers, etc.) having to create ethnic-specific scripts with ethnic-specific roles and hence having to find ethnic-specific actors to play such roles, they can take advantage of the "fudge factor" and write scripts, create roles, and cast characters in accordance with a logic that all Asians are the same. Although Asians and Asian Americans are finally being depicted, it is in a manner that assumes that all Asians are the same, requires a small number of roles that do not stray from the assumed knowledge about them, and do not differ from ethnicity to ethnicity, even within the US context.

Finally, given the pervasiveness of media among youth, it is worth mentioning here the use of implicit yellowface in video games, as well as to describe another variant of implicit yellowface. Indeed, in order to play many games, people are invited to take on an Asian or Asian American identity, but that identity is highly stereotypical and problematic. Anthony Sze-Fai Shiu describes how two video games, *Duke Nukem 3D* and *Shadow Warrior*, allow for white players to play Asian avatars and thus perform "as a racial other for the sake of game play" (2006, 109). Both games are designed and programmed by white men. The problem is that the goal of *Duke Nukem 3D*, set in "post-apocalypse" multiracial Los Angeles, is for the white characters "to save the white women whom the aliens target for 'breeding' " (ibid., 110). Thus, the game relies on "fears of miscegenation, 'biracial' offspring, and murderous black men" and on the premise that "the white race . . . is under attack" (ibid., 111) in order to advance a need for "the regeneration of white power, pride, and identity" (ibid., 112). On the other hand, *Shadow Warrior*, set in Japan, allows gamers unfamiliar with Japan to play an Asian character, while the game mocks Asian/Asian American men as lacking sexual virility.

Each of these three types of implicit yellowface – Asian or Asian American actors performing Asianness, cross-ethnic Asian performance (including mixed-race Asian Americans playing monoracial parts), and people being invited to perform Asianness as part of playing a video game regardless of the player's own racial identity – emphasizes the way in which yellowface produces an Orientalized Asianness. And, like explicit yellowface, each draws attention to the *constructed* nature of representations of Asians and Asian Americans.

Yellowface and Ambivalence

To make sense of yellowface and, in particular, to make sense of the construction of Asian and Asian American characters to the exclusion of Asian and Asian American actors, it is important to recognize the neocolonial context in which these representations are made. That is,

the power relations that ensure Asian American subordination in relation to white dominant superiority in media are part of a broader colonial logic in which other racialized minorities are positioned. We
suggest that, not unlike African Americans, Native Americans, and
Latinas/os, Asian Americans are represented ambivalently within
US media culture through the practice of yellowface. In his postcolo-
nial work, Homi Bhabha attempts to explain the psychic portrayals
of colonized people by the colonizer. He suggests that race is structured ambivalently, that minoritized subjects are constructed through
both a fear and a loathing, on the one hand, and, on the other, according to a desire for and an attraction to the other. The concept of the
stereotype therefore depends fundamentally on an oscillation or fluctuation, if you will, between a kind of racial love on the one hand and
a racial hatred on the other.

Thus, from this perspective, the yellowface performances of Micky
Rooney and Eddie Murphy are ambivalent. On the one hand, a representation of Asianness is desired, or else the yellowface role would not
exist at all. On the other hand, an Asian or Asian American actor
playing that role is undesirable and, hence, is excluded. The excessive
and caricatured performance of a particular notion of Asianness by
non-Asian American actors is ambivalent, both valuing Asianness as a
racial signifier and also fixing it as an essentialized image without
complexity or respect for lived Asian American people and their
experiences. Additionally, the cross-ethnic performance of Asians
and Asian American actors playing roles of Asians and Asian
Americans who do not share the same ethnic cultural experiences
of their character is also ambivalent, both foregrounding the story
of a particular Asian American experience (e.g., the Korean American
family in *All-American Girl* and the Japanese family in *Heroes*)
and yet also demonstrating that the actual ethnic and national experience of Asians and Asian Americans is ultimately irrelevant and
unimportant.

This vacillation, fluctuation, shuttling between and across a
desirous, attractive, and alluring representation and the representation of the degraded Asian and Asian American character is definitive
of the ambivalent construction of the stereotype, the creation of alternative poles neither of which embeds the racialized subject with
humanity, complexity, feelings, or a point of view. Both kinds of representation are objectifying. Yet to some extent both are necessary to the
construction of the stereotype.

Yellowface Logics

The history of Asian Americans in media has been one of various versions of yellowface. Not unlike the history of blackface, the history of yellowface is the projection of non-Asian Americans, a mocking description of how non-Asian Americans have thought about and used the power to create, project, and disseminate representations of who Asian Americans are. While yellowface representations may give us an externalized image to let us know what non-Asian Americans think of Asians and Asian Americans, it is not an Asian American self-representation. *Yellowface logics*, then, are the logics that assume that it is okay for the dominant mainstream to project an image of Asians and Asian Americans that it finds interesting, amusing, demeaning, off-putting, or simply worth projecting. It is the image projected outward for popular consumption, consideration, or discussion – the logic that privileges dominant stereotypes and representations over Asian and Asian American self-representations. The projection of yellowface logics offers up a mask of a people as a definition of the people themselves. It assumes the amusement of a non-Asian audience through false depictions, the equivalence of all Asian and Asian American groups, and the irrelevance of resistance and protests of these groups of such representations. Yellowface logics are demeaning and degrading but illuminate the longstanding power imbalances between whites and Asians and Asian Americans and other racially minoritized groups. In essence yellowface is a performative display that emphasizes unequal power relations and tends to highlight, almost as a sort of ironic depiction, the degree to which Asian Americans are disempowered and unable to create and control their own self-images. It serves as a reminder of Asian American disenfranchisement and disempowerment and the inability to change the United States in accordance with an Asian American vision of it. Yellowface is about inclusion – are Asian Americans to be included or not? – and draws out important issues of identity for Asian Americans.

While yellowface logics assume white authority to produce and distribute representations of Asians and Asian Americans and rely on an assumed power differential (indeed, help to reproduce that power differential), another aspect is that Asian Americans have been forced to view themselves in the media through the vision of the colonizer. The concept of yellowface draws upon and reaffirms Asians and Asian Americans as forever foreigners. And, in terms of the developmental psychology of people, how does an Asian American child figure out who they are by watching a white actor "playing Asian" in yellowface? To be told that you are not good enough to take on a role performed by a Caucasian playing you, and that neither you nor your race can act

– not even as characters meant to represent you – leaves a strong psychological impression.

While we have already discussed several types of yellowface here, we also want the concept to be a useful way to understand a variety of additional types of representations of Asians and Asian Americans, and to encourage students and scholars to test the limits of the logic. We have already mentioned the example of Bruce Lee being unable to land the lead in *Kung Fu* because he looked too Asian. We would argue further that currently there exists a constraining tendency to create Asian and Asian American medical roles. This form of typecasting limits the roles that Asian and Asian American actors can play, essentially walling off other parts for which they have the expertise. Here, the limited career options, opportunities, and representations reveal yellowface discrimination and exclusion. On college campuses across the nation, sumo wrestling contests and geisha parties employ yellowface logics;[26] participating in such events requires compliance with normativized and racialized performances. Even cartoons can be understood through yellowface logics, as in Abercrombie and Fitch's representations of caricatures of Asians/Asian Americans with squinty eyes.

Conclusion

In essence, yellowface is part of a long history about Asian and Asian American inclusion/exclusion. Just as Asians were restricted from migrating, and just as Asian Americans were refused citizenship status, yellowface and its attendant logics helped enforce their limitation, restriction, and exclusion. While perhaps *seeming* to invite and embrace inclusion of Asians and Asian Americans, yellowface ensures the distancing and ultimate abnegation of them.

By not attributing any specificity to Asian Americans, yellowface is ambiguous and aggregative. It helps white viewers feel comfortable and simultaneously be at ease with something they understand to be a diametrically oppositional other, quintessentially alien and inscrutable. Inscrutability is an effect of structural yellowface, the denial of Asian American subjectivity and complexity, which provides no insight into lived realities and experiences. Hence, when people encounter Asians and Asian Americans in their daily lives and compare them to the images on screen, there is a misalignment, a lack of parallel. We understand just how inhumane such images are when we, as Asian Americans, are greeted with "ching chong ching chong" or people breaking out into Bruce Lee martial arts moves at the sight of us. We ask, How can those who have never encountered or met an

Asian or Asian American relate when there is no repertoire of humane images of them from which to draw?

In this chapter, we explained how yellowface has a historical base in Asian and Asian American exclusion in labor, representation, and cultural practice. By looking at explicit yellowface, we saw that Asian and Asian Americans actors and actresses were excluded from working in Hollywood while simultaneously being mocked and made fun of in a form of racial masquerade. Explicit yellowface becomes both a signal to Asians and Asian Americans of their inferiority and a joke from which non-Asian and non-Asian American audiences can take pleasure. We also see the prevalence of yellowface logics in representations of implicit yellowface, where an "authentic" Asian look is determined by non-Asians and where all Asians are assumed to look, sound, and *be* the same and are thus cast as such. We discussed yellowface as part of a larger ambivalent discourse and representation of Asians and Asian Americans. Finally, we explained the logic of yellowface within the larger process of representation in media culture, showing how yellowface logic subjugates and marginalizes Asians and Asian Americans within the dominant media and reminds them of their disenfranchisement.

The entire practice of yellowface not only reveals Hollywood's participation in the social surveillance of miscegenation, but it also implies the superiority of white actors in even acting "Asian." Moreover, having these representations be *the* representation sends the message that this is what Asians and Asian Americans have to do/be in order to make it in the acting profession.[27] There is a relationship between Orientalism and yellowface: the arrogance of Westerners telling the story of the Orient better than "Orientals" is replicated in the arrogance of believing that Asians cannot act; therefore, white people must show them how to do it. Perhaps, also, white actors playing Asians and Asian Americans reveals an assumption that audiences *prefer* and are more comfortable with white actors.

Historically, because of anti-miscegenation laws and also because of Hollywood's own rules regarding interracial romance, Asian Americans were unable to play romantic leads in films before the regulations were changed in the 1950s. Additionally, however, the anomalous films discussed by Hye Seung Chung (2005) – *Daughter of Shanghai* (1937) and *King of Chinatown* (1939) – are indeed that – anomalous – in their depiction of romance between two Asian Americans, but were simultaneously an effect of rules against white–Asian romantic relations.

The inclusion of Asian Americans even to this day is fraught with ambivalence. It is not clear whether or not mainstream media really want Asian Americans. The promise to immigrants of participation in and having a part of the "American dream," therefore, is an ambivalent one. With "inclusion" comes the experience of "exclusion." We base this argument on the ambivalent inclusion of Asian Americans and the lack of cultural specificity, recognition, respect, and appreciation given to actual ethnic and cultural diversity. For Asian Americans, "inclusion" often entails a performance of yellowface tropes, representations, and stereotypes within dominant mainstream media. Ironically, this inclusion produces the Asian and Asian American as forever foreign.

The ambivalence about their inclusion in the media sends a strong message about identity to Asian Americans. Not seeing pictures that look like you up on the silver or plasma screen implies a lack of importance and relevance. Not seeing actors given roles suggests that producers do not think Asian Americans can act, or perhaps speak fluently, and possibly that they are not attractive and would not make good role models. The psychic dimension of an accumulation of experiences of being non-existent in media over one's life time no doubt has the potential to have a complex and powerful effect on the psyche of Asian Americans. The psychic effects may include the lesson that Asians and Asian Americans do not know how to perform *themselves* on screen or in real life. If whites know best how to play Asians authentically, as the logic of yellowface goes, then Asian Americans must be tutored to learn what they do not know about their own authenticity.

Seeing oneself in a mocking pose repeatedly is a dehumanizing experience, one that tells people over and over they are objects, that they have no control over how their representation appears in public, and that others have the right to control that image and tell stories and make physical jokes at their expense. Moreover, as we have suggested, such images also imply one needs to act in this way in order to be accepted in the mainstream, or to be accepted at all.

CHAPTER 04

Problematic Representations of Asian American Gender and Sexuality

In beginning a study of Asian and Asian American gender representations, one might assume from the outset that dominant media portray Asian and Asian American men differently from Asian and Asian American women, and thus one might search for contrasting media representations. After all, as Laura Kang suggests, historically dominant mainstream culture has imagined Asian and Asian American men and women to be very different.[1] Asian women were constructed as "aesthetically pleasing, sexually willing and speechless" as well as "dark" and "primitive" (2002, 74). As Kang suggests further: whereas Asian women were "exotic and enticing, the men were almost always portrayed as predatory figures . . . as ugly or loathsome" (ibid., 75),[2] as "tyrannical and lecherous, cruel in their treatment of their women while lusting after the Euro-American woman." They are an "enemy rival" who is "inferior in both physique and ethics" and bent on "territorial conquest" (ibid., 77).

Thus, on the one hand, while Asian women were often depicted as passive objects, men were constructed as villains. After realizing that representations do differ, however – indeed, that differences between Asian and Asian American men and women have been conspicuously foregrounded – it is possible to make two additional observations: first, *both* men and women are represented in troubling ways; and second, representations of Asian and Asian American men and women may be *cut from the same cloth* and therefore may *work in concert*.

One purpose of this chapter, then, is to understand the way media represent Asian and Asian American men and women differently. However, simply juxtaposing images of Asian American men with those of Asian American women is not sufficient to explain why media have produced derogatory images of *both*. We suggest that when media highlight gender in order to differentiate men from women, as we will show, they draw attention away from the interrelated phenomena of gender, sexuality, and race. Thus, in order to highlight their interrelationship, we take an *intersectional* approach that attempts to understand race, sexuality, and gender as logically interlocking social phenomena.[3] Such an approach has been central to work in women's and gender studies; however, intersectional analysis has been less often used in media studies research.

One reason Asian and Asian American men and women have been represented differently, and interrelatedly, has to do with the history of colonialism. Colonial logics have been fundamental to the way people of color have been represented in Western media.[4] The juxtaposition of the sexually alluring and available Asian and Asian American woman with the villainous and therefore undesirable Asian and Asian American man suggests two things: First, it implies that the woman is free to enter into a romantic relationship with someone other than the Asian and Asian American man (i.e., the white man). Second, it suggests that the Asian and Asian American man, prominently featured as undesirable if not loathsome, will be found to be an inferior romantic competitor, and therefore, within the storyline, justifiably forgotten or eliminated. Thus, her desirability combined with his undesirability ensures his eliminability.

Moreover, because the Asian and Asian American man is so undesirable, indeed barbaric and uncivilized,[5] not only is the Asian and Asian American woman available, but there is grounds for her rescue from the grips of Asian and Asian American male patriarchy, an escape from a most horrible fate (Kabbani, 1986, 27).[6] This particular construction of Asian masculine savagery parallels that of colonial narratives of Native Americans. As Rana Kabbani has written about colonial stereotypes of Native Americans, "The forging of racial stereotypes and the confirmation of the notions of savagery were vital to the colonialist world view. In colonial America, for instance, there was a systematic attempt to portray the Indian as an abductor of women, a killer of children, and a collector of scalps, as an apology for white brutality against him" (ibid., 4). Just as the Native American woman required rescue from the "savage Indian," so too do white women and coveted Asian and Asian American women need to be saved from the deceptive, barbaric, and abusive Asian and Asian American men, justifying their rescue by white men.[7]

It is important to understand that media work to construct men and women differently and that such representations are part of a longstanding colonial logic that constructs men and women's representations interrelatedly. Still, scholars of gender and sexuality have begun to rethink the way gender representations operate. Thus, this chapter discusses the complex ways in which media represent whiteness as well as the ways they have produced generalizing stereotypes. Additionally, the chapter provides both historical and contemporary examples and complicates our study of stereotypes through an intersectional analysis of Asian and Asian American gender and sexuality. We use the example of online pornography to illustrate how gender and sexuality are interrelated and also focus attention on the way masculinity, in particular, is constructed. Throughout the chapter we provide a re-reading of gender representations using an *intersectional* scholarly approach that sees relationships among race, sexuality, and gender and complicates the historical gendered[8] model of how media stereotypes work to explain how today's gendered representations are, indeed, also racialized and sexualized.

Gender, race, and sexuality are all part of an interlinked system of representation that helps describe and define who has power in relationship to others. In this interlocking system, some are constructed as having power and dominance, and others are depicted as being powerless and submissive, and sometimes subservient. The subordination of some is requisite for the empowerment of others.[9] In this world of media representations, visible differences are highlighted and sometimes accentuated so as to clarify who has power and who does not. Whiteness comes to have meaning in relation to the representation of racialized others. As the late Ruth Frankenberg suggested, whiteness is a product of *negative difference*; people come to understand themselves as white through a process by which they know who they are by what they are not. Thus, Frankenberg suggests, the only way white people can understand themselves as white is by contrasting their experiences with those of people of color (1996). Another way of saying this in relation to Asian and Asian Americans is that whiteness becomes meaningful when contrasted to Asianness. Whiteness is therefore a default racial identity, an identity that does not come from the inside so much as being defined by what is not observed to be constitutive of the other. We suggest further that, like whiteness, gender is also a product of negative difference; gender is meaningful when contrasted to what it *is not*. So, gender, race, and sexual representation help create a map or template that one can study and examine in order to find out who is in power and, relatedly, who is powerless. People are taught and reminded of their social position through all three kinds of representation – race, gender, and sexuality – which is why we need to study media representations intersectionally.

Ambivalent Representations of Asian and Asian American Women

Throughout the history of US media, common stereotypes of men and women have emerged. It is worth considering those repetitive and dense representations, or what Patricia Hill Collins and Darrell Hamamoto both call "controlling images,"[10] as they appear so often, even in contemporary media representations of Asian and Asian American men and women.

To understand all three kinds of representation, it is important to consider representations of women in media as part of an *ambivalent dialectic*, two contrasting portraits that appear to be opposite but in fact function together to represent women in problematic ways; for white women, it is the dialectic of the virgin and the whore. This notion that women must either be chaste or perpetually sexually available constructs women's sexuality through heterosexual masculine normative desire for control and possession. For African American women, the ambivalent dialectic is the happy to serve "mammy" or the sexually tempting "Jezebel." Again, both media representations of women define her as available to serve men, and each side of the dialectic helps solidify the other: the virgin and the mammy become alternatives to the whore and the Jezebel and, as such, gain definition and meaning through their interrelationship.

For Asian Americans, the reigning stereotypes for women related to the virgin and whore dialectic have been the Lotus Blossom[11] and Madame Butterfly, on the one hand, and the Dragon Lady, on the other. The Lotus Blossom and Madame Butterfly are depictions of women as sexually attractive and alluring and demure, passive, obedient, physically non-imposing, self-sacrificial, and supplicant (especially to white male suitors). Thus, Asian and Asian American women are constructed both as sexual objects and as lacking power; indeed, the lack of power is intrinsic to the representation of sexual desirability. The primary distinction between the Lotus Blossom and the Madame Butterfly is that the latter is tragically self-sacrificial. She is so self-sacrificial that she is ultimately willing to take her own life either to save a child or children, or for the sake of her man.

On the other side of the dialectic is the Dragon Lady, who is sinister and surreptitious and often functions as a feminized version of yellow peril. She is untrustworthy, deceitful, conniving, and plotting, and she may use sex or sexuality to get what she wants, including the object of her sexual desire. She is a dark force, whose sexuality may be masculinized, whose heterosexuality may be cast as either incomplete, unusual in some way, or simply unattractive. Whereas both the Lotus

Blossom and the Dragon Lady representations configure women as sexually available, the Lotus Blossom image renders sexual availability passive and non-threatening and the Dragon Lady construction imagines sexual availability as a threat.

It is important to state here that, while the ambivalent dialectic of Lotus Blossom/Madame Butterfly and Dragon Lady is a useful one in describing broad patterns of media representation, not all roles an actor plays may fall within the stereotype. However, a given actor may be more or less typecast in stereotypical roles. Additionally, as Peter Feng (2000) and Cynthia Liu (2000) have suggested, audiences may have very different reactions, interpretations, and understandings even of stereotypical performances, depending on the social, cultural, political, or historical context.

Despite the complexity of representation, it is nevertheless the case that the image of the Lotus Blossom appears notably during the historical era following World War II. In that period, both films and television shows constructed Asian women as subservient, obsequious, and willing to sacrifice themselves for the pleasures of men.[12] Their own desires and interests – in a sense their subjectivities – are not even secondary to men's; they are simply non-existent. For example, Nancy Kwan, who played the title character in *The World of Suzie Wong* (1960), was the quintessential "hooker with a heart of gold," constructed as willing to do anything to win her white male suitor's affection.[13]

In the 1957 film *Sayonara*, we see both the Lotus Blossom representation and a version of the Madame Butterfly variant. Set in 1951 Japan, *Sayonara* is a story about a decorated air force pilot who falls in love with a famed Japanese Matsubayashi Girl, a dramatic stage performer. The couple, Lloyd (Marlon Brando) and Hana-Ogi (Miiko Taka), are separated by cultural anti-miscegenation on both sides. On his side, the air force doesn't want men to fraternize, or even be seen in public, with "indigenous" Japanese women. On the other hand, Matsubayashi Girls, too, have strict rules against fraternization. Even more powerfully, Americans killed Hana-Ogi's father and shot her brother. But, even as Lloyd and Hana-Ogi challenge anti-miscegenation through their commitment to interracial romance, Hana-Ogi's freedom comes in the form of a liberation out of strict gender behavior into gendered domesticity. Thus, as she says at one point, her dream is to be a woman, a mother, and a lover.

While the film centers this primary narrative of Lloyd and Hana-Ogi's romance, a second romance informs the first. In it Joe Kelly (Red Buttons) has fallen in love with Katsumi (Miyoshi Umeki), and they marry, despite the military's discouragement of such relations. The military then attempts to ship Kelly back to the United States without his wife Katsumi. After watching a Kabuki doll tragedy in which a man and his wife die together rather than live apart, Kelly and Katsumi mutually commit suicide, dying in each other's arms. Prior to this suicide, Katsumi appears in several scenes that position her more as an object and less as a subject. In one, after they have been married, Red Buttons asks Lloyd to kiss Katsumi to congratulate her, which he does on the lips. In another, Katsumi makes food for both Kelly and Lloyd. Kelly ultimately convinces Lloyd that Japanese women are desirable romantic objects by using Katsumi as an example of the benefits of being served. Thus, in one important scene, shown in part in *Slaying the Dragon* (1988), Katsumi gives Kelly a bath, during which he says to Lloyd, "This is the life, ain't it, Ace?"

Despite the strong social message challenging racial discrimination and anti-miscegenation, the depiction of women as selfless and sacrificial, and as commodities for white US military personnel, remains overriding in the film.

In contrast with the Lotus Blossom and Madame Butterfly controlling images, Anna May Wong was typecast in film roles that came to personify the Dragon Lady stereotype. In one of her early films, *Daughter of the Dragon* (1931), she plays the daughter of the arch-devil Fu Manchu – hence the progeny of the icon of yellow peril. Before that, in 1924, Anna May Wong was cast in the role of an accomplice to the male Mongol villain in *Thief of Bagdad* (1924). Not unsurprisingly, in perhaps her most famous role, in *Shanghai Express* (1932), she plays a Dragon Lady figure, seen in shadow throughout much of the film. Perhaps the most memorable part of her role is when she stabs the man who has raped her, the Chinese villain, in the back.[14] While this act ends up saving the white characters from the villain, she is able to take that action only because of her own duplicitous nature; Shanghai Lily (Marlene Dietrich), for example, is also sexually compromised in the narrative (constructed as whore) but does not kill the villain when he attempts to engage her sexually. Thus, her compromised sexuality is redeemed in part through its contrast with Anna May Wong's more frightening, dark, and violent sexuality. The irony is that it is Anna May Wong's character, not that of Marlene Dietrich, whose rape becomes the exigence for the rapist's murder.

Roles conforming to the image of the Dragon Lady continue, even today, decades after Anna May Wong played parts that helped create it. While she does not play only Dragon Lady roles, and while there are many ways to interpret them, Lucy Liu has appeared in such parts in *Payback* (1991) and *Kill Bill* (2003), as well as in *Ally McBeal* (Greco Larson, 2006, 71). In *Payback* she plays Pearl, a dominatrix/hit-woman. Pearl is in bed with Val (played by Gregg Henry) when confronted by Porter, Mel Gibson's character. During the scene Pearl invokes her dominatrix side, touching and groping Val. However, when Porter readies to

Figure 4.1   Anna May Wong in *Daughter of the Dragon*

pistol-whip Val, Pearl stops him and says, "Allow me," and starts abusing and beating him. In *Kill Bill*, Liu plays O-ren Ishii, who kills her father's murderer while on top of him before sexual intercourse. Even in dramedy television, the Dragon Lady emerges; for example, we will show how Lucy Liu's character Ling Woo on the television show *Ally McBeal* epitomizes the Dragon Lady.

Ling Woo is a no-nonsense lawyer who is sexually forward, what Rachel Dubrofsky describes as a "sexual viper" (2002, 274); when she comes on screen the music for the Wicked Witch of the West from the *Wizard of Oz* plays. At times, she appears to be overly litigious to a fault. Ling both uses sex as a tool and is constructed ultimately as an object.

As Dubrofsky writes: "[Ling] constantly maintains that she has no interest in sex except as a tool to hold onto a man. In fact, it is hard to figure out why Ling would want a man because she treats all men with utter contempt. . . . she will go to great lengths to reify her sexual currency as a woman" (ibid., 273).

Ling Woo is constructed as having, if not mystical, then unusual, inventive, and unique sexual abilities and potentially threatening sexual desires. In a slightly different role, Lucy Liu's recent cameo spot on *Ugly Betty* positions her character initially as sexually unattractive and bookish. Later, however, she not only becomes sexually assertive and vamp-like, but sexually dangerous in her desire for revenge.

Laura Kang suggests that such images exist even in many other Hollywood films, such as *Come See the Paradise* (1990), *Year of the Dragon* (1985), and *Thousand Pieces of Gold* (1991). Despite the many differences among these films, all of the "three narratives revolve centrally around an interracial sexual relationship between a white male and an Asian female" (2002, 78).[15] What is key is the way those relationships parallel the historical, colonial media representation of gender – each film ultimately reaffirms "the primacy of the white male over both the Asian woman and the Asian males of her community" (ibid.).

In examples of the Lotus Blossom and Madame Butterfly, it becomes clear that racial representations are gendered and that they pivot on the interplay between gendered people as either threat or desirable object. Their gender renders them as a convenient sexual object, and their race as exotic. That the suitors in these films were often white US military personnel suggests a particular colonial relationship between the Lotus Blossom image and the US war encounters with Asian nations. Like the Lotus Blossom's construction of women's non-agency, and indeed irrelevance, Asian and Asian American women more generally are represented as substitutable, as simply a placeholder or stand-in for all Asian and Asian American women. Renee Tajima writes, "Asian women in American cinema are interchangeable in appearance and name, and are joined together by the common language of non-language-that is, uninterpretable chattering, pidgin English, giggling, or silence" (1989, 309). When women are constructed as endlessly substitutable, they are meaningless as individuals, and have meaning only when serving as iconic representations of a generic type. As such, variants of stereotypes of Asian and Asian American women in media have historically been quite limited.

Asian American Men and Media

We have seen how stereotypical representations of Asian and Asian American women are well ensconced within mainstream representation; representations of Asian and Asian American men, too, are constructed in quite limiting ways. As we discussed in chapter 2, Asian and Asian American men have often been characterized as a yellow peril, as physical threats, gangsters, or martial arts foes. However, they are also largely constructed as asexual and nerdy, as delivery boys or computer geeks, and ordinarily as physically unattractive. Once again, we can see a representation of the ambivalent dialectic, with yellow peril discourse requiring emasculation as a way to cover over anxiety over power relations. An example of the representation of Asian and Asian American men as asexual is the character of Long Duk Dong in the film *Sixteen Candles* (1984). Long Duk Dong, played by Gedde Watanabe, is a geeky foreign exchange student with a heavy Asian accent, unaware of US social norms, who lives with Samantha, the lead character (Molly Ringwald), and her family.[16] Long Duk Dong does not attract the typically beautiful girl; rather, he courts the large-breasted, masculine, female jock named "Lumberjack" (Debra Pollack). In one scene, Lumberjack is riding a stationary exercise bicycle and Dong is sitting on her lap. Afterward, Dong is riding the bike while Lumberjack is lifting barbells. Thus, the gender roles are switched; Dong is feminized, does exercises stereotypically configured to be feminine, and rides on Lumberjack's lap. On the other hand, Lumberjack is masculine, both larger and stronger than Dong. While this representation aims to provide comic relief, it both feminizes Asian American men and simultaneously constructs alternative gender and sexuality as aberrant. Similarly, the Asian American character in the film *The Goonies* (1985) is the clumsy yet nerdy and crafty Data. A lovable character, Data nevertheless still provides bumbling comic relief, much like Mr Yunioshi from *Breakfast at Tiffany's* (1961) and Long Duk Dong.

This representation of the asexual, geeky computer nerd continues to appear in contemporary media representations. In the television show *Beauty and the Geek*, many of the geeks are Asian American men romantically interested in the typical, often white, "beauty." Even films that complicate or debunk the portrayal, such as *Harold and Kumar Go to White Castle* (2004) and *Better Luck Tomorrow* (2002), use the representation of failed Asian and Asian American masculinity in order to set up the movie and the joke before deconstructing it. Overall, the dominant culture constructs Asian and Asian American men as desexualized, hence as less powerful than and inferior to all other men, be they white, African American, Latino, or other.

In his study of the film *Showdown in Little Tokyo* (1991), Thomas Nakayama illustrates this relational aspect of Asian and Asian American men in the media. His analysis illustrates particularly well the importance of studying race, gender, and sexuality simultaneously rather than as discrete and separate social phenomena. Nakayama suggests that the representation of the Asian American man in the film functions to reconstitute white masculinity. Thus, Detective Kenner (Dolph Lundgren) works with Johnny Murata (Brandon Lee) to fight crime.[17] It is by reading this interrelationship between the representation of the two men in the film that Nakayama is able to argue that Murata's representation serves to bolster Kenner's; hence, through the depiction of Murata as physically inferior to Kenner, heterosexual white masculinity is reaffirmed. While the film constructs Asian masculinity as threatening, drawing a connection between Asian men's bodies and violent Yakuza ganghood, phallic white heterosexual masculinity ends up being physically superior and ultimately wins the day. As Kenner's buddy, Murata is constructed as the less virile, feminized sidekick who, in contrast to both Kenner and the yellow peril villains, helps by way of contrast to make obvious Kenner's massive power and potency.

In the film *Deuce Bigalow: European Gigalow* (2005), Asian male sexuality and inferiority function as a joke. When trying to quit his job, Lil Kim, the Asian male prostitute played by Topper, is instructed by T. J., his African American pimp, played by Eddie Griffin, to "go make me some money." Lil Kim replies, "No way. I take my three inches elsewhere." Here, the stereotype of Asian male sexual inferiority works alongside a recognition of Asian American racial inferiority to produce a punchline for the joke, meant to be funny for non-Asian and non-Asian American viewers and an insult to Asian and Asian American audiences.

The construction of white masculinity through the impotence of Asians continues to be widespread in media. In a commercial for Priceline, William Shatner plays the samurai-trained "Negotiator." While not in yellowface, and although wearing a business suit, Shatner nevertheless uses his "natural" martial arts skills to outflank the one nameless opponent sent to fight him, flings a throwing star expertly at the leader of his foes, pinning his robed arm to the table, and easily catches two darts thrown at him with his hands, while his foes, Asians clustered around a computer at a table, are unable to think of an affordable way to buy a hotel room for every member of their martial arts team. The Negotiator magically appears at the dojo, uses these symbols of Asia in expert and superior ways, and presents Priceline as the solution to the complex problem none of the large grouping of arbitrary Asians could solve.

Within Asian American studies, longtime activist, writer, and scholar Frank Chin has worked to reclaim masculinity for Asian

American men.[18] Railing against the dominant racist media depiction of Asian and Asian American men as asexual, ineffectual, and the like, Chin argues in favor of an "heroic" authentic Asian masculinity in contrast to the "fake" masculinity also represented in the work of Maxine Hong Kingston and Amy Tan, for instance. In arguing against such a position, Cynthia Liu suggests that, "in arguing that the racism of early Hollywood filmmakers maligns images of Asian American men even as the same racism 'benignly' co-opts, sexualizes, and domesticates Asian American women's images, the implicit critical project becomes one of propping up hetero-normative, Asian-masculine desirability" (2000, 26). Jachinson Chan maintains Chin "is problematic precisely because he does not challenge mainstream myths of manhood" (2001, 13), myths, we would argue, that have served to construct Asian American men as asexual and inferior. Thus, aligning himself with King-Kok Cheung, who argues for a more complex notion of Asian and Asian American sexuality, Chan looks for "different models of Chinese American masculinities [that] will lead to a strategically indeterminate, non-committal masculinity that embraces selective socially constructed feminine roles without fears of effeminization and homosexualization" (ibid., 20).

As is clear in Liu's and Chan's comments, in challenging dominant colonial imagery of Asians and Asian Americans, the goal should not simply be to reclaim a version of dominant white masculinity for Asian and Asian American men; nor should it be to find an historical masculinity that in some ways allows for a parallel structuring of gender within Asian and Asian American communities to that of dominant white society and culture; nor is it to diminish or even overlook ways Asian and Asian American masculinity functions to dominate Asian and Asian American women. Rather, our goal is to challenge the traditional way dominant media culture has constructed gender of both Asian and Asian American men and women and then to chart out an approach that encourages consideration, appreciation, and celebration and critical analysis of a multiplicity of racial, gendered, sexual, and classed identities.

In April of 2004, *Details* magazine published an issue with a one-page spread picturing an Asian American man with the caption "Gay or Asian?" Asian American organizations, LGBT organizations, and individuals protested the image. For instance, Asian Media Watch contacted officials at *Details* objecting to the item. As Asian Media Watch indicates, Daniel Peres, editor-in-chief of the magazine, published an apology statement on April 16, 2004, that read:

> Over the past three weeks, I have received an unprecedented number of letters regarding the "Gay or Asian?" piece, which ran in the April issue of *Details*.

It has been made abundantly clear to me that this story, which is part of an ongoing series challenging male cultural stereotypes, was insensitive, hurtful, and in poor taste – an obvious point that I regret not recognizing prior to publication.

There's a line that should never be crossed in any satirical humor, and *Details* crossed it. I, on behalf of the magazine, deeply regret this misstep, and apologize to those who were offended.

Sincerely,
Daniel Peres[19]

On April 21, members of the Asian American LGBT community met with *Details* for further discussions. At the meeting, they objected to the fact that the article made gay Asian Americans feel they had to choose between the gay community and the Asian American community – that it strongly suggested that gay Asians and Asian Americans were not part of both communities. They also argued that it made them feel they did not exist or were not seen to matter, and suggested that the article increased the level of homophobia and reproduced negative images of the Asian American community.[20] Gay Asian & Pacific Islander Men of New York (GAPIMNY) maintained the item was homophobic, drew on stereotypical ideas about Asian Americans, implied Asian Americans were not American, suggested people could not be both gay and Asian, and perpetuated the invisibility of gay Asian Americans within society.[21]

The trouble over *Details* suggests Asian and Asian American men's sexuality continues to matter in terms of feelings of inclusion, citizenship, empowerment, and belonging. The article rhetorically drives a wedge between heterosexual and gay men, demeaning both and reminds us that dominant culture regularly constructs homosexuality as deviant. Within that, it constructs Asian American gay men as unusually deviant. And it suggests Asian American men are de facto homosexual. As a whole, then, the article works to put into question gay sexuality *and* the sexuality of Asian and Asian American men (including gay Asians and Asian Americans) more broadly. It also encourages heterosexual Asian and Asian American men not to identify with the experiences of gay Asian and Asian American men and to downplay and to close off homosexual desires, care for men, and sexual feelings in general, hence contributing to a heteronormative and homophobic culture.

Asian Americans in Internet Porn

Studying gender representations in mainstream media is one thing, but one of the most, if not the most, powerful media industries is that of pornography. Pornographic images are found throughout society as well as the increasingly dominant medium of the Internet. Thus, it is important to consider at least briefly the way in which gender relations function in pornography. To do this, we draw on scholars who have examined Asian and Asian American media representations in pornography, each of whom have clarified how gender functions in pornography in a similar way to how it functions in mainstream media. In her essay about Asian Americans and pornography, Thuy Linh Nguyen Tu suggests that "the presence of Asian bodies" is in part responsible for the "phenomenal success of the online adult industry" (2003, 267). Speaking of the presence of porn sites on the World Wide Web, Tu claims that "Asian porn sites are, according to some statistics, pulling in 25 to 30 percent of [the online adult industry's] revenue" (ibid.). She suggests that such sites are rather unimaginative in their depiction of Asian women, relying on assumptions such as "they are exotic and hold limitless sexual knowledge, yet docile and eager to please" (ibid., 268).

While the power of the pornography industry to define Asian and Asian American sexuality is immense, it is important to note that, despite this tremendously powerful image machinery, critical responses to such representations are possible. Tu discusses Mimi Thi Nguyen's website "Exoticize This," which provides feminist resources as an alternative for those looking for Asian porn (2003, 269).[22] Similarly, as Tu demonstrates, others such as Prema Murthy, Kristina Wong, and Greg Pak have created web alternatives that challenge prevailing notions of gender and sexuality, working from stereotypes that might lead Internet users to their site and then challenging them.[23]

In his examination of gay male pornography, Canadian filmmaker Richard Fung (1991) suggests a gender relations factor in the way male–male sex is mediated, with Asian men consistently constructed as the "bottom" for white men. Thus, Asian men are portrayed in the feminine role, as passive, vulnerable, and weak. They play the parts of the subordinate laborers and are constructed for the look of the gay white male. While Fung does not say this, what we can infer is that Asian and Asian American desire is not central to these pornographic plots. As Jachinson Chan writes, "Fung's critique of the ways in which gay Asian men are represented in gay porn parallels the ways in which heterosexual Asian men are portrayed in mainstream media" (2001, 16).

Indeed, Greg Pak critiques the pornography industry's (and possibly mainstream media's) treatment of Asian and Asian American men and women. Specifically addressing the lack of Asian–Asian sexual relations, Pak's short film *Asian Pride Porn* (2000) is a satirical infomercial that touts the presence of "smart Asian women and sexually empowered Asian men." As if in response to Fung's inference that Asian and

Asian American desire is not central in most pornography, Pak's *Asian Pride Porn* centers Asian and Asian American desire, despite its heteronormativity.

Looking at the pornography industry and critiques of it, particularly of gay male pornography, highlights the importance of considering race, gender, and sexuality together, as well as possible locations for critical analysis and response to dominant imagery, as we will show.

Re-reading Gender through an Attention to Sexuality

Despite the powerful gendered representations of Asian and Asian American women and men in mainstream and pornographic media, recent scholarship on sexuality allows us to rethink the binaries of gender and to imagine new possibilities for gendered representation. To conclude this chapter, we analyze Bruce Lee as someone who challenged the dominant media representation of masculinity and reperformed and re-represented Asian and Asian American masculinity. Thus, he offered a new powerful representation of Asian and Asian American men as martial artists. That image challenged the representation of physical inferiority and weakness of an earlier era. Yet such a portrayal became its own kind of controlling image.

Recent scholarship, however, has worked to rethink the "hardness" of Bruce Lee's image and to reimagine his representation in ways that challenge gender and sexual norms. Bruce Lee, a powerful martial artist and *sifu* (master) and later a movie star of international prominence, became part of popular cultural lore, with intense fan followings that continue to this day around the world. For example, he has been memorialized in Mostar, Bosnia, where a statue was erected in tribute to him and perhaps as a model to smooth political tensions, as he represents strength, peace, and heroism. Additionally, he has been memorialized as a figure in Madame Tussaud's wax museum in Hong Kong. While many things account for Bruce Lee's mythic status, Vijay Prashad argues that he was a powerful anti-imperialist icon for poor and suffering peoples worldwide. As Prashad writes, "With his bare fists and his *nanchakus*,[24] Lee provided young people with the sense that we could be victorious, like the Vietnamese guerrillas, against the virulence of international capitalism" (2003, 54).

"Lee was born in San Francisco's Chinese Hospital on November 27, 1940" (Chan, 2001, 75), and entered pictures when he made his first film, *Golden Gate Girl* (1941), at the age of three months. He went to college at the University of Washington, Seattle, where he gained first-hand knowledge of Asian American life by working as a busboy and as a martial arts instructor of Wing Chun kung fu. He left college and

Figure 4.2   Bruce Lee's Figure in Madame Tussaud's in Hong Kong

married Linda Emery; soon thereafter their son Brandon was born and then their daughter Shannon. As a *sifu*, he trained Chuck Norris, Roman Polanski, and Kareem Abdul-Jabbar, among many others. Before gaining fame in pictures later in his career, Lee played the masked role of Kato in the 1966 television series *The Green Hornet*. He was arguably the conceptual designer for the television series *Kung Fu*, but producers denied him the part as the lead, instead giving it to white actor David Carradine.[25] Not unlike Anna May Wong, who was passed over for the lead in *The Good Earth* (1937), Lee left the United States, moved to Hong Kong, and eventually starred in twenty films there before returning home. Two of these films were particularly memorable: *Fist of Fury* (1971) and *The Chinese Connection* (1972). As Chan suggests, after these blockbusters were released, Hollywood producers changed their tune, and offered Lee "million-dollar movie contracts and guest appearances on talk shows such as *The Tonight Show* starring Johnny Carson" (2001, 74). Lee joined hands with Raymond Chow to form Concord Productions and co-produced his final two films, *Return of the Dragon* (1972) and *Enter the Dragon* (1973). He died at the age of only thirty-two, in 1973, and every year people come from all over the world to view his shrine in Seattle.

Chan suggests Bruce Lee offered an image that allowed for sensuality and sexuality, anchored by his martial arts, centered the Chinese male body, and offered "a disengagement of his masculine identity from the patriarchal society he inhabits in his films by exuding an ambi-sexual identity" (2001, 18). Chan sees Lee as constructing a marginalizing masculinity because he was not accepted by US culture. At first glance, some might imagine Lee constructs a macho, physical, manly "hegemonic masculinity." Certainly, his martial arts profession would suggest as much; he is, after all, "a hero who dominates his opponents by using excessive violence" (ibid., 77). And it is certainly arguable that Lee inadvertently became the progenitor of a stereotype that still exists for Asian American men, and to some extent Asian American women, as born martial artists. Still, as Chan suggests, his characters "are not typically patriarchal or misogynistic[; they] do not oppress the female characters nor do they exhibit an exaggerated James Bond-like heterosexism" (ibid.). For Chan, Lee has an ambiguous masculinity, indeterminate in its meaning, and resistant of patriarchal and hegemonic masculinities.

However, while Lee self-consciously displays his body in sometimes sexually desirable ways and is on display for broad admiration of his Chinese body, and while he neither flaunts heterosexism nor binarizes heterosexuality and homosexuality, one could read his ambivalence, which Chan sees as "unresolved" (2001, 91), as a kind of asexuality. Mimi Nguyen suggests: "The lack of sexual conquest or encounter is a striking feature of his cinematic oeuvre, through which the Lee character is inscribed with asexuality or quasi-Confucian asceticism" (2007, 273). For Nguyen, Bruce Lee provides a "hard masculinity," a "muscular fighting body that precipitates the resolution of conflict" (ibid., 281). In contrast, as Nguyen discusses, Lynne Chan, through her alter ego JJ Chinois, produces a "a new body that 'corrects' an absence with a virile but also subversive presence" (ibid., 282). Thus Chan performs as JJ Chinois, who performs as Bruce Lee, "to conform to but also challenge the possibilities for superpersonhood" (ibid., 283). Nguyen describes the importance of Chan's remasculinization of Bruce Lee when she writes, "Rearticulating Bruce Lee's hardness, Chan theatricalizes racial masculinity and explores its erotic potential divorced from the perceived rights and privileges of hegemonic, but also cultural nationalist, heteronormativity. JJ Chinois's is a superstar Asian masculinity that is flexible, performative, glamorous, self-aware, exotic, and hard but also vulnerable and, importantly, queer" (ibid., 282).

Conclusion

In looking at US media historically, we see the production of well-defined stereotypes of men and women, and while those stereotypes continue to reappear contemporarily, a new era of exciting scholarship in media, film, and Asian American studies suggests that those stereotypical images cannot only be challenged and critiqued, but also be viewed differently/queered; additionally, the Internet can be used creatively in order to critique, as well as to offer new and revised representations of Asians and Asian Americans.

We began this chapter by suggesting that representations of Asian and Asian American women and men were interlinked. Scholarship on colonialism has argued that the interlinking of these dual depictions is part of a larger construction of colonial relations, thus providing historical rationale. We then turned our attention to the representations of Asian American women as Lotus Blossoms, Madame Butterflies, and Dragon Ladies, tracking a variety of historical and contemporary ways these stereotypical roles have emerged, and to stereotypical representations of Asian and Asian American men. We also discussed gendered representations in both heterosexual and gay pornography. Finally, we drew on contemporary scholarship on Bruce Lee to suggest ways stereotypes and masculinity more broadly can be challenged and reimagined. Such new scholarship in Asian American studies, film, and media studies provides those of us conducting critical media investigation with methods to challenge such representations and their historical emergence. Thus, one can come to understand any new representations of Asian and Asian American masculinity and gender and do so with strong awareness of the historical gendered representations that have had and continue to have such a strong effect on Asians and Asian Americans. This scholarship provides an alternative, critical vocabulary for understanding the complex system of gender and sexual relations as they exist within dominant media culture. The next step would be to see some of this scholarship translated into more images, such as those of Lynne Chan, that then work to transform broader publics and institutions.

CHAPTER
05

Threatening Model Minorities: The Asian American Horatio Alger Story[1]

IMPORTANT early work in the field of Asian American studies noted that, in the 1960s, amid protests for civil rights, educational equality, and social justice, mainstream media began characterizing Asian Americans as model minorities. In his pivotal essay "Asian Americans as the Model Minority: An Analysis of the Popular Press Image in the 1960s and 1980s" (1988), Keith Osajima suggested that this concept was, in fact, used by the popular news media to refer to Asian Americans in the mid-1960s. Osajima discovered that the term first appeared in 1966 in an article by William Petersen in the *New York Times Magazine*, "Success Story: Japanese-American Style,"[2] and then later that same year, this time in an article focusing on Chinese Americans, in *U.S. News and World Report*, "Success story of One Minority in the U.S."[3] News media discourse characterized Asian Americans as having high test scores and financial success and being unlikely to commit crimes. Osajima sought to debunk the model minority myth, suggesting that this image pitted Asian Americans against African Americans, constructed Asian Americans as racially exceptional yet not of the mainstream, and suggested they needed no social services or federal support, in contrast to other racial minorities. Thus, model minority discourse drove a political wedge between racially disadvantaged groups and undermined legitimate struggles, activism, and legislation for social justice by describing the "model" minority as one who is quiet, hardworking, stays out of trouble, listens to elders, and takes upon themselves the responsibility for change rather than assigning blame and advocating for social change to the government.

More recently, Deborah Woo has described additional elements of the model minority stereotype and demonstrated that it continues in present-day news media discourse. Articles assert that Asian

Americans are highly educated, have successful careers and high employment, and experience low rates of divorce, mental illness, and rates of crime (2000, 23). Woo describes model minority discourse as drawing on the myth of Horatio Alger and applying it to Asian Americans as immigrants overcoming obstacles on the road to success. As she writes: "Underlying it all is a theme of hard work and determination reminiscent of stories told by Horatio Alger (1832–1899), a Harvard-educated ordained minister with celebrated stories about penniless boys who pulled themselves up by their own 'bootstraps'" (ibid., 24). Woo suggests that media stories about Asian American entrepreneurial success abound within the mass media, ranging from the narrative of billionaire Jeong Kim, who made his way from rags to riches, to stories of hard workers such as David Tsang and Chong-Moon Lee, who gained success in the high tech industry.

While both Osajima and Woo describe important aspects of the model minority stereotype as it functions in public discourse, recently Yuko Kawai (2005) has highlighted the significant effect of one variant of the model minority media discourse – the model minority as yellow peril. The subtext of this variant, which we discuss in more detail later in this chapter, is that Asians and Asian Americans who have become successful in fact pose a looming threat to the US nation-state.

In this chapter, we trace scholarship, as well as contemporary and historical media representations, of the model minority stereotype.[4] First, we discuss it historically, then contemporarily, beginning with an examination of Charlie Chan, an early example of model minority imagery. Then we consider the stereotype of Asian and Asian Americans as journalists and medical personnel and assess the model minority image as it appears on Asian and Asian American TV food programs and in discourse about mixed-race Asian Americans. Second, we trace ways model minority discourse doubles as a yellow peril discourse. In particular, we look at the theme of educational over-achievement, which simultaneously constructs Asians and Asian Americans as threats to universities and ultimately to the nation. This particular doubling of the model minority and yellow peril produces a racial ambivalence, one that appears to compliment Asians and Asian Americans and yet constructs their success as a threat to the nation, and builds a divisive, competitive discourse about racial minorities. Ultimately, we argue that the model minority myth overtly masks racist policies, attitudes, and representations by alternating between admiration for and fear of Asians and Asian Americans, thereby dishing up tired problematic stereotypes such as yellow peril masquerading as flattery, and by doing so rending it difficult to challenge and critique such representations.

The Asian American Horatio Alger

While, as Osajima demonstrated, the concept of the model minority as applied to Asian Americans emerged in the 1960s in public news discourse, Jachinson Chan (2001) has suggested that Charlie Chan[5] was an early precursor to the model minority stereotype.[6] Unlike arch-villain Fu Manchu, who is the ultimate embodiment of yellow peril, Chan is dedicated to the United States and to its people. He gets along well with others and, as such, is a successful example of immigrant assimilation. He is also dedicated to his family and, unlike Fu Manchu, does not challenge the "hegemonic hetero-masculine order" (2001, 53). Sexually, he is an "emasculated breeder," the father of ten children, but thoroughly stoic, submissive, and lacking sexual potency and agency. As Chan suggests, "Chan's asexuality is consistently juxtaposed against the sexual exploits of the protagonist. It can be argued that Chan's subordinate role is an essential element in his popularity: he is an intelligent, culturally different, ornament that adds color to a monocultural society" (ibid., 63). Finally, his language skills, which do not improve over time, mark him indelibly as unassimilable. He serves as a representative of a particular social and class position, that of the social servant, a "detective-sergeant," someone successful even as he is disempowered. Thus, Charlie Chan represents an early version of the model minority stereotype, one who does not challenge the dominant social order and who is submissive, obedient, sexually nonthreatening, intelligent, competent, and dependable, thereby providing a decorative and exotic flavor for monocultural dominant white US society.

More recently, two other kinds of Asian and Asian American model minorities have appeared: one, a stereotype of journalists fashioned after the successful news anchor Connie Chung; the other, a typecasting of TV characters as medical professionals. Connie Chung, as a successful TV journalist, unwittingly became a representation of the model minority myth for women. News organizations considering hiring Asian American women as newscasters deployed her image as one to which prospective newscasters would have to live up to. In the film *Slaying the Dragon* (1988), Emerald Yeh, a former anchor for San Francisco's KRON-TV, recounts a past interview with CNN in which someone commented, "You look different. You've cut your hair." Yeh states that CNN wanted her to look more like Connie Chung and to be more "exotic." Emil Guillermo, an editorialist for the SFGate (the online portal for the *San Francisco Chronicle*) and columnist for *Asianweek.com*, writes, "So now there's a Connie stereotype in every city, in every market. Wherever there's a TV newscast, you'll find one."[7] Thus, the model minority myth continues to be Connie Chung, limiting possibilities for Asian and Asian American women journalists, even as it might also provide for opportunities.[8]

The discourse of the model minority also extends to prime-time television representations. A study of prime-time television representations of Asian Pacific Islander Americans in 2004 found that, "Of the eight APIA characters with known occupations, five hold advanced degrees, often in the medical sciences." While in early media Asians and Asian Americans were often typecast in a variety of roles – Fu Manchu, Charlie Chan, Lotus Blossom, Madame Butterfly, and the Dragon Lady – today's mainstream media stereotype, the model minority, appears in the form of a medical professional.

Whether it is the real Dr Sanjay Gupta, the famous medical correspondent for *CNN*, the fictional Mahesh Vijayaraghavensaty-anaryanamurth ("Bug") (Ravi Kapoor), famed forensic entomologist on television's *Crossing Jordan*, surgeon Neela Rasgotra (Parminder Nagra) in *ER*, Cristina Yang (Sandra Oh) in *Grey's Anatomy*, forensic psychiatrist George Huang (B. D. Wong) in *Law and Order: Special Victims Unit*, Ken Jeong as Dr Kuni in *Knocked Up* (2007), or geneticist Mohinder Suresh (Sendhil Ramamurthy) in *Heroes*, all of these Asian and Asian American characters are conspicuously members of the medical profession.[9]

It is instructive to spend some time considering the roles of Ming-Na Wen and Sandra Oh, two female actors who have played high-profile roles as medical professionals on television, in order to understand the way their characters figure in relationship to the model minority stereotype.[10] Ming-Na Wen is well known for her voice-over narration and her role as Jing-Mei "June" in Wayne Wang's film *The Joy Luck Club*,[11] and for her performance as a series regular, a medical student and then a doctor, in *ER*. We will first look at her character Deb Chen, in the television show *ER*, and then discuss Sandra Oh's character Cristina Yang in *Grey's Anatomy*. By examining the similar yet different ways the characters embody a model minority stereotype, we can begin to understand its ambivalent nature.

In his essay about the television narrative in *ER*, Michael J. Porter discusses the episode "House of Cards," in which one substory in the episode concerns two medical students, Deb Chen (Ming-Na Wen) and John Carter (Noah Wyle). Carter is the primary character, through whom audiences are to understand the story. As Porter suggests, "John serves as a thematic foil to another medical student, Deb Chen." Whereas Carter is interested in the patient, Chen "seems more concerned with the science of medicine" (1988, 147–8). The episode allows us to learn more about Carter's character and to understand the stark differences between Carter and Chen. When Chen finds out she has not completed as many procedures as Carter, she worries she will fail as a medical student and sets out to perform more procedures. As a result she becomes envious that Carter is allowed to conduct a difficult procedure and then, without being asked, performs one on her own on a patient after bribing the nurse to leave the room. Of course, Chen endangers the patient by doing this, but other doctors, who take over once her attempt at the central line has failed, are able to remedy the situation. Later in the episode, Chen is at her parent's home, apparently there while her parents are throwing a lavish party. She tells Carter she is quitting and says, "I didn't care about the patient, I just wanted the procedure." She continues, "I like the science of it. But the patients, the sickness, sometimes it almost scares me" (ibid., 149). Even she compares Carter, who she sees as caring about the patients, to herself.

This narrative constructs Chen in stereotypical fashion as the Asian American model minority, but with the additional characterization of her being more interested in science than in people, rich, shamefully competitive, and desperate to get ahead. What is implied is that she is incapable of being the kind of doctor who cares about patients in the way that Carter can and does. In this episode, then, the white man becomes the "ideal doctor," and the Asian American woman is bright, but too unconcerned about the welfare of patients to succeed. Indeed, while we use this example here to demonstrate the construction of the model minority stereotype in media, one can see that there is also a degree of threat implied in Deb Chen's representation (which we will discuss at length later on in the chapter) that goes something like this: "If more competitive, unscrupulous, career-driven Asians and Asian Americans become doctors, patients will be in danger, because such doctors really do not care about the patient's life." Thus, Asians and Asian Americans are a threat in so far as they become too successful, or perhaps too bent on success. Additionally, because she lacks empathy, does not put people ahead of herself, and is career-driven rather than compassionate, Deb Chen also figures as a failed woman, and a failed Asian American woman at that.

Interestingly, the role of contemporary film and television phenom Sandra Oh in *Grey's Anatomy* is similar in important ways.[12] In fact, one narrative thread in *Grey's Anatomy* is strikingly similar to that of *ER*. In one episode of *ER*, after giving birth to a mixed-race African American–Chinese American baby, conceived during a one-night stand with an African American man, Jing-Mei (Deb)[13] Chen painfully gives up the baby, fearing her parents will not approve. In *Grey's Anatomy*, Cristina falls in love with Dr Preston Burke, an African American medical colleague, chief cardiothoracic surgeon and her superior. She becomes pregnant by Burke and schedules an abortion without telling him, only then to suffer from an ectopic pregnancy. Thus, at least in these early seasons, Cristina directly references Jing-Mei on the show.

Figure 5.1   Cristina Yang (Sandra Oh) in a public, yet intimate shot with Preston Burke (Isaiah Washington) in *Grey's Anatomy*

As with Chen in *ER*, Yang's romantic interest is not another Asian American. Nor is it someone white, which might reinforce the stereotype of Asian and Asian American women as romantic objects for white men but on the other hand would fly in the face of anti-miscegenationist views.[14] Indeed, the representation of Cristina (while brilliantly played by Oh) has changed little since Chen's role in *ER*. Cristina is a highly competitive medical student whose main romantic interest is an African American man. She worries about what her mother thinks about her and even goes so far as to hide the fact that she and Burke are together.

Some might argue that it is better to be portrayed stereotypically as a doctor than to be played stereotypically as a villain. However, as we have shown, the model minority stereotype is not a compliment, but a divisive discourse, one that in fact constructs Asian Americans as "exceptional" minorities, but minorities nevertheless, hence not of the mainstream. Furthermore, as we show later, representing Asian Americans as overachievers in media functions as an implicit threat, a villainy of a different magnitude.

Even in the show, itself, being good at one's job is not viewed as admirable. For instance, both Cristina and Deb are treated as robots within the hospital. Deb wants to build her technical skill at the expense of the patient. Cristina attains the most proficiency in cardiothoracic surgery because of her robot-like skill and is well known for being the best among the interns. She is so robotic that one of the new doctors is unimpressed, because she lacks the emotional skills and interactions to be a good surgeon. One example of this representation of "smart but robotic" is the film *Akeelah and the Bee* (2006), where the primary competitor of the lead character, Akeelah, is an Asian American boy, Dylan Chu. In one scene, Dr Larabee, Akeelah's mentor, teaches Akeelah new vocabulary by having her read a passage written by W. E. B. DuBois. Akeelah becomes upset, stating that, "in the time it took to learn that one word, Dylan probably learned twenty." Dr Larabee replies, "And those twenty words won't mean anything to him. He's just a little robot memorizing lists of words." Thus, the implication is twofold: both that Asian Americans like Dylan do not know the significance of words and that such word memorizers are little robots, more machine than human, rote learners who will struggle to apply their knowledge because they are simply widgets on the assembly line of modernist, capitalist, industrial society.

Thus, as Kawai (2005) suggests, the role of the doctor can double, ambivalently, for the villainous yellow peril image of yesteryear. In other words, by overrepresenting Asian Americans as doctors while underrepresenting them overall, the media evoke anxiety about a potential Asian "takeover" of yet another set of US jobs. It is clear that roles are still incredibly limited for Asian Americans, that single-occupational typecasting significantly restricts possible jobs for Asian and Asian American actors, and that limiting actors to such roles radically reduces the ability to represent Asians and Asian Americans as diverse human beings.

Horatio Alger stories generally appear in PBS biographies of famous Asian Americans, not only in the specific cases of Asians and Asian Americans as media personnel on TV, as in *ER* and *Grey's Anatomy*. The film *Searching for Asian America* (2003)[15] represents Governor Gary Locke (of Washington) and Lela Lee (creator of *Angry Little Asian Girl*) as having "made it." Gary Locke emerges as a political hero by not falling in line with political interests and lobbying, but by working hard. And Lela Lee does not have a mainstream cartoon, but continues efforts to establish herself as an Asian American who does not speak the standard line. The film *Maya Lin: A Strong Clear Vision* (1994) also follows the Asian American Horatio Alger narrative. Architect Maya Lin, who was chosen in a competition to design the Vietnam Veterans' War Memorial, demonstrates courage, forthrightness, and determination, going against great odds to win the right to make an artistic work that represents the nation's continuing dis-ease with the history of the Vietnam War. In the end, what is implied by this representation is that, while they may struggle as racial minorities, and in the case of Lin and Lee as minority women, these three do not need the help of mainstream society (as do other minorities) to succeed; rather, they and other Asians and Asian Americans like them can do it on their own, by sheer dint of determination, hard work, and intelligence, and by maintaining good moral values.

Even television shows about food are not immune from Asian American Horatio Alger myth-making. According to Anita Mannur (2005a), model minority representations of Asians and Asian Americans also appear in live or seemingly live televisual contexts, such as cooking shows. These images construct a desire for "fusion cuisine," which is seen to cross borders between East and West, and through the use of multicultural themes such shows assert America is a democratic place, offering full and equal access to immigrants. Mannur suggests in her study of Ming Tsai and Padma Lakshmi, however, that these images mask exclusion, conflict, and resistance. According to Mannur, Ming Tsai, of *East Meets West* and *Ming's Quest*, is represented as being thoroughly comfortable in the worlds of both East and West. He is often depicted in high-class settings, appears to blend in easily, and is figured as the ideal US transnational citizen of the future. His brand of food offers a hybrid of both Eastern and Western cultures. He and his food are hybrids.

Padma Lakshmi, of *Padma's Passport*, offers another version of model minority. Mannur suggests that Lakshmi is Orientalized and eroticized. Access to her sexuality is constructed as being interconnected with access to the food she prepares. Unlike Tsai, Lakshmi is not comfortable in the kitchen, and her representation as exotically ethnic draws attention away from her cooking. Cooking, in this case, is not central to her marketability. Her portrayal as a model minority is dependent on her bodily construction as erotic and sexually available. As Mannur writes, "Lakshmi is the alluring temptress who is a cosmopolitan world traveler and still remembers her roots. Ming Tsai is the hyperassimilated Asian American but is also comfortable with his traditional upbringing in an immigrant Taiwanese American family" (2005b, 82).

Perhaps no other Asian or Asian American represents the "American dream" and the myth of Horatio Alger better, however, than Tiger Woods. A child phenom in golf, born on December 30, 1975, in Cypress, California, Woods is reputed to be one of the greatest golfers of all time, if not the greatest. He burst onto the scene at a time when he was not allowed to play on some golf greens because of the color of his skin. He was the youngest player to win the Master's tournament, at Augusta, Georgia, a course that had one of the longest histories of racial restrictions, and he was the first racial minority to win a major golf event (golf being considered by many to be the whitest of sports). In addition to his golfing success, his image as a

multiracial celebrity who identifies himself as mixed race was successfully used as a catalyst for the policy efforts to include mixed
racial identification options on the 2000 US Census. In June 1995, he
voiced his opinion on the matter of his racial identity in a press
release, claiming his pride in being multiracial. While more about his
father and his African American heritage has been made by media, he
is also a popular figure in Thailand and among Thai Americans and
Asian Americans, more generally.

Since the media have gone to great extremes to play up his African
Americanness, some might wonder why we are discussing Woods here
as an Asian American. In addition, historically, people of mixed racial
heritage have been represented tragically as products of cross-racial
rapes, as maladroit specimens contaminated by tainted racialized
blood, or as psychologically deranged or mentally afflicted because of
the inevitable biological degeneracy that emerges when the racial line
is crossed by sex. How did mixed race move from the category of faulty
and inferior biological offspring to today's representation of Tiger
Woods as the great mixed-race hope?

Perez (2005) suggests Woods shuttles between race consciousness
and race elision. On the one hand, Woods himself coined the term
"Cablinasian" – Caucasian, black, Indian, and Asian – to describe the
white, African American, Native American, Chinese, and Thai parts of
his identity. On the other hand, Perez suggests, Woods figures as a
Horatio Alger figure and is mythically read into a narrative of America
as a multicultural nation where the racial future will be universally
color neutral. Unlike Woods's race-conscious moniker, the Horatio
Alger mythology is premised on an organized forgetting of racism and
racial harm and suffering in the United States. As Horatio Alger, everyone can imagine themselves to be a Tiger Woods. Thus, Woods hails the
arrival of race as no longer mattering at all.

Similarly, historian Henry Yu (2002) suggests Woods is constructed
as a fantasy figure who single-handedly promises the elimination of
racial problems from the past. Woods's mixed raceness becomes a
metaphor for America's as-yet unattained future. Through commercialization, his image promises people from different racial groups
will get along; if one buys the right products, the illusion of racial
wholeness can be attained and maintained.

It is important to discuss mixed-race Asian Americans like Tiger
Woods when considering the model minority stereotype. Students have
often commented that Asian American men do not become models
unless they are mixed race. Thus, media appear to strive for representations of Asian Americans that appear closer to the Anglo-Saxon norm.
Mixed-race figures such as Keanu Reeves, Dean Cain, Jimmy Smits, and
Rob Schneider come to be acceptable stars, even heroes, in contempo-

rary media. And yet, despite their heritage, little is made of their Asianness and Asian Americanness. It is as if they become stars and heroes, in part, because general audiences do not know of their Asian backgrounds.

Perhaps this is the reason why there is a practice of "outing" within the mixed-race Asian American community (Nishime, 2005). Because of their feeling of a lack of representation or acknowledgement, perhaps because of the culture's broader inability to see them as "whole," because their "Asian" and "Asian American" identities are suppressed, and hence because of feelings of indeterminacy, some mixed-race Asian Americans strive to "out" stars of mixed-race Asian American identity, to call attention to their status and to challenge the media's masking of their complete racial identity. In short, some mixed-race Asian Americans make mixed-race racial identity matter.

Despite these challenging and resisting strategies, mixed-race Asian Americans in media will continue to face the trend toward being characterized as model minorities. Their status of appearing in the media as the hope for the future, thus offering utopic possibilities for the racial future of the nation, should be challenged, as should the larger Horatio Alger mythology.[16] Critical work should be undertaken to draw attention to the way the model minority myth divides, to show that Asians and Asian Americans are typecast in limiting ways, and to suggest that the model minority is a discourse that participates in historical and continuing racism, rather than challenges that legacy, our present, and our future.

Threatening Model Minorities

While it is clear from the discussion in the previous section that stereotypical model minority imagery is alive and well (indeed, we argue that it is the prevailing stereotypical discourse of Asians and Asian Americans), one variant that has much significance is of the model minority who pose a threat, very often to the US nation-state. Thus the stereotype is problematic, because it disguises an assertion of fear, distrust, and danger as a compliment (one that, as we have argued, is in fact a putdown).

Yuko Kawai (2005) has suggested that there is an ambivalent discourse at work, with the model minority stereotype being tightly interwoven with another racialized representation of Asians and Asian Americans, yellow peril.[17] Kawai notes how pervasive the model minority stereotype is today, and she sees both international and national representations of both stereotypes. Thus, on the one hand,

Asian Americans as the model minority represent well-educated, familial, submissive minorities and are economically competitive; on the other hand they are a threat and pose a danger to the West and to the United States specifically. In her article Kawai analyzes the film *Rising Sun* (1993), tracing both model minority and yellow peril themes.

Kawai suggests *Rising Sun* emerges "in the background of Japan's economic threat to the United States and 'Japan-bashing' in the 1980s" (2005, 111). While it appears to be a yellow peril film, it is Kawai's contention that it also functions to reproduce the model minority myth. As she argues, "The Asian man in the film is a 'good' guy in the sense that he is willing to assimilate to the White rules of the game (i.e., dressing exactly like the White cowboys do and attacking them in a 'cowboy style') but is a 'bad' guy who disrupts what the White cowboys attempt to achieve (i.e., taking away their woman)" (ibid., 120). In addition, Japan figures as both model minority and yellow peril country to the United States. For instance, the film juxtaposes "Japan's affluence and America's poverty" (ibid., 121). However, this representation is not unproblematic. As Kawai notes, while the film stresses Japan's superiority, it simultaneously "exaggerates the [country's] foreignness" (ibid., 122). It pits African Americans against Asian Americans and aligns African Americans with white America,[18] and "It is surely an advantage for White America to have African Americans to protect its interests" (ibid., 125). Essentially, whites benefit from blacks despising Asians, which prevents minorities from joining hands against white supremacy. According to Kawai, the model minority image is implicated in the depiction of Japanese as villains and gangsters, since "the Japanese characters are associated with 'passivity' and 'docility,' which are part of the model minority stereotype, even when they are gangsters" (ibid.).

Building on Kawai's theorization of model minority discourse doubling as yellow peril discourse, we discuss two articles about Asian and Asian American educational success, both of which use success to develop a model minority mythology that simultaneously characterizes Asians and Asian Americans as threatening the US nation-state. A November 19, 2005, *Wall Street Journal* article tells of two Silicon Valley high schools where white students are fleeing because of an influx of Asian students (Hwang, 2005). The story suggests that, while "white flight" historically was used to refer to the way whites moved from inner cities into the suburbs when the inner cities became "overrun" by racial minorities, primarily African Americans, this new "white flight" refers to white families leaving top-notch academically superb high schools because of the influx of highly competitive, educationally superior Asians.

As this story goes, white parents have taken their children out of these two schools and sent them "to private schools or . . . whiter public schools." According to the white parents, the Silicon Valley schools "are too Asian." The article maintains that both some white and some Asian parents think the environment in the schools is too intensely competitive and that such competition creates "an unhealthy cultural isolation." It also suggests that the phenomenon of white parents taking their kids out of Asian-dominated public schools is not specific to the Silicon Valley and exists at other competitive public high schools in the United States: at "Wootton High School in Rockville, Md., known flippantly to some locals as 'Won Ton,' roughly 35% of students are of Asian descent." The school is stereotyped, and so are Asians as being "good at math." The article suggests, "Some parents and students say these various forces are creating an unhealthy cultural isolation in the schools."

Such discourse, while focused in the *Wall Street Journal* article on Asians and Asian Americans in elite high schools, also exists in discourse about public university education. For instance, an article by Timothy Egan titled "Little Asia on the Hill," in the "EducationLife" section of the *New York Times* newspaper in January 2007, asks, "Is this the new face of higher education?"[19] The article is the cover story of the section of the newspaper, with a front headline that reads "The Asian Campus," and with pictures of only Asians and Asian Americans.[20] The article describes how "Asian" UC Berkeley is. While it provides a "balanced" assessment of the overrepresentation of Asian and Asian American students at Berkeley and at US colleges and universities more generally,[21] its main emphasis is on creating an image of Berkeley as beset by an overabundance of Asians and Asian Americans. It reads,

> This fall and last, the number of Asian freshmen at Berkeley has been at a record high, about 46 percent. The overall undergraduate population is 41 percent Asian. On this golden campus, where a creek runs through a redwood grove, there are residence halls with Asian themes; good dim sum is never more than a five-minute walk away; heaping, spicy bowls of pho are served up in the Bear's Lair cafeteria; and numerous social clubs are linked by common ancestry to countries far across the Pacific. (Egan, 2007, 24)

The article goes on to question Berkeley's "diversity," implying that having so many Asians and Asian Americans makes it un-diverse. Egan then comments on the face of public universities in California and writes, "But it is the new face of the state's vaunted public university system. Asians make up the largest single ethnic group, 37 percent, at its nine undergraduate campuses" (ibid.). The article further implies that the large Asian and Asian American population at Berkeley creates an image problem for the university: "Berkeley is freighted with the baggage of stereotypes – that it is boring socially, full of science nerds, a hard place to make friends."

Not only does the article trot out well-chiseled, yet also well-weathered, stereotypes of Asian Americans as cloistered ("selective self-racial segregation" in Egan's phrase) or ghettoized in Little Tokyos or Chinatowns, but it also reproduces contemporary stereotypes of Asian Americans as computer nerds and study geeks, as if college is not about studying. It insults Asians and Asian Americans as boring people, with narrow interests in academics to a fault, rendering Berkeley un-fun, like a rectory or monastery. Not only are Asian Americans limited socially, according to Egan but also they tend not to speak in class, tend to revere authority, do not want to buck the system, and emphasize book and computer "learning" over the "back-and-forth Socratic tradition" associated with traditional US classroom participation.

Perhaps what is even more troubling in the article is the reproduction of the forever foreigner stereotype. Egan describes "numerous social clubs" that "are linked by common ancestry to countries far across the Pacific." He says that, more and more, Berkeley is turning "toward the setting sun for its identity." His description diminishes the experiences and cultural lives of Asian Americans in favor of images of distanced Asians "far" from America. The article emphasizes that 95 percent of the *parents* of the students from the first-year class come from Asia, hence downplaying the fact that the students "are pre-dominantly first-generation American," hence *American citizens* (Egan, 2007, 26). It implies that one of America's vaunted institutions of higher learning, populated by so many first-generation students, is somehow more Asian and hence less American.

This reference to Asian, in an article largely about Asian Americans, is part of historical model minority discourse,[22] as Thomas Nakayama suggests. In his study Nakayama finds that "Asian Americans who have lived in this country for generations [are] treated, discursively, as identical to Asians who have never left Asia." The media articles he looks at distinguish Asian Americans from "Americans." As he suggests, "Implicit here is the claim that Asian (Americans?) are not Americans." Thus, the discourse "returns" to Asia to make sense of why Asian Americans are succeeding, hence marking them as forever foreigners (1988, 68).

While there are historically black colleges, tribal colleges, Jewish-sponsored universities, Hispanic-serving institutions, Baptist, Catholic, and other religious colleges, and of course innumerable informal historically white colleges and universities, there is not a comparable Asian American-sponsored college or university in the United States.[23] Yet, Egan's article relies on the problematic notion that there are too many Asians and Asian Americans at Berkeley, that Berkeley is not the "real America," that being Asian or Asian American is not being American. Thus it implies that doing well in school, using computers, and not partying or carousing is a bad and boring thing; in essence, the cultural life Asians and Asian Americans have created at Berkeley is dismissed out of hand. It is not seen as something positive that contributes to the success of the university or the United States, and ultimately benefits *all students* who attend Berkeley. Egan does not consider that being studious at one of the world's leading public institutions of higher learning ought to be admired rather than disparaged.

Egan's article also does what Keith Osajima argued early writing that defined Asian Americans as "model minorities" did: it attempts to drive a wedge between Asians and Asian Americans and blacks, Latinos, and Native Americans. He writes, "What is troubling to some is that the big public school on the hill certainly does not look like the ethnic face of California, which is 12 percent Asian, more than twice the national average," and "In California, the rise of the Asian campus, of the strict meritocracy, has come at the expense of historically underrepresented blacks and Hispanics" (2007, 24). He also suggests that "highly credentialed Asian applicants" are being chosen over "students of color with less stellar test scores and grades" (ibid.) and that increasing enrollments of Asian Americans occur simultaneously with rollbacks of affirmative action policies. Thus, rather than examine carefully the way poor and urban minorities, including Asian Americans, suffer from a lack of access, the article positions Asians and Asian Americans as against *all* other groups, including (but not saying so outright) whites.

This kind of article is not directed toward Asian Americans as readers and carries the message that Asian Americans are, once again, taking over. It functions by highlighting the dramatic, surprising, and possibly shocking realization that Berkeley and the UC system, indeed elite universities broadly (the article mentions Stanford, Harvard, Princeton, MIT, Amherst, Johns Hopkins, Dartmouth, Carnegie-Mellon, Stony Brook (SUNY), the California Institute of Technology, Cornell, Cooper Union, Wellesley, the University of Texas at Austin, Columbia, and Rutgers), are either no longer predominantly white or have relatively large Asian and Asian American student enrollments. The article downplays the fact that only recently has white dominance in higher education in California's top public schools changed. While it sprinkles some nods to the positives created by the Asian and Asian American feel of the campus, especially referencing Asians and Asian Americans saying so, the bulk of the article does not see the Asian and Asian American presence as a contribution but rather as a threat to Berkeley, the education system, and ultimately white students. How such an article can assert that Asians and Asian Americans have increased the studious atmosphere and educational competition on campus and how this can then be cast solely as a liability, not something that should be revered, celebrated, and embraced as a positive move toward higher education; how the essay can imply in the strongest terms that it is well-qualified Asians and Asian Americans and not rich, privileged, well-connected, and highly educated whites who are edging out African Americans and Latinos; and how it can imply that Berkeley is less attractive for non-Asians and non-Asian Americans because of the large numbers of Asians and Asian Americans suggests the powerful way a neo-conservative, yellow peril discourse continues to reverberate in the mainstream US media.

Model Minority Discourse as Exclusionary Discourse

Given our discussion of model minority yellow peril discourse, it becomes clear that racism has not gone away, and that there is no progression, not even a slow one, toward a better representation of Asians and Asian Americans in mainstream media. Instead, as is apparent in the article "Little Asia on the Hill," what is constructed as "overrepresentation" of Asians and Asian Americans on college campuses masks the continuing mass underrepresentation and effective exclusion of Asians and Asian Americans in management and leadership positions, in literature, arts, and humanities fields, in federal social service and welfare programs, in sports, in the legal profession, and, for the purposes of this book, the mainstream media.

While, educationally, Asians and Asian Americans have greater representation in some areas, in the media, despite dramatic discourses of yellow peril, it is clear that representation is still at exclusion-era and segregation-era lows. The Asian American Justice Center found that,

> In 2004, the estimated APIA population numbered approximately 14 million, or 5% of the total U.S. population. However, the percentage of APIAs in prime time television consistently falls below that of the actual population. The public tends to rely on characterizations from the media to formulate beliefs about racial groups with whom they have little contact. Thus, many television viewers may believe that APIAs in prime time are representative of APIAs in the United States. (2006, 3)

The study examines prime-time APIA regulars on the six national television networks during fall 2005 and compares those findings with that of the earlier 2004 report, *Asian Pacific Americans in Prime Time: Light, Camera and Little Action*. The many findings in the report are that

"APIAS comprise only 2.6% of all prime time television regulars," that "among the 102 prime time programs, only 14 feature at least one APIA regular, and only one program (ABC's *Lost*) includes more than one," and that "only 16 APIAs are featured as regulars on prime time television" (ibid., 4–5). If we were to compare "Little Asia on the Hill" to this report, then college students in the University of California system have vastly more opportunities to interact and be influenced by a variety of Asians and Asian Americans than to gain access to famous and not-so-famous Asians and Asian Americans on network television. Thus, the *underrepresentation* of Asians and Asian Americans emphasizes how the model minority myth works to disavow the continued exclusion of Asian Americans. And the number of examples of Asian Americans in the media that we discuss help us show how the model minority myth functions alongside and in concert with yellow peril discourses.

What these statistics also suggest is that Asian Americans continue to be little represented on mainstream television. Indeed, one could argue that they are not represented in most mainstream media – television, radio, film, newspapers, and journals. One must begin to wonder, after the Asian American movement of the 1960s and 1970s, after changes that have taken place in parts of society, if it is even possible to change the situation in commercial visual media, given the degree of stereotyping and negative representation, and the prominence of a model minority stereotype that preaches Asian American success and suggests that Asian Americans have no problems to worry about.

As we saw in this chapter, the model minority stereotype is more than simply "Asians and Asian Americans are smart and good at math." Rather, it is a complex and problematic representation which, at the surface level, appears to compliment Asian and Asian American achievements but in fact functions as a yellow peril discourse. First, we explored the historical bases for the model minority, from Charlie Chan and its manifestation as an enduring Asian American Horatio Alger myth. From this arose the model minority representations of successful journalists, successful doctors, and successful students, but not without the added insult of being robotic, uncaring, and asocial. We saw that the myth crosses the boundaries of fictional television and non-fictional and reality televisual contexts, as in PBS specials and the food television genre. However, the model minority/Asian American Horatio Alger is aptly embodied by Tiger Woods and mixed-race Asian Americans, who read into the narrative of a color-neutral United States. The masking of the Asian and Asian American part of their racial identities would seem to explain why mixed-race Asian Americans "out" other mixed-race Asian Americans, and thus draw attention to discriminating aspects of model minority discourses. In the end, the model minority representation, as Kawai (2005) has argued, is ambivalent, doubling with a yellow peril discourse that permeates such films as *Rising Sun*, as well as educational discourses in the United States.

As we stated earlier, racism has not gone away. Asians and Asian Americans are underrepresented and when represented are constructed in troubling and limiting ways. Media suggest that they are succeeding in education, distinguishing them from other minorities, but, as a result, they should be feared and possibly eliminated. Model minority discourse as it has been applied to Asians and Asian Americans both saturates the media landscape and serves as an obstacle to those who wish to challenge and protest continuing discrimination, racism, and racial exclusion. In its Asian and Asian American guise, the Horatio Alger myth continues to be a threatening one.

PART II
STRIVING FOR MEDIA INDEPENDENCE

CHAPTER 06

Asian American Public Criticisms and Community Protests

THIS chapter examines explicit critiques of offensive dominant media representations of Asians and Asian Americans. These criticisms serve as an ideal transition, because they are both about the dominant media and simultaneously oppositional to it. As Ono and Sloop (1995) argue, it is crucial to give as much critical and analytical attention to resistant and vernacular representations – those produced by localized communities – as to dominant representations – those that circulate broadly within corporate, commercial, and public spaces. Thus, while we are highly critical of mainstream representations (while still allowing space for appreciative and negotiated readings of dominant figures such as Nancy Kwan [e.g., Feng, 2000] and Bruce Lee [e.g., Nguyen, 2007]), as previous chapters demonstrate, we have invested equally in bringing critical attention to independent, activist, and critical representations, in part to help carve out a critical space for such representations in the larger media landscape.

We examine public protests, particularly responses to troubling media representations of Asian Americans. Yen Le Espiritu (1992) calls Asian American public protests a "reactive solidarity"; Asian American panethnicity and solidarity emerge in response and reaction to outbursts or occurrences of anti-Asian and anti-Asian American sentiments. Espiritu uses the case of Vincent Chin as an example of anti-Asian violence that spurred Asian Americans into a reactive solidarity, which unifies Asian Americans through a "common burden that racist antagonists can't tell us apart."[1] For example, one could consider the collective and Internet-mobilized outing of mixed-race actors as an example of reactive solidarity, one that seeks not to challenge explicit racism, as in the Vincent Chin case, but to respond to and challenge the implicit racism produced by invisibility when mixed-race Asian Americans are not cast in mixed-race roles.

After discussing the concepts of mimicry and mockery as theoretical frames through which to view some media representations, we look at an historical example of media activism surrounding a controversy that emerged around the Broadway production of *Miss Saigon*. Then, in order to highlight the continuing importance of media activism, we examine two contemporary representative events of reactive solidarity and public protest against the implicit embodiment and enactment of Asian stereotypes: comments by Rosie O'Donnell in *The View* and a six-minute prank call on JV and Elvis's radio program. Rosie O'Donnell's brief ching chong comments were televised nationally, and JV and Elvis's skit about a telephone caller ordering food from a Chinese restaurant went out over the radio airwaves, as well as on the Internet. Both examples draw on and reproduce racist stereotypes of Asians and Asian Americans – specifically Chinese and Chinese Americans. In particular, both use the forever foreigner stereotype and make fun of Chinese and Chinese American language. We analyze both together in order to illustrate that resisting mockery continues to be relevant contemporarily across a variety of media, each with different degrees and means of distribution, and with different levels of offense, from an off-the-cuff remark to a carefully planned and lengthy prank. In the end, we argue that Asian American activism calls attention to the problems of current media representations and racial oppression against Asians and Asian Americans. Finally, we address the effectiveness and victories of media activism, as well as point to the difficulties of media activism in the future.

Not Missing *Miss Saigon*: A Case of Asian American Activism

The protest of the Broadway premiere of *Miss Saigon* in 1991 continues to be regarded as a landmark instance of Asian American activism against derogatory representations. Cameron Mackintosh, the show's producer, asked Jonathan Pryce, a Caucasian British actor, to reprise his role as the Vietnamese pimp in the New York production. However, Asian American activists protested the yellowface portrayal by Pryce, in addition to other Western misrepresentations of Asians, such as the stereotype that Asians are submissive "Orientals," that men are sexually impotent, and other Orientalist depictions of Asians appearing in the production.[2] In response to Asian American protests, the Actors' Equity Association initially refused to grant Pryce the documents necessary for him to work in the United States, although they eventually reversed their decision. Nevertheless, protests continued both in New York and across the country. In Minneapolis–St Paul, Minnesota, a multiracial coalition including Asian Americans conducted teach-ins and demonstrations and distributed pamphlets, while the Asian American

Renaissance put on counter-performances in response (Kondo, 1997, 233). LGBT Asian Americans in New York also protested, especially when a prominent lesbian and gay organization, the Lambda Legal Defense and Education Fund (LLDEF), decided to use *Miss Saigon* in their annual fundraiser, against the wishes of Asian American gay and lesbian organizations in the area (Yoshikawa, 1994). According to Yoshikawa, the Asian Lesbians of the East Coast (ALOEC) and the Gay Asian and Pacific Islander Men of New York (GAPIMNY) launched a large-scale effort against *Miss Saigon* and LLDEF, involving two demonstrations by a coalition that critiqued the show and its use in the LLDEF fundraiser. When LLDEF refused to cancel their benefit, the coalition expanded to take in others within the gay and lesbian community, particularly LGBTs of color, to protest at the benefit. A second demonstration was planned for opening night. This led to a coalition within the Asian American community, incorporating other Asian American organizations, including but not limited to the Asian Pacific Alliance for Creative Equality, Youth for Philippine Action, and the Pan Asian Repertory Theater, despite Yoshikawa's initial hesitation not to organize with members outside the LGBT community. As Yoshikawa recounts, there was no outright homophobia in the coalition, but she does recall experiences of the "conservatism and homophobia of our own Asian and Pacific Islander communities" and was wary of those who might try to downplay the LGBT origins and membership (1994, 290). Despite this initial hesitancy, the coalition went through with the second protest, and this time mainstream media arrived to cover it. In the end, *Miss Saigon* continued on Broadway, and the coalition eventually disbanded. The media coverage, however, ensured that the protests at least had the effect of providing information to the larger public.

In addition to giving an overview of the *Miss Saigon* events, Kondo looks at the film *Rising Sun* (1993)[3] and the theater productions *Face Value* and *The Mikado* as instances of dominant media abuses and activism against them via the arts. Each of these instances illustrates activism against offensive anti-Asian media representations. Histories of Asian American activism typically lump media activism together with activism in general (some common examples of traditional Asian American activism are the Vincent Chin case and the Third World strike).[4] However, media activism is part of, although different from, Asian American activism in general: media activism participates in a contest over symbols, language, and representation – hence, its primary emphasis is to challenge the politics of representation; activism more generally, while sometimes including a contest over representations, often emphasizes the material and the symbolic outcomes arising from material acts.

The protest of *Miss Saigon* was both activism of the traditional kind and media activism. It dealt centrally with the politics of representation, of who plays what, and who has the right to play what, but it also had to do with the medium of theater as a forum for the communication of ideas and its pedagogical and informational role in educating theater-goers about Asian Americans.[5] If the various *Miss Saigon* protests were taken purely as an instance of Asian American activism, it would be fair to say that they failed, as they did not stop the show and did not, in the end, alter the employment of actors. Yoshikawa concludes, however, that the protestors never thought they would be able close down the show (1994, 293). Thus, while ending the production would have been ideal, the goal to challenge stereotypes and offensive casting, to shift the meanings of representations in the production, to provide an Asian American perspective on the show, to call for a more complex and nuanced version of Asian Americans, and to do all of this publicly, was itself a significant achievement.

On the other hand, activists in the Vincent Chin case protested his murder, the justice system's unjust response, and the mild treatment of the murderers. Although the media played an important role in constructing the event and participated in the fomenting of anti-Japanese fervor in Detroit, as well as in the nation at large,[6] and although a critique of the media coverage of the case was a part of the activism surrounding Chin's murder, the primary emphasis in that case was on what Ebens and Nitz and the courts did.

The Persistence of Mimicry and Mockery

In order to understand Asian American media activism and what is at issue historically for those who challenge what they see as unjust and offensive media representations, we discuss what has become a common, indeed, recurring representation of Asians and Asian Americans: mimicry and mockery. Additionally, the two primary case studies we examine in this chapter both activate mimicry and mockery of Asian Americans as a form of humor. We suggested in chapter 3 that yellowface was a kind of ambivalent representation that requires the audience to know the actor playing Asian is not Asian or Asian American in order to get the mocking humor of the performance. In *Miss Saigon*, protests erupted in response to yellowface mockery, for example. And in 1995 Judge Lance Ito, who presided over the O. J. Simpson murder trial, became famous, but was then subject to mimicry and public mockery.[7] Such incidents suggest that mimicry and mockery are common media frames used to represent Asians and Asian Americans. By applying Homi Bhabha's concepts and discussing them in relationship to media activism, we can see how mimicry and mockery, while derogatory and while reproducing colonial and racial relations, nevertheless do leave open a space for resistance, which Asian Americans have occupied and utilized.[8]

As Bhabha suggests, mimicry is an "elusive and effective strategy" for reproducing colonial power and knowledge and for maintaining colonial relations, since the colonial power holder "repeatedly exercises its authority through the figures of farce" (1994, 85). In order to maintain colonial relations, colonial regimes produce images of the colonized as the Other, thus as different (ibid., 86). Whereas mimicry is a performance that makes difference into a spectacle and highlights unacceptable qualities of the Other, mockery is an act that distinguishes between who is in power and who has the power to name and regulate appropriate and inappropriate behavior. The act of mockery through mimicry reminds colonial subjects of their unequal position within society. The representation of the difference of the Other becomes a process of disavowal; the Other's difference is the reason for its inferiority, but through repeated mimicry the ability to protest unequal treatment because of that difference is denied. For example, in the act of mocking welfare mothers and poor people, their difference as it appears in media representations is based on a tautology: on the one hand their lack of money is constructed as the reason for their inferiority; on the other their inferiority is constructed as the reason for their lack of money. However, despite the fact that difference is foregrounded in media, mockery denies protests that could be pursued based on the recognition of difference, i.e. people refuse to believe that poor people need help more than others, even though it is acknowledged that they are poor and will continue to be so. But Bhabha argues that mimicry also provides a space of resistance for the colonized. While the colonized may well be aware of the colonizer's representations of them, the colonizer does not understand the degree to which those representations do not, in fact, describe the lived identities of the colonized. Thus, the colonized can use this knowledge as a space of resistance. Just as Cameron Mackintosh might have thought he was having the best actor portray the Eurasian pimp in *Miss Saigon*, Asian American groups recognized this as mimicry and mockery and used their knowledge of the unjust and discriminatory history of yellowface performance to protest.

Across the years 2006 and 2007, two important instances of Asian mockery in the dominant media elicited significant protests from Asian Americans: Rosie O'Donnell's use of "ching chong" speech on the daytime television show *The View* on December 5, 2006, and a prank phone call by the radio talk-show hosts JV and Elvis on April 5, 2007. We choose to examine these two instances in more detail for two primary reasons. First, O'Donnell's ching chong comments are not uncommon in dominant media representations. For example, comedian and talk-show host Adam Corolla and NBA superstar Shaquille O'Neal have each previously made ching chong comments in reference to Asians and Asian Americans.[9] What we call ching chong speech can be subsumed under what Elaine Chun calls "mock Asian" stylings – discourse and language that "marks racial otherness" and "overtly marks Asian racial difference" (2004, 264). Various permutations of mock Asian stylings appear in such places as the 2002 Abercrombie and Fitch T-shirts and the puppet character Kim Jong-il in the film *Team America: World Police* (2004). O'Donnell's is just the most recent high-profile case at the time of writing. Second, Asian American responses to these two instances occurred within a year of each other, thus highlighting the persistent presence of Asian American activism in response to offensive racist media representations. These examples occurring within a year are strong evidence that media continue to represent Asians and Asian Americans in derogatory ways and that activists continue to respond to these representations.

Rosie O'Donnell Ching Chonging on *The View*

Rosie O'Donnell's ching chong comments originally aired on the December 5, 2006, episode of *The View*. *The View* is a daytime talk-show program featuring celebrity women co-hosts of different backgrounds and ages informally discussing current events. The show has had a history of co-hosts coming and going; however, as part-producer and part-owner, Barbara Walters is the one consistent host. Rosie O'Donnell's comments came during her stint as a co-host of the show. In reference to Danny DeVito's inebriated appearance during the November 29 episode of *The View*, O'Donnell was commenting on the seemingly absurd amount of national and international attention that it had commanded. She stated, "The fact is that it's news all over the world. You know, you can imagine in China it's like, 'Ching chong, ching chong, Danny DeVito, ching chong chong chong chong, drunk, *The View*, ching chong." The audience and fellow co-host responded with laughter,[10] but many Asian Americans had a much different reaction.

Asian American activists protested O'Donnell's comments soon after they aired. Protests took on many different forms: organizations and prominent political figures released public statements, and magazines printed and bloggers posted their own opinions on the issue. John Liu, a member of Queens (NY) City Council, sent a letter, dated December 9, to Walters, blasting O'Donnell for hitting a "raw nerve in our community" (Cruz, 2006). In addition, the Asian American Journalists Association criticized O'Donnell, stating that ching chong comments give the "impression that Asian Americans are a group that is substandard to English-speaking people" (Campbell, 2006). The Organization for Chinese Americans (OCA) released a statement demanding an apology from Rosie O'Donnell and *The View*, saying, "We hope that Rosie O'Donnell, the producers of *The View* at ABC, and the public recognize the insensitivity shown through the remarks and reactions. Our community demands, and deserves a very public apology."[11] The Asian American Justice Center (AAJC) also released a statement, in which its president and executive director, Karen K. Narasaki, said, "Ms. O'Donnell's comments show how much ignorance exists about Chinese and Asians in general. The fact that neither she nor her producers understand how that phrase has been used to denigrate Asians and Asian Americans – to the extent that it has become a racial slur – is appalling" (Campbell, 2006).

O'Donnell's response to the Asian American activists' critiques was not well received. Her spokesperson Cindi Berger released a statement saying, "I certainly hope that one day they will be able to grasp her humor" (Hutchinson, 2006). On December 8, O'Donnell posted a response on her blog declaring, "It was not my intent to mock just to say how odd it is that danny drunk was news all over the world even in China."[12] Eventually, as a result of continued protest, on the December 14 episode of *The View*, O'Donnell put forth another and more public apology:

> So apparently "ching-chong," unbeknownst to me, is a very offensive word or way to make fun, quote unquote, or mock . . . Asian accents . . . Some Asian people have told me it's as bad as the N-word. To which I was like, "Really? I didn't know that." But to anyone who felt offended at my Chinese, Asian, pseudo-Japanese, sounded a little Yiddish accent that I was doing, ya know, it was never intented to mock . . . and I'm sorry for those people who felt hurt or were teased on the playground."[13]

She followed this with the warning that "there's a good chance I'll do something like that again, probably in the next week – not on purpose, only 'cause it's how my brain works" (Carlson, 2006). The audience applauded the apology, and the broader dominant media attention to this issue died down.

However, the apology did not placate all Asian Americans. Rather, it stimulated more Asian American activism. O'Donnell's apology was not a heartfelt one in which she admitted her mistake; nor was it likely to improve public perceptions of the situation; it actually had the effect of putting the blame for racial harm on the victims for not having an appropriate sense of humor, not being able to take a joke.

The apology started with co-host Elisabeth Hasselbeck recalling that she and her Chinese acupuncturist talked about the incident, at which point O'Donnell begrudgingly chimes in, "Okay, we *have* to talk about it." She provides a recap of the events which culminates in her replaying the video of the December 5 episode. O'Donnell then says she initially thought of it as her just doing accents as usual, until she was notified that "this apparently is offensive to a lot of Asian people." Afterwards she goes on to state that she checked with Judy, an Asian woman who works in hair and make-up, who confirmed the general Asian sentiment by stating that "people did tease me by saying 'Ching chong.'" Thus she begins by constructing herself as innocent, unknowledgable, and unaware, then moves to being surprised to learn that what she said was offensive. Next, she suggests the harmful part of her comments were unintentional, and finally, she offers an apology. However, the apology takes the form of a justification for future trangressions, while simultaneously blaming the victim – which unfortunately downplays the offensive nature of her comments and the sentiments of those who challenged them by suggesting that those who felt insulted were like adults who could not grow beyond childhood scars. She also said that she felt "sorry for" instead of being "sorry to," communicating that she regrets that those incidents happened instead of apologizing that she made an offensive remark. She suggests that, because her comments were unintentionally made, they are somehow excusable because of their accidental nature; thus, she is not responsible for the harm they caused. Furthermore, by framing the whole issue as a personal and psychological/emotional one, she ignores the degree to which such racist language is structurally embedded within institutions and practices of everyday life, such as a mainstream media organization like hers and "the way her brain works." Finally, her last comment indicates that she did not learn from the situation, as she is apt to do the same thing again and apologizes for it in advance, as if it were to protect herself from future scorn when once again she utters racist comments.

Karen Lincoln Michel, president of Unity: Journalists of Color Inc., commented that O'Donnell's words "didn't sound like an apology to me" (Carlson, 2006). Esther Wu, in a *Dallas News* editorial, states that the words have so much power, because "it goes to the core of who we are. They also serve as reminders that no matter how long we've lived in this country, we may never be accepted; we will continue to be looked upon as foreigners, different, strange, exotic" (Wu, 2006). In addition, she states that the AAJC's audit of anti-Asian violence often starts with similar racial taunts. The OCA criticizes O'Donnell's ignorance of the connection between language and violence, stating that she does not realize "how this type of language can manipulate itself into much more serious and potentially violent acts" (ibid.). *Reappropriate*, a blog written from the perspective of an activist Asian American woman, says, "this is further insult. Asian Americans and race activists all over had better not accept this superficial lip service towards placation" (Jenn, 2006). O'Donnell did not reply to these statements or critiques.

On February 22, 2007, Beau Sia, an Asian American poet, uploaded a *YouTube* video called "An Open Letter to All the Rosie O'Donnells," in which he recounts a racist history and connects taunts such as O'Donnell's to hate crimes, drawing an analogy between diversity within the Asian American community and the queer community, and calling for an actual heartfelt apology from O'Donnell (Sia, 2007). This video prompted O'Donnell to post an apology on her blog on February 24, 2007, stating, "I apologize for any and all pain caused to any and all by my comments ignorance lack of compassion – empathy under-standing. U [you] r [are] right. i didnt get it. i know my intent was not to harm, yet obviously i did."[14]

O'Donnell's commitment to social issues (kids' rights, gun control, LGBT issues) distinguishes her from many previous perpetrators of ching chong comments. Thus, the disconnect among the vernacular use of ching chong speech as taunting, her mockery, her denial of such insults, and her hesitancy to apologize surprised much of the Asian American activist community. In his previously mentioned letter, John Liu commented, "It's so repulsive . . . that it's absurd. Coming from someone who herself has been indignant when she has felt that certain comments insult a community" (Cruz, 2006), and Karen Narasaki, in her statement on behalf of the AAJC, stated, "What is even more troubling is her response when the issue was brought to her attention. The sad irony is that Ms. O'Donnell, herself a personal cham-pion of fighting intolerance on the basis of sexual orientation, is unable to see beyond her own bigotry" (Campbell, 2006).

Protest of the ching chong incident worked on at least two levels: first, it critiqued O'Donnell's comments and ignorance, the micro-individual level of enacting racist speech and humor; second, it chal-lenged the media production, since Barbara Walters and other producers of the show did not distance themselves from the incident but rather remained silent, thereby implicitly supporting O'Donnell's statements. Asian American activists started to challenge the institu-tional responsibility of the networks, who support the perpetuation of racial mockery by providing a media space for its consideration nation-ally. Statements by Liu and Narasaki argue that Walters, other produc-ers, and ABC are equally at fault for allowing such insulting comments about Asian Americans, and by remaining silent about them. Unity: Journalists of Color also released a statement that was directed at Walters and the network, stating, "When one of the co-hosts demeans and mocks the language of an entire race of people on national television, it warrants an explanation by the show's producer at least, and by the network at most. ... By allowing O'Donnell's cheap jab at Chinese Americans to go unchecked, the network is essentially condoning racial and ethnic slurs" (Makwakwa, 2006). Thus, Asian American activists, in this case, recognize that media representations are not just the sole responsibility of individuals who portray or impersonate Asians and Asian Americans, but the institutional responsibility of both networks and producers who allow for such actions to occur.

"The Dog House" versus a Chinese Restaurant

Whereas O'Donnell's repeated use of the words "ching chong" played out on national television and in the public eye, another derogatory incident against Asian Americans took place on the radio talk show *Doghouse with JV and Elvis*, hosted by two disc jockeys known as Jeff Vandergrift, who is JV, and Dan Lay, who plays Elvis (McShane, 2007). "The Dog House" was a daily morning show on New York City's WFNY-FM station on CBS Radio and was also available via streaming radio on the Internet. The prank phone call segment first aired on April 5 and was rebroadcast on April 19, 2007.[15] In this skit JV and Elvis play upon Asian American stereotypes of the forever foreigner, male sexual impotence, the sexually submissive, exotic woman, and Asians as unable to follow humor in English.[16]

The premise of the skit is that Jeff calls a New York City Chinese restaurant to place an order. His voice is cold, robotic, and monotone; it sounds computerized and occasionally makes odd pauses when speaking. Whereas O'Donnell's offensive act consisted of a short improvised joke, this phone call lasted roughly six minutes, was purposeful and premeditated, and involved an extended interaction with three different Asians, presumably all Chinese employees of the restaurant.

The skit begins when an Asian woman answers the phone. The racialized and gendered circumstances of the prank become clear when Jeff asks, "Hi, how are you, Asian lady?" The "computer" voice carefully enunciates each word for emphasis. Because it is unclear what Jeff is ordering, or in fact what his motive for calling is, the woman employee hands the phone to a man, who then later hands it back to her. Jeff asks the female to speak up because he "can barely hear [her] ass." Jeff continues making sexually harassing comments, asking her if he should pick up the food so he can see her naked. When she is speaking he sometimes interrupts her with apparent comments such as, "naked ... or maybe I can pick it up ... that way I can see your hot

Asian spicy ass." Because she responds to Jeff as if he is an earnest cus-
tomer, not some rude sexually harassing, racist caller, it is unclear to
the listener whether or not she understands the meaning of Jeff's comments. She persists in trying to complete Jeff's order, but, unable to do
so, she passes the phone to a Chinese man, who also attempts to complete the order. The man gets further than the woman was able to do
and confirms the caller's order of an egg roll and sweet and sour pork.
The man gives helpful instructions to Jeff, telling him to be sure to mix
the sauce and pork together at home so that the food stays fresh and
does not get "soggy." However, Jeff mistakenly hears the word as
"faggy," and repeats "faggy" three times before changing topics,
having linked homophobia to representations of Asian American
men's impotence. Jeff then compliments the man, saying, "You are
very nice Chinese man." The Chinese man continues to try to complete
the order, but Jeff interrupts him and states, "I swear to fucking God.
Probably can't drive for shit but who cares?" The man at the restaurant
ignores this comment and then asks "Alright, anything else?" Jeff
responds by saying, "I need shrimp flied lice," pronouncing the letter L
instead of the letter R in the words "fried" and "rice." Jeff then asks the
man at the restaurant to tell him about his "tiny egg roll," implicitly
referring to his genitals. The phone call ends with Jeff confessing that
he is also Chinese, has trained in "kung fool," and that he would like
to have sex with the "hot Asian girl that answer the phone."

The second broadcast of the skit drew a response from Asian
American activists. The Organization for Chinese Americans (OCA)
became the largest critic of the JV and Elvis show. In a statement
released two days after the rebroadcast, the OCA demanded an apology
from the two hosts and CBS Radio and that they and their producer
should be fired. Florence Chen, OCA-New Jersey chapter president,
threatened a boycott, stating "we will be calling on the strength of the
Asian American market to urge advertisers to pull their support." Ben
Fong, a radio critic for the *San Francisco Chronicle*, also insisted JV and
Elvis be fired.[17] Even California State Senator Leland Yee joined the
campaign against JV and Elvis.

Then, on April 23, Karen Matteo, CBS Radio spokeswoman, stated
that JV and Elvis were suspended indefinitely without pay.[18] She also
said that Jeff Vandergrift apologized twice on the April 23 show.[19]
However, OCA and others argued that, after CBS's Imus scandal, indefi-
nite suspension would not suffice, and that JV and Dan Lay needed to
be fired. Vicki Shu Smolin, president of the New York City chapter of
the OCA said, "If they don't fire the DJs, it will be a double standard."
On May 12, Mateo announced that "The Dog House with JV and Elvis
will no longer be broadcast" (McShane, 2007). The show was taken off
the air, and the two DJs lost their jobs.

Asian American activists participated in the protest by picketing the show and making public statements.[20] They argued for apologies from the hosts and producers, foregrounding the need for both micro- and macro-level changes in media representations, and threatened CBS with a boycott, while simultaneously calling for the firing of JV and Elvis. They also compared Asian and Asian American racial marginalization in the media with that of African Americans by using the incident of Don Imus, who had been fired for referring to members of the Rutgers women's basketball team as "nappy-headed hos,"[21] as a justification for firing the disc jockeys; if Imus was fired for racist comments against African American women, JV and Elvis should also be fired for an offensive radio skit about Asians and Asian Americans.

A theme that arises in Asian American public protest of derogatory media representations is a comparison with other racial groups, as here. For example, a studio director of AAJC asked, "Had Rosie faked ebonics or exaggerated a lisp to imitate gays, would she expect people to be quiet?" (Hua, 2006). When protesting media, Asian Americans must also challenge the model minority stereotype, both to educate the audience about the problematic nature of such events and simultaneously to break down the model minority stereotype, the submissive and quiet Asian, to mobilize other Asian Americans.

Mimicry, Mockery, and Mobilizing Resistance

Rosie O'Donnell's ching chong comments and the JV and Elvis prank draw on stereotypes of Asians and Asian Americans. Both rely on racially essentialist ideas that connect Asians and Asian Americans to the punchline of the joke and the humor of the prank. When O'Donnell mentions Chinese reporters and mocks the Chinese language, she unintentionally and indirectly draws upon and highlights the forever foreigner stereotype and the experience of exclusion and otherness of Asians and Asian Americans. Her joke hinges upon the dominant culture's perception of Asian languages, the historical description of Asian languages as "ching chong," and the conflation of all Asians speaking with an incomprehensible accent.

JV and Elvis's prank draws upon three primary stereotypes of Asian Americans. First, it objectifies Asian women as submissive sexual objects. Second, it ambivalently emasculates Asian men while bestowing on them inherent martial arts knowledge. Finally, it reifies Asian and Asian American status as forever foreigners through its mockery of non-native English speakers. The prevalence of the word "Asian" throughout foregrounds racial components of discourse and stereotypes within the dominant media. Both instances rely on Asian

American marginalization in society and foreground them with a mocking rhetoric in dominant media. As we have suggested throughout the book thus far, representations like these become issues of power: Who has the ability to represent whom, and how are they represented?[22] In mimicking what they see as "Asian," both O'Donnell and JV and Elvis demonstrate their power to represent Asians in the media through mimicry and mockery; whether they intended (as the case of JV and Elvis) or did not intend (as in the case of O'Donnell) to mock Asians is irrelevant, it is the ability to mock Asians and Asian Americans that demonstrates their power in the dominant media.

As Bhabha suggests, however, there is a space where resistance is possible, where a response to mimicking and mocking acts and events can occur. It is in this space, or gap, between the mimicking and mocking image and the lived experiences of Asians and Asian Americans where activists can challenge the degree to which dominant stereotypes are offensive and fail to address the experiential reality of Asians and Asian Americans.[23] The responses by activists illustrate effective means of protesting dominant media abuses. First, both protests make clear the media's role in airing discourse that impacts the experience of Asians and Asian Americans, whether it is through mock speech or an extended prank call, and how these trangressions specifically apply to Asians and Asian Americans. In doing so, these media protests specifically center Asians and Asian Americans being offended, not just "race" more broadly. Second, both protests launch critiques at both the level of the individual, i.e. O'Donnell and JV & Elvis, and at the level of production, i.e. the networks who produce the shows. In doing so, the protests attempt to change or pressure those who allow for such representations of Asians and Asian Americans and recognize that the institutions and organizations that permit mocking actions are also responsible. Both also work at the level of representation *and* materiality, the JV and Elvis example most effectively. Both protests manage to achieve what protests of *Miss Saigon* were not able to do: get the dominant media to apologize and in the case of JV and Elvis, stop the show of the perpetrators.

Neither activist moments, however, was able explicitly to show or to explain "real" Asian Americans. Neither was able to explore the complexity of Asian and Asian American people or the complexity of Asian and Asian American culture; rather, each successfully drew attention to the way stereotypes of Asians and Asian Americans were false and inadequate representations of Asian and Asian American lives. They were not able to argue that, while some Asian Americans may speak with an accent, all are not all the same and are not foreigners to the United States. Also, they were not able to argue for alternative representations or to challenge the institutional and structural media industries, beyond a given program or network, that supports such discourse across time and space. Neither protest necessarily shifted the meaning and perception of Asian Americans in dominant media, which is something that the protests of *Miss Saigon* were able to do.

In the end it might be that protest, grassroots or media-mobilizations, might be productive spaces to draw attention to Asian and Asian American marginalization in society and media overall. However, "reactive solidarities" may suffer from being "reactive," versus proactive. As a result of being caught behind the eight ball, and having to respond to derogatory representations setting the terms and grounds for a debate, activists may not have the space to theorize, historicize, and contextualize adequately why racial harm exists, what racial injury means historically, culturally, socially, and politically, and how such injury functions more broadly in power relations among Asians and Asian Americans, dominant white society, and other racialized minorities. To do this would require time, proactivity, and a complexity of research, thought, and analysis that may not be fully possible in a reactive solidarity, but is possible in Asian American studies as a field, in Asian American organizations (media organizations in particular), and in alternative media productions. In the next chapters, we will see how Asian American independent media are making proactive efforts to influence media representation, putting forth resistant, but also sometimes self-defining, images of Asians and Asian Americans.

Asian American Media Independence

In previous chapters, we examined mainstream media representations of Asians and Asian Americans, and in particular stereotypes or "controlling images" that appear recurringly within dominant media contexts. Specifically, we discussed yellow peril, yellowface, gender and sexuality, and model minority representations. And in chapter 6 we examined protests of such representations. However, Asian Americans have also created representations themselves in and through independent and alternative media.

We suggest that the dominant representations in the mainstream make up only one site, one archive, for how Asian Americans have been and can be represented. Asian American filmmakers, media centers, and media advocacy programs and organizations have sought to create their own art and institutions and set up a site for the imagination, generation, and establishment of their own representations. Artists strive for *media independence*, independence from the mainstream, dominant, corporate, and sometimes capitalist influences. This broader goal of instituting a space where Asian American art can be produced and a forum for its distribution is key to Asian American media independence.

The focus of this chapter is Asian American independent media. In the first section we define independent media and then examine media that independent artists have created. This is followed by a discussion of different media artists and how they understand, and how their work functions as, independent media. In the final section, we conceptualize Asian American independent media as a vernacular discourse and provide some examples.

Defining Independent Media

Even though a fair amount of scholarship attends to Asian American independent media,[1] often "independent media" (or indy/indie media) goes undefined, and as yet no attempt at a comprehensive theorization has been attempted in print. When we say "independent," we refer to the non-mainstream production of media, with the recognition that the independent does have a relationship with the dominant and mainstream; sometimes it not only converges with the dominant and mainstream media but also, at least at times, cannot be distinguished from them. Independent media, therefore, exist in a close interrelationship with dominant media.

Typically, the concept independent media also refers to a "DIY" or "do it yourself" artistic ethic. Independent media are sometimes conceived, written, directed, produced, and even funded by the same person, or by a small group of people working together. This allows for artistic freedom and agency, in which one person or a small group of people will make decisions concerning writing, editing, directing, and sometimes advertising and distribution.

Additionally, independent implies that artists work free of corporate capital and dominant mainstream influences and constraints, and that their own whims and desires drive the creation of media products.[2] Deirdre Boyle argues that independently produced videos are free from "commercial constraints, conventional styles, and traditional interpretations fostered by mainstream media and the dominant culture" and have the ability to explore multiple voices and styles (1992, 16). To be free from commercial constraints often means that, in order to produce independent media, writers and directors must obtain capital from community members or rack up personal debt.

However, the term "independent" does not simply mean having independent funding, as some independent media are at least partly funded by corporations. For example, the television show *Project Greenlight* documents the making of an independent film. There is a competition for best screenplay and a separate competition for best director; both are selected from a nationwide pool of scripts and directors, respectively, and the director then gets to make the screenplay, which they have never seen, into a film. This television show was sponsored by such major companies as the cable station Bravo, the studio Miramax, Coca-Cola, Honda, Stella Artois, and the computer company Hewlett Packard. Yet it is generally understood to be an independent production. Thus, the term independent refers to funding, marketing, and production but also to other aspects, such as the audience, content, and context.

Independent also implies being alternative to the mainstream, emphasizing off-center themes, styles, and experimental forms. Film school films, documentaries, short themes, short films, avant-garde, first-person perspective, or personally narrated documentaries would fall under the general category of "independent," for example.

Asian American independent media cut across television, print, film, and radio. Only recently have studies appeared that pay attention to new media, such as the Internet.[3]

Additionally, however, independent media may come to be defined as independent simply because they are created by racial minorities. There is an assumption that racial minorities provide a perspective that is alternative to the mainstream, especially if the themes of their films focus on racial, ethnic, or cultural life, and even if they obtain funding from corporations. Auteurism, or the creative role of the director, plays a part in whether or not a given film is understood to be independent or not. So, if an Asian American writes, produces, and/or directs a film, then it may be deemed independent, even if it was financed in part or even fully by corporations. Despite his success in the mainstream and within dominant media industries, well-known director Ang Lee may be considered independent, because he is understood to be Asian or Asian American and because his early films, such as *The Wedding Banquet* (1993), were independently financed, even though his films were marketed and distributed in the mainstream.

However, Ang Lee is a good example of a director who does not explicitly identify as being Asian American.[4] Thus, in his case, media have constructed him racially, characterizing his work as more independent than his recent mainstream film resumé would suggest. Despite the mainstream success of his work, he continues to be viewed, in large part, as an independent filmmaker.

Similarly, because of its topical focus on Japanese Americans, the made for TV movie *Farewell to Manzanar* (1976) certainly has independent elements. John Korty, a Caucasian male, wrote and directed the film, which was adapted from the book of the same name written by Jeanne Wakatsuki Houston, a Japanese woman, and her white husband, James D. Houston. The film explores the Japanese American incarceration experience during World War II and employs Asian American actors. It is aimed toward a general public, as well as Asian Americans, but it is often included on Asian American film lists and on Asian American film course syllabuses. Its focus on Japanese Americans, on the unjust circumstances of the incarceration, and its predominantly Japanese American acting cast, as well as an anti-racist director, render this made-for-TV show independent in character, especially as it challenges mainstream television and film in important ways.

Musicologist Joseph Lam (1999) puts forth a way of looking at Asian American music that we adapt here to help define Asian American independent media. To avoid being restricted to stylistic and racially essentialist discourses, Lam argues for a consideration of the contexts of production and reception.

Music scholar Oliver Wang frames this consideration of production and reception as "who makes the music and why?" along with "how is the music used, how is it understood?" (2001, 442). Wang states that media, specifically music (but we extend his comments beyond music), are sites where "Asian American communities could be imagined symbolically" as opposed to materially (ibid., 443). That is, Asian American communities can be imagined through symbols and not just the physical and geographical constraints of neighborhood enclaves. Thus, Asian American independent media can serve as a constitutive rhetoric,[5] constructing an Asian American community through and around media products such as film, music, and art. One purpose and effect of Asian American independent film is to constitute an Asian American community abstractly. For example, Peter Feng (2002a) states the Asian American cinema serves to construct the current identities of Asian America by attending to the theme of historicity. In constructing and refining identities, Asian American independent media also construct a community made of refined identities.

What Independence Means to Independents

While it is beyond the scope of this book to conduct an ethnographic study of filmmakers, we will discuss possible reasons why Asian Americans may be producing independent media by considering how directors, producers, and artists have employed particular topics and reviewing other scholars' notions of what defines Asian American independent media. In her collection on Asian American artists, Kara Kelley Hallmark (2007) posits that the common theme and experience of racism in the United States unites Asian American artists and is a reason why they produce independent art. Thus, artistic work grows out of collective political and cultural struggles. That is, being Asian American is to be uniquely situated within what Oliver Wang describes as the "particular historical context of race, gender, class, and immigration experiences that have shaped people's experiences" (2001, 442). These unique experiences may lead Asian American independent producers to address topics such as, but not limited to, activism, immigration, adoption, civil rights, US colonialism, youth culture, multiracial heritages, ancestry, culture clashes, and performance, along with intersections of these topics.[6]

For example, filmmakers Eric Byler and Kip Fulbeck explore and redefine identity in their own films. Both directors have addressed the presence of an Asian American dynamic identity, especially in the case of mixed-race children. Byler's film *Americanese* (2006) focuses on a romance between an Asian American man and a mixed-race woman and the difficulties that arise when these "complex individuals . . . encounter race issues."[7] Fulbeck's *Banana Split* (1991) is an exploratory account of his own experience of being mixed race, recounting, among other issues, his experiences as a child and of dating in college. Both films illustrate the self-conscious, self-representational redefinition of identities that often permeates Asian American independent media: this self-representation explores, challenges, and refines identities in an attempt to deconstruct Asian stereotypes in dominant media films.

Daryl Chin posits that Asian American independent media in the early 1990s had a dual purpose: to "reinforce a sense of shared experience among Asian Americans of diverse backgrounds," while also informing and enriching the "larger society with authentic Asian American voices and viewpoints" (1992, 47). Wayne Wang's film *The Joy Luck Club* (1993) is a good example of fulfilling this dual purpose. Asian American independent media provide a site of reidentification or primary and secondary identification, both in the mainstream media and within the specific community. *The Joy Luck Club*, adapted from Amy Tan's book of the same title, is also a good example of a film that, while financed by Hollywood, engages with issues emerging out of Chinese and Chinese American experiences, and is made by a director widely known for his many successful independent films.

To think of Asian American independent media purely as products of Asian American directors, writers, artists, and creators narrows the conceptual lens too much. In referencing Asian American artists, Elaine Kim states that we should instead look at art "as a process, not exotic artifact or investment item, so that we can appreciate both the political identities it expresses and the aesthetic processes that are inseparable from these identities. "Such art," she suggests, inspires the creative expression of "Asian Americans who have felt excluded by particular forms of racialization from conversations about American culture" (2003, 46). In addition, artistic products, in the form of video, film, fine art, drama, music, etc., connect the past to the present and construct a future. Such works may recognize that identities, both political and cultural, are fluid and shifting and not fixed and static; thus, the old foundations of racial essentialism, identity politics, and explicitly activist media work are shifting into the realm of explorations of representation and identity.

Asian American Independent Media as a Vernacular Discourse

Up to this point, we have defined independent as being outside the dominant and mainstream media system. Importantly, Asian

American independent media have historically attended to topics of Asian American history and experience, serving both the Asian American and the non-Asian American public, and being better viewed as a process, not a product. Now we wish to expand upon these notions and develop certain ideas more fully, such as defining as well as further theorizing Asian American independent media in terms of pastiche and "vernacular discourse." We look first at the relationship of the independent with the dominant through the concepts of pastiche and subculture and then at Asian American independent media as a vernacular discourse through a variety of examples in order to help us analyze what Asian American independent media entail, how they relate to dominant media, and what Asian American independent media can mean for Asian Americans and media overall.

Although the focus on Asian American experiences within independent media is one of the features that distinguishes the independent from the mainstream, one way of thinking about independent media is that they only exist because of the presence of the dominant and mainstream media.[8] Asian American independent media interact with dominant media through a form of pastiche.[9] Pastiche is the creation of a unique artistic form or product constructed out of bits and pieces of a dominant or other culture (Ono and Sloop, 1995, 20). Thus, Asian American independent media borrow from mainstream texts, and sample and recombine them. In addition, independent media, for the most part, adhere to some of the format constraints of the dominant media. For example, Feng explains, "Even an independently funded movie must be aware of the requirements of distributors and exhibitors for products that conform to established parameters, such as the thirty-minute and sixty-minute blocks that govern broadcast television" (2002a, 7). As much as Asian American independent media, or independent media in general, may tend to operate from the margins, they are still related to, and sometimes restricted by, the dominant discourse.[10]

One can think of Asian American independent media as a kind of subculture in relation to dominant culture. Despite all of the problems one might imagine as inherent to the concept of subculture, we use it nonetheless for the heuristic reason that subculture sometimes subtly challenges dominant culture. Here, we draw upon Dick Hebdige's notion of subculture, as the "expressive forms and rituals of . . . subordinate groups" that simultaneously indicate the "presence of difference" to dominant culture, while becoming "icons" and "signs of forbidden identity, sources of value" for subordinate groups (1988, 2–3). Hebdige's theory is useful in conceptualizing Asian American independent media's activist and oppositional stance, in contrast to dominant media's derogation of Asians and Asian Americans via representation and stereotype.

In his work, Hebdige stresses the relationship between subculture and dominant culture; subculture challenges the dominant ideology and hegemony, not explicitly but rather indirectly. His examples include punk, mod, and teddy movements in the 1970s. Despite the fact that these subcultures were not united, and were disparate/ and sometimes unaffiliated with one another, they were all anti-mainstream and oppositional to the dominant culture in which they were, as Hebdige states, "ostensibly defined" (1988, 73). Thus, subcultures have oppositional qualities to the mainstream and represent a "noise" and disruptive presence in the process of mediating events through representation.[11] Hebdige argues that subcultures express "a fundamental tension between those in power and those who are condemned to subordinate positions and second-class lives" (ibid., 132). While we do not see Asian Americans as condemned to subordinacy, and thus as fated to living second-class lives, for the purposes of analysis, if we view Asian American independent media as a kind of subculture, this implies that current dominant media representations of Asian Americans are incongruent with their lives and with what it means to be Asian American. Subcultural expression involves a struggle over signs and signification and the power to control them. Engaging in the contest over what signs mean is political activity in and of itself. As George Lipsitz suggests, the politics over signs is as important as politics per se: "Politics and culture maintain a paradoxical relationship in which only effective political action can win breathing room for a new culture, but only a revolution in culture can make people capable of political action. . . . Most often, however, culture exists as a form of politics, as a means of reshaping individual and collective practice for specified interests" (2001, 16–17).

Given what we know about subculture, Asian American indie media might also be considered a subculture within the media industry, battling over the signification of Asian Americans and asserting the significance and signification of new signs to contest and challenge more limiting stereotypical representations of gender, sexuality, and beauty. Indeed, individual expressions and actions, although not intended to be oppositional, may inadvertently take an oppositional stance.

However, if we understand Asian American independent media work only within the theoretical framework of subculture, this would suggest that Asian American independent media are *inherently* oppositional and challenging to dominant media. However, sometimes independent media are created without regard for the dominant, and sometimes independent media also reify and reproduce stereotypes of Asian Americans.[12] Asians and Asian Americans can align themselves, intentionally or not, with anti-Asian sentiments or be complicit in propagating derogatory media images. Thus, as we move beyond Hebdige's oppositional framework, we also recognize indie media production of individual expressions, the ability to constitute community, and their unique form of and ability to create expression that centers Asian Americans and/or contributes to the notion of being Asian American.[13] Images of Asian Americans from Asian American and anti-white supremacist standpoints transform the environment in which simple stereotypes emerge, thus complicating the image instead of simplifying it.

We argue that Asian American media independence and products that develop from independent media work have the potential to serve the community and insert themselves within dominant culture in a resistant way; however, they are not always solely resistant. We theorize a purpose for Asian American independent media in which discourse from marginalized communities, while perhaps counter to the dominant discourse, does not always center opposition or work from opposition as a starting point, but serves the function of constructing and reaffirming cultural identities and community ties. In essence, Asian American independent media might well serve what Richard Gregg (1971) calls the "ego-function of the rhetoric" that focuses on group self-identification rather than opposition to dominant media. Traditionally, Asian American media attended to certain Asian American themes in an attempt to address Asian American audiences.

Asian American film festivals, such as the San Francisco International Asian American Film Festival or the Visual Communications Film Fest in Los Angeles, are organized primarily by Asian Americans, show films for Asian Americans and the broader public, and are generally about Asians and Asian Americans. Many scholars have attended to numerous aspects of what they deem to be "Asian American independent media." For instance, Daryl Chin regards them as speaking to diverse experiences of those who identify as Asian American, while documenting overlooked, suppressed, and misrepresented histories and also humanizing the bureaucratized experiences of immigration and assimilation (1992).[14] Asian American independent media, much like Asian American studies overall, seek to expand the breadth of knowledge regarding Asian Americans within United States cultural and social histories. A classic example that voices the multiple experiences of Asian Americans is the documentary *Who Killed Vincent Chin?* (1987), which explores the complexity of the Asian American experience by discussing issues such as Lily and Vincent Chin's immigration and acculturation, their racial humiliation, and the racial injustice leading to Vincent's death.

Similarly, *The Fall of the I-Hotel* (1983) tells the story of elderly Filipino men being forced out of their living space in San Francisco, the I-Hotel, because certain corporations wanted to use that space for expanding commerce. The story is as much about the activism this action generated among a broad, diverse community as it is about the tremendous struggle these men will experience upon losing their homes. Not only does the film humanize Filipinos, it also provides an historical lesson about the longstanding contribution Filipinos have made to US society and culture.

Asian American independent media work might oppose and resist stereotypical representations of gender, beauty, sexuality, and identity, but may also reify, amplify, comply with, and reinforce other stereotypical and traditional notions of identity and racial essentialism, while also serving self-representational and self-affirmation purposes, such as in autobiographical documentaries.[15] Thus, it is presumptuous to assume that Asian American independent media will be inherently oppositional and resistant to dominant culture. Rather, we argue that media portrayals, when produced by Asian Americans, have the potential to provide more complex narratives and images than we have seen in the dominant media. In addition, the independents may help decolonize media by reinscribing onto cultural memory Asian American images in place of objectifying white supremacist ones and, thus, change the landscape of dominant media overall.

We posit that, despite their lack of wide distribution and resources for production, one purpose of Asian American independent media is to illustrate the complexity of the Asian American experience, to help create new places for production and distribution, and to change the ideological field by introducing new symbols and metaphors. To illustrate the complexity of the Asian American experience, they may employ a variety of aesthetic strategies, such as narrative fictions, literal documentaries, experimental films, etc.[16]

Thus, Asian American independent media might knowingly or unknowingly influence the ideological field of dominant media. Hallmark argues that writing Asian American art into art history "does not change how we value art" (2007, xiv).[17] However, the recognition of Asian American art is the opening of a new classificatory set, in which, as Stallybrass and White argue, "new sites of symbolic and metaphorical intensity in the ideological field" begin to emerge (1986, 25).

Whether intentional or unintentional, by creating a presence, and thus by creating a space for production, Asian American independent media help influence the way that Asians and Asian Americans are represented within dominant media. To help us understand their role within the community itself and in relation to the mainstream and dominant media, we posit two ways of approaching Asian American independent media. One perspective draws upon the seminal work of the volume *Moving the Image*. This viewpoint assumes a self-representational stance of Asian American media; that is, drawing upon their own experiences, communities, and collective memories, Asian Americans intervene with a "camera, pen, or sound recorder" to put forth their ideas and concerns regarding dominant media misrepresentation or the lack of representation, while simultaneously providing their own image of Asian Americans (Leong, 1991, xiv). This perspective takes a more political and activist position on Asian American independent media work and presupposes that it is inherently oppositional, akin to Hebdige's notion of an oppositional subculture, while serving as a rhetoric of community reaffirmation, which is a characteristic of the vernacular rhetoric. Hebdige's notion of subculture allows us to analyze and deconstruct the activist perspective of Asian American independent media within dominant culture, while Ono and Sloop's vernacular rhetoric frames the message within the community. However, by looking purely at independent media productions, we also ignore the independent filmmaker's, musician's, and artist's forays into dominant media and cinema industries.

In this context, Asian American independent directors may produce, direct, or act in dominant media features while also participating in the production and creation of independent works – for example, the director Justin Lin or the actor Kal Penn. Justin Lin directed mainstream movies such as *Annapolis* (2006) and *The Fast and the Furious: Tokyo Drift* (2006) before creating his social satirical movie *Finishing the Game* (2007). Kal Penn acted in two movies released in 2006: the major studio movie *Van Wilder 2: The Rise of Taj* (2006) and the independent film *The Namesake* (2006). Often, the independent media circuit becomes a place for recognition,[18] allowing for the transition to dominant media industries and highlighting the relationship between dominant media financial infrastructures and independent media creative benefits.

We also argue that audiences, critics, and media construct Asian American independent media identities and associations.[19] Critics, media, press, and other public discourse categorize, for the public, the type of filmmaker and type of film, regardless of the self-representational or Asian American-produced aspects. One effect of public discourse is to fix and stabilize a fluid Asian American identity by simplifying complex identities. Although an artist, television show, or movie may not identify with the politics associated with the term "Asian American," dominant discourses or subcultural, marginal, or community discourses may take up a filmmaker such as Ang Lee as Asian American. We analyze filmmakers who take up, purposefully or not, Asian American issues even as they may or may not identify overtly with Asian American independent work that the now classic *Moving the Image* initially defined.

In summary, Asian American independent media are an alternative to dominant media and posit complex images and visions of Asian Americans that may be oppositional to dominant media. They are also vernacular, Asian American friendly, specific, and political on some level, and operate as an ego-function to inspire. Asian American media are diverse and wide ranging, uniquely situated in the cultural, political, and social experiences of Asian Americans. They are constructed by both vernacular identifications and dominant discourse categorizations. Asian American independent media are not truly "independent" of dominant media but are in relationship with them, through pastiche and through the economics of media production and distribution.

Leong reminds us that "Alternative media can imprint images and carry voices in the form of the film letter, film poem, film essay, film pamphlet, and film report" (1991, xix). Independent media provide a space and forum for different and alternative voices. However, film is not the only alternative and independent medium. In the exploration of how and why Asian Americans engage in independent media, we also extend our analysis into other commonly overlooked media spaces, such as Asian American music, comedy, and art.

In future chapters, we seek to answer how Asian Americans self-represent themselves through independent media products and how these independent media artifacts relate to dominant culture, whether they reify and reinforce or challenge and resist problematic historical representations of Asian Americans. Asian American media do not separate themselves from dominant media but rather engage with them from a variety of perspectives. By looking at independent media artifacts, we can see the difficulties of self-representation, the potential for changing and reconfiguring problematic images, and the style of Asian American media independence.

CHAPTER
08

The Interface of Asian American Independent Media and the Mainstream

İN this chapter, we discuss different examples of Asian Americans who produce independent media, from Mike Park's record label, to Margaret Cho's TV show and stand-up comedy performance and Justin Lin's independent film work. In his article "Encoding/Decoding," Stuart Hall has suggested that audiences may have a variety of interpretations of media products, ranging from dominant, to negotiated, to resistant readings. Dominant readings accept the current ideological and hegemonic status quo, often reproducing preferred interpretations and receiving the message in the way it was encoded (Hall, 2006, 171), whereas negotiated readings require some acceptance of the dominant message, but are accompanied by personal resistance and modification, reflecting the reader's own political and ideological position (ibid., 172). Resistant readings, however, do not subscribe to the hegemonic codes but rather, when observing and consuming dominant media texts, bring in oppositional frames of reference and thinking (ibid., 173).

We adapt Hall's work on audiences and apply it to both texts and auteurs. We look at ways media texts reproduce dominant representations, how representations are sometimes negotiated, and how sometimes they are even resistant. We also examine such independent artists as Park, Cho, and Lin to suggest that producers themselves do not simply resist dominant representations of Asian Americans but also work along a continuum from oppositional to resistant. Asian American independent media makers borrow from and participate in both dominant and vernacular culture. Thus, in our approach, we focus on the producer, recognizing that a rhetorical move is required, whether explicitly resistant or a more subtle move that involves an insertion into the mainstream and a shift in how one sees a particular medium, art form, or representation.

We begin with Mike Park's Asian Man Records (AMR) label and his side project, the band The Chinkees. Then, we examine his influence as an Asian American upon the ska–punk hardcore music scene, drawing attention to an Asian American presence within what is predominantly a white subculture. We start here to see how an Asian American musician operates using an independent music label of his own creation and how his music serves as a rhetoric of Asian American media independence.

Then we transition into a discussion of independent media that occupies, interacts with, embodies, and inhabits the space between independent and mainstream media by discussing Margaret Cho and her experiences in mainstream television and stand-up comedy. Finally, we look at *The Fast and the Furious: Tokyo Drift* (2006) and discuss Asian American independent film director Justin Lin and his making of a mainstream film. Through these cases, we see how Asian Americans in media generate mixed and ambivalent results through their opposition to and reification of Asian American stereotypes.

Asian Man Independence

Officially started in May 1996, Asian Man Records is the brainchild of Mike Park. A small and independent label by choice,[1] it operates out of Mike Park's parents' garage, has one employee besides himself, and conducts sales by mail-order and in "punk rock mom and pop" stores. Despite its meager resources, AMR is important in the indie music community and has had a huge influence on the ska and punk music scene, in particular by promoting new bands and resurrecting and releasing classic albums. For example, its catalog has re-released early albums by Screeching Weasel and the Queers while providing current popular bands, such as Alkaline Trio, with their first exposure.

AMR now supports fifty bands, although not all of them are Asian American, and lists more than 100 releases in its catalog (Haucke, 2003). Modeled after Dischord Records in Washington, DC, it conducts all business transactions through handshakes and verbal agreements, relying upon friendship, trust, and a common vision about the purpose of music to maintain and dictate the nature of business relationships (Moskowitz, 2005). The label only works with bands that are explicitly "ANTI-RACIST, ANTI-SEXIST, ANTI-PREJUDICE, and that support the ideas of peace and unity". Additionally, all compact discs released by AMR are available for $8 or less, thus keeping music affordable for the fans.

One must think of AMR as an outgrowth of Mike Park. However, as much as it is defined by Park, Park is not solely defined by the label. He has also founded the non-profit Plea for Peace (PFP) organization, formed the B. Lee Band and The Chinkees ska–punk groups, and released a solo acoustic record as a joint venture with Sub-City Records, called *North Hangook Falling*.

Although not well known in the mainstream music scene, Mike Park and AMR are well respected by indie musicians and fans alike. According to Louis Posen of Hopeless/Sub City Records,[2] Park is regarded as a "visionary and leader in the punk and music community," and is known quite simply as "The Man" (Moskowitz, 2005).[3] He serves as a role model for Asian American musicians and others in the punk scene, infusing his music with meaningful, political, and intellectual messages, and runs an independent record label and non-profit organization whose purpose is progressive social change. In the vein of punk's DIY ethic, Park created AMR as a means of releasing his own music along with that of his friends and friends of friends (August, 2005), suggesting one way in which Asian Americans have laid claim to media independence.

As is evident from his band names, song titles, and record label, Mike Park identifies himself as an Asian American and often foregrounds his identity as an integral component of his work as an entrepreneur, artist, and activist.[4] In an interview with Asia Pacific Arts, Park answers questions and talks candidly about being an Asian American musician and working within the medium of music: he created AMR out of necessity but also as a resistant and oppositional act within the music industry when he realized that "the music business was something that I had little in common with and the hope that I could make my own rules and be involved in music under my own guidelines."

Since the informal and open nature of independent music allows for Park's DIY ethic to flourish and thus enables him to present a different model of making and distributing his work, eschewing contracts and a purely for-profit company model. Park is able to correct what he sees as one of the problems with the mainstream music industry: the lack of Asian American musicians and role models, because the major corporations "don't want to invest the money" in making an Asian American pop star. At the same time he says, concerning the mainstream ignorance of mixed-race Asian Americans such as Karen O, from the popular music group the Yeah Yeah Yeahs, "You have the Karen O's who are half Korean, but their face isn't Asian, so you don't look at them and go 'Asian.' You look at them and go 'white.' So it [an Asian American popstar] doesn't exist."[5]

In addition to operating outside mainstream business practices, AMR and Mike Park inject a dose of culturally syncretic Asian Americanness into independent music, particularly within the sub-culture of punk rock. Park's music demonstrates an awareness of Asian American experiences, attending to themes of racism, social injustice, and growing up Asian American. His groups The Chinkees and The B. Lee Band often focus on Asian American themes, particularly racism, personal experiences of Asian immigrant family expectations, and social injustice, as we will see in songs "Asian Prodigy" and "Don't sit next to me just because I'm Asian."

Park also drew on his Asian American experiences with his earlier band, Skankin Pickle, for which he was lead singer, for example performing songs that are in Korean, that concern his relationship with his father, that are about being Asian American, and that discuss Asian American popular figures such as Margaret Cho. Even after Skankin Pickle disbanded, Park's musical endeavors foregrounded his Asian American experience.

Park's first solo production, *The B. Lee Band*, a ska album with punk influence made with the group Less than Jake as the back-up band, consisted primarily of songs about friends such as "Gerry is strong," and the pressures of being a musician, such as "Song #3 part 2," and contained popular culture references to people such as "Mr Hanalei." His second side project, The Chinkees, is also a ska band that built upon the B. Lee Band and incorporates organs and solo acoustic guitar. Their first album, titled *The Chinkees are Coming*, deals with the same themes of friendship and artistic struggle but also expands into Asian American themes and social justice issues of peace and unity.

The music of these two bands points to a growing resistance to the dominant discourse, along with an emphasis on vernacular discourse and self-affirmation from an Asian American perspective. The names of the bands themselves indicate an awareness of the Asian American stereotypes that permeate society and the media. The B. Lee Band was originally the Bruce Lee Band, drawing on the stereotype of Asian martial artists, until trademark and copyright infringement charges were filed. As for The Chinkees, the name highlights the racial slurs specific to Asian Americans. Park states that the name "is not meant to be a racial slur, but just the opposite. It's meant to be a direct look at racism and the reality of its presence . . . Organ-driven ska, led by Mike Park, great songs about equality, racial issues and personal experiences!" Thus, the band's name can be read as a reappropriation of a racial ethnic slur, equivalent to feminist reclamations of "bitch" and LGBT reclamations of "queer." However, both names can be problematic, since both names also reproduce a stereotype and racist language. Can recontextualization override the iconic, like Bruce Lee, or the historic, as in the case of the slur "chinkee," meanings prevalent in the dominant media? Or can recontextualizing bring about awareness of issues of racism and the Asian American experience and promote social change?

Second, both albums contain songs that are in Korean: "Hongulmamotaya" (I can't speak Korean) and "Komsomida" (Thank you very much) on *The B. Lee Band* and "Norehapshida" (Let's sing together) on *The Chinkees are Coming*.[6] The songs are public demonstrations of Asian Americanness, specifically Korean American identity, merging personal experiences with American ska–punk musical stylings. As a result, these song titles create Asian American-influenced ska-punk independent music, drawing in non-Asian and non-Asian American fans and asserting an Asian American voice into the ska–punk subculture.[7] Other songs, such as "Asian Prodigy" and "Don't sit next to me just because I'm Asian," challenge the model minority stereotype from both a private–public and a personal–social view. "Asian Prodigy" describes the pressure Park felt from his parents to be an "Asian prodigy" when he would rather be a musician. "Don't sit next to me just because I'm Asian" explores people's assumptions that Park is smart because of his Asian ethnicity and his experience with the superficial friendships that arise from those assumptions.

Finally, Park samples audio from other media texts, both public and personal. The song "Our Country," from the Chinkees' album, opens with a recording of a woman leaving a message on an answering machine for "Mr Park," which is likely to refer to Mike Park's father. She is trying to sell a product to the Park family and is referencing an earlier event in which Mr Park did not react kindly to her sales pitch. She says,

> There's a lot of people Asian in our country, and I'd like to think well of them. And, uh, what are you doing for your people, is that, is setting a tone of unfriendliness and letting us know that you do not like us, and we've been bad in this country . . . We certainly like you. We let you into our country. So I think the least you can do is let me know your PO box or your home address and I can send you . . . through the mail. The plan that I wanted to show you and talk to you in a friendly and receptive manner . . .

The message seeks to get Mr Park to give this woman personal information, ostensibly in order to sell him something. In doing so, it threatens him by suggesting Americans will not accept him if he does not comply. The message serves as a passive aggressive threat to Mr Park, implicitly arguing that his unfriendliness might and will be perceived as a dislike of Americans. It does not include Mr Park as an American and implies that "American" is, in reality, white people. The woman continues with the passive threat, stating that this unfriendliness will affect his business, and that he should do this for his family or else go back to his homeland or country. When she states "We let you into our country," Mike Park interposes in a low whispering voice in the background, strumming a guitar and employing a sardonic and ironic tone, "Thank you for letting us into your country." In this song, Park's use of irony subtly highlights the racism and xenophobia the caller uses against Mr Park and, if we extrapolate from this case, against Asians and Asian Americans throughout the United States.

The beginning of "Brother, Brother," from *The B. Lee Band*, and the ending of "The Chinkees are Coming" utilize audio samples from movies that highlight Asian representation in the dominant media. "Brother, Brother" samples a segment from the 1982 film *They Call Me Bruce*, which also responds to the "all Asians look the same" stereotype. This sample recalls a conversation between Jun, the Korean cook, and his boss, who decides to call him Bruce. When Jun seeks to correct his boss and asks why he calls him Bruce, the latter responds by saying, "You all look alike, anyways." At the end of "The Chinkees are coming," Park inserts an audio sample from *Pulp Fiction* (1994), in which Christopher Walken's character recalls his time in a Vietnamese POW camp. However, Park also edits the sample, repeating the section where Walken's character says "damn the greasy slopes" and "the gooks." Thus, Park isolates the racial slurs and conversations to highlight what those sections communicate about Asians and Asian Americans. In the latter example particularly, these snippets communicate a dominant discourse about Asians' and Asian Americans' position in the media as "gooks" and "all the same," and as being cursory subjects and villains.

Park and AMR show how music, which may not be profitable in the end, can allow for creative freedom that embraces multiple voices and is artistically and politically challenging. Park foregrounds and emphasizes the political nature of his music, going against the stereotype of Asian American political apathy, youth culture, and mainstream pop-punk bands.[8]

The major shortcoming of Park's independent record lable is its limited audience, restrained by the resources and the goal to maintain the small size of the label. As Park stated in response to denying co-optation by major distributors and major labels, "A bigger label means bigger and more problems." However, the flexibility of an unencumbered small independent label does allow him to put out messages about Asian Americanness that are not limited by dominant mainstream media.

In the AMR case study, we attended to the more explicit and resistant productions of independent media which work to redefine and reposition Asian American representations in relation to mainstream, dominant culture, while affirming their particular identity and experiences. However, Asian Americans also continue to operate on the margins and in niche markets to construct resistant and oppositional representations that benefit a small audience but have the potential to reach a wider public.[9] In the next section we look at Asian American media artifacts that transition into a mainstream audience, yet encounter resistance from the dominant media because of an explicit Asian American representation.

The Margaret Cho Show[10]

We will use Margaret Cho's television show *All-American Girl* and the video release of her tour *I'm the One that I Want* as examples of artifacts that transition into the mainstream media while still explicitly representing an explicit Asian American oppositional representation.[11] *All-American Girl* suggests certain difficulties Asian Americans face when bridging into the mainstream. *I'm the One that I Want* recalls Cho's experience working with dominant media in producing the sitcom, and illustrates the tensions of externalizing and internalizing Asian Americanness within the dominant media.

First aired on September 14, 1995, *All-American Girl* is famous for having the first all-Asian American sitcom cast. Based loosely upon Margaret Cho's experiences growing up, it is about a 21-year-old Margaret Kim, a Westernized Korean American, and her family, which includes a pushy and overbearing mother, a laid-back father, a model minority brother, and a brash Americanized, yet understanding grandmother. The stories often revolve around the tensions between Korean and American cultures and values and Kim's negotiations of these tensions. The television show suffered consistently weak reviews and also garnered harsh criticism from the Asian American community, in part for the use of ethnic yellowface.[12] In their study of twenty Asian and Asian American men and women viewers of *All-American Girl*, Rona Halualani and Leah Vande Berg (1998) found varying responses.[13] On the one hand, many viewed the show as progressive and as an exemplar of a positive, non-stereotypical depiction of Asian Americans. Some viewers saw the Kims as representing the prototypical American family and the show as being equivalent to *The Cosby Show* for African Americans (1998, 218). Others perceived the show as providing a positive representation of Asian and Asian American women, a counter to demure Madame Butterfly and Lotus Blossom representations of cinema's past (ibid., 220). Still others saw it as breaking new ground for Asian Americans (ibid., 221), as obliterating the barriers facing Asians and Asian Americans in mainstream programming.

Others, however, viewed *All-American Girl* more negatively and saw the programs as reproducing Orientalist images, the model minority stereotype, a Horatio Alger-like figure overcoming adversity (Halualani and Berg, 1998, 222), and stereotypes of subservient women (ibid., 225). A Korean American man saw the representation of Korean American men as insulting and oppressive and the representation of the Korean American mother as particularly degrading, since Margaret, the main character, is represented as wanting to be nothing like her (ibid., 226). Another viewer considered that the show constructed Korea as backward and repressive and the United States as a site for freedom. As Halualani and Vande Berg write about one viewer, "She 'read' the series' promotion of American ideals in the narrative content as reinforcing Anglo superiority and a non-threatening Asian inferiority" (ibid.). Yet another viewer saw the grandmother character as representing a desire for total Americanization and a rejection of her Asian identity, hence "complete assimilation to American culture" (ibid., 226–7). After one season *All-American Girl* was cancelled, and its last episode aired March 15, 1995.

By analyzing Cho's material in *I'm the One that I Want*, we can see beyond the descriptive accounts of the events and television show and examine the influence of the dominant and mainstream media representation on a young Asian American who became famous through her independent stand-up comedy show. Thus, we can see Cho's personal accounts of the difficulty of transitioning to the mainstream media and situate it within a larger context/history of mainstream media representation.

I'm the One that I Want: Beyond *All-American Girl*

I'm the One that I Want (ITOTIW)[14] is one of Margaret Cho's solo stand-up performances centered on her professional life, particularly her rise to stardom and fall from grace in *All-American Girl*. Here we will conduct a close textual analysis of two sections of *ITOTIW* that concern her experience with the dominant media. First, we will analyze her account of getting the part in *All-American Girl* to see the effect of making the transition into the mainstream dominant media. Then we will turn our attention to Cho's account of the production of the show to illustrate the tensions that arise from working within the constraints of dominant media and to analyze the film of the tour as challenging and resistant media activism.

Approximately twenty-seven minutes into her performance, Cho tells a touching story about seeing her 95-year-old grandfather. Lamenting the declining ability of her grandfather to remember her, she states "he's like my primary father figure. My real father was deported when I was three days old. . . . my grandfather was always my main man." However, this time, Cho states, "he really saw me." Her grandfather, wrought with emotion, grabs Cho's hand and says, to an uproarious laugh from the audience, "What happened to your television show?" Here, Cho switches topics and says, "Once upon a time, I had my own TV show called *All-American Girl*," and explains that it "featured the first all-Asian American family on television. It was a groundbreaking show, and I was the young star." Then, she recounts the hard life of a traveling stand-up comic before continuing her account of *All-American Girl*. She states, "I was trying to get off the road and I got a deal to do a sitcom, so I went back to Los Angeles and my manager had me meet with all these different sitcom writers. . . . We met one guy that my manager really liked. Yeah, this guy is fucking hot! He just came off *Empty Nest*." The writer was Gary Jacobs, whom Cho states "took five minutes of my standup comedy and stretched it out into a half-hour pilot about a rebellious daughter growing up in a conservative Korean household." Juxtaposing the fictional sitcom idea with her real life, Cho says further that "the real story was that I had moved back home, after a brief stab at independence, and I had to live in the basement because my father didn't want to watch me come down off crystal meth. Now that would have been a great sitcom."

During her first screen test for the show, Cho describes her encounter with the gendered beauty norms of dominant media: "I got a phone call that night from the producer of the show. A woman named Gail. Somebody who I had really come to love and trust. And Gail called me up in a panic." Reenacting the phone call, and performing the part of Gail, Cho continues, "The network is concerned about the fullness of your face. They think that you're really overweight." And Cho, switching to a narrative voice, says, "I believed it. I believed it because I didn't know better. I was twenty-three years old. I didn't know who I was. This network seemed so huge and so smart, and they had money and everything and I was so insecure because, when I was growing up, I never saw Asian people on television. Oh except on *M.A.S.H.* sometimes." She then discusses Asians and Asian Americans on TV, using the example of *Kung Fu*: "But that doesn't really count because David Carradine, the star of *Kung-Fu*, was not Chinese. So that show shouldn't be called *Kung Fu*. It should be called *Hey, That Guy's Not Chinese*."

Later on, Cho recounts the first episode of *All-American Girl*. Its story was about Cho's character, who is also a stand-up comic, publicly embarrassing her family, only to learn her lesson and vow never to do it again. Switching back to narration, Cho sarcastically comments that her boyfriend at the time, the famous indie film director Quentin Tarantino, stated, "you fucking live to embarrass your family in real life."

Understood through Bhabha's concept of mimicry, *All-American Girl*'s racialized production served as a barricade to the white audience; they could not possibly understand this Orientalist mimicry made up as Asian authenticity, and thus the show simply offended Asian and Asian American audiences. First, the transition to *All-American Girl* caused a "watering down" of Cho's comedy, especially as it was the "first" show with an all-Asian American cast. By participating in it, Cho relinquished some creative control, and the show did not draw or build upon the edgy material and performance style of her stand-up comedy – the comedy that made her famous in the first place. The disconnect between Cho and Jacobs is evident in the final product, where Cho's stand-up comedic humor is sugar coated in the sitcom format. Second, in asking Cho to perform their concept of Asianness, the network effectively had her play yellowface and subjected her to psychosocial damage, symbolically saying that, "*Even though she is Asian, she is not Asian enough.*" In the end, *ITOTIW* draws a distinction between Cho's personal independent persona and the character that mainstream media and network television wanted and created for *All-American Girl*. Thus, the production of *All-American Girl* was a failed attempt by the mainstream media to produce an explicitly Asian American show without real knowledge of Asian Americans. Despite being the first show to feature an all Asian American cast, *All-American Girl* failed to bridge the gap between the dominant media and Asian Americans.

Performing the Independent Ethic: Cho's oppositions and realizations

ITOTIW allows us to see Cho's critique of dominant media in relation to her experience. In this next section, we discuss what it says about the challenges and dangers of working within the dominant media systems. However, we are not the only scholars to discuss Margaret Cho's performance; so, we draw here upon Rachel Lee's analysis of *ITOTIW*.[15] In her analysis of Cho's stand-up in general and *ITOTIW* specifically, Lee argues that she uses a "theatre of the body" that stages and situates histories of transnational migration, the borders of the body, and demands upon racialized and queer bodies (2004, 126). Whereas Lee's perspective comes from theater and drama studies, and sees Cho's performance as an example of the national abjection of Asians, we take a more rhetorical approach, looking at what her performance says about Asian and Asian Americans within Hollywood. Lee states that her argument is "not that Cho is unable to find home through Hollywood development but that home itself has become unsettled, revealed as a spatial arrangement whose ideality rests upon imprisonment" (ibid., 109–10).

However, we have seen Hollywood's problematic representation of Asians and Asian Americans, how Hollywood imagines and represents Asianness, and its various effects on Margaret Cho.[16]

In *ITOTIW*, Cho launches a critique of the dominant media, in particular through the examples of *Kung Fu* and *M.A.S.H.* and their lack, or weak portrayal, of Asian Americans. As a genre in dominant media, the sitcom focuses primarily on white characters.[17] Cho draws attention to how *All-American Girl* depicts a Korean American family and uses cultural tensions to drive the plot line. Her sardonic remark about her manager loving Gary Jacobs puts into relief Cho's own off-center perspective as an Asian American woman stand-up comedian. Such a perspective does not fit easily into a mainstream media production intended for a white audience, such as *Empty Nest*. We suggest that, rather than connecting with them, the mainstream media mimic and mock Asian Americans in *All-American Girl*, albeit perhaps unintentionally. By becoming an Asian American version of *Empty Nest*, *All-American Girl* does not capture Cho's experiences as an Asian American; rather, it is the dominant media's image of those experiences, an inadequate white-washed version of Cho's life, that makes it onto the small screen.

Cho describes the way she was pressured to play Asian: "Oh, yes, because I was fucking it up so bad, they had to hire somebody to help me be more Asian." However, she imitates the consultant who told her to speak "more Asian," to use "chopsticks," to put chopsticks in her hair, and to use an abacus – the things that the dominant media see as authentic markers of Asianness.[18] In its representation of characters through this racially troubling image of Asianness, *All-American Girl* was not marketable to any community.

According to L. S. Kim, Cho has effectively "mapped out a road of rejection and invisibility" that Asian Americans have traveled in their excursion into the dominant media (2004, 125).[19] Kim also states that, despite the difficulty of working within the dominant media, where her creative control was compromised in order to cater to white audiences and their notions of Asianness, Cho has also "illustrated, demonstrated, and demanded respect for herself, Korean Americans, and others who have been marginalized" (ibid.). However, Kim importantly says that Cho's experiences and performances ask Asian Americans to "recognize their active role in the ways television programs are made and to take up a more proactive role in our own representation" (ibid., 142). Indeed, Cho's experience in All-American Girl and Kim's call for Asian Americans to recognize their agency when it comes to media representation echoes Dorinne Kondo's question, "For what kind of Asian roles are we competing?" (1997, 231). In the next section, we turn to Asian American media productions that have spanned the boundary between independent and mainstream media culture, but also vigilantly asking "at what cost?"

The (Asian American) Fast and the Furious

We examine *The Fast and the Furious: Tokyo Drift* (2006) for three reasons. First, this film is directed by Justin Lin, an independent Asian American director best known for *Better Luck Tomorrow* (2002). Second, Asian American characters and actors play a significant role in the film, which is set in Japan, figuring a Japanese product of the transnational and global capitalist culture. Finally, it is a mainstream film that incorporates aspects of Japanese and Asian American culture while also being constrained by historical and contemporary dominant media norms.

In this section, we turn our attention to the presence of Asian Americanness, both in the production process and in the film itself. *Tokyo Drift* opened on June 16, 2006, to mixed reviews from critics. Roger Ebert says that Lin "takes an established franchise and makes it surprisingly fresh and intriguing"; whereas Richard Roeper, Ebert's counterpart, said "the whole thing is preposterous. The acting is so awful, some of the worst performances I've seen in a long, long time."[20] Despite these mixed reviews, *Tokyo Drift* opened to great fanfare and netted $23,973,840 during its opening weekend.

The characters of *Tokyo Drift* differ in significant ways from the characters of the previous *The Fast and the Furious* movies. The film's narrative revolves around Sean, played by Lucas Black, a young man sent to Japan to live with his father in order to avoid jail time. In Tokyo, a foreign place to him, he encounters Twinkie (Bow Wow), and eventually becomes involved in the underground world of street compact car racing and drifting, which is the art of sliding a car sideways through turns by alternating acceleration with braking in order to preserve high speeds. Sean meets Neela (Nathalie Kelly), but comes into conflict with the drift king DK (Brian Tee). DK's business partner, Han (Sung Kang), who soon takes Sean under his wing, shows Sean the ins and outs of Tokyo, and teaches him how to drift. As Sean and Neela's relationship blossoms, so does DK's disdain of Sean. However, DK's uncle, a member of the Yakuza – a Japanese organized crime syndicate similar to the stereotype of an Italian Mafia – discovers that Han must be cheating them out of money. DK confronts Han, which spawns a Tokyo car chase that ends with Han's death in a fiery car crash, with Sean watching. In an effort to clear his name, Sean challenges DK to race and eventually wins.

We argue that an Asian American independent media ethic exists within *Tokyo Drift*, as a part of the production of the film, along with its nuanced representation of Asians and Asian Americans. Here, we draw upon Kandice Chuh and her challenge to Asian American studies to "imagine otherwise" and to extend beyond topical discourse and into the realm of the epistemological. Chuh addresses the problem of solely interrogating "representational objectifications of Asian-raced peoples in the United States" and "dehumanizing images that affiliate certain object-ive meanings to certain bodies" (2003, 9). She challenges Asian American studies to look beyond Asian American themed culture, Asian American identities, and the examination of Asian American objects, and to look at what Asian Americans have to say and how the unique response is "Asian American." Thus, we use *Tokyo Drift* as an example of what a bona fide independent Asian American director might do when charged with directing a film within a mainstream franchise, and how Asian Americanness emerges in such a film. We will attend first to the representation of characters and then to the production of the film. *Tokyo Drift* addresses Asian American themes, particularly Orientalist notions of othering and challenges dominant media representations of Asians and Asian Americans.

The character of Han functions under the sign of Asian American. Speaking accentless English and exuding an American cool, Han is neither indebted to nor controlled by DK, but rather operates on his own, with his own gang. He invites Sean, the new American, into his group. Han displays a fierce individualistic and "devil may care" attitude, not fearful of DK and not necessarily controlled by the social norms of Japanese society. While standing on top of a roof, overlooking the streets of Tokyo and a mass of people crossing the street, Han tells Sean to "Look at all those people down there. They follow the rules for what. They're letting fear lead them." "What happens if they don't?" asks Sean. Han replies, "Life is simple, you make choices and you don't look back." Although the film centers Sean, Han shepherds Sean into Japanese society. Han is neither the hero, nor the bumbling sidekick, nor the "Charlie Chan." Rather, he is cool, collected, and respected. On the other hand, DK, the antagonist in the film, often incites conflict with Sean out of jealousy of his budding romance with Neela. Despite being the villain, DK, himself, is not portrayed as the "Fu Manchu" or Asian gangster. Rather, he is a wannabe gangster, a poser, a person who wants the social status of gangster but is unwilling to live that dangerously or to participate in dishonorable activities. More appropriately, he is popular, respected, and feared because of his drift king status and his cursory relationship with the Yakuza.

Han and DK complicate mainstream and dominant representations of Asians and Asian Americans when compared with the previous *The Fast and the Furious* films. DK distorts the representation of Asian villainy. He is not the one-dimensional Asian American gangster who terrorizes white business owners but rather is an insecure drift king who makes friends and enemies through his skills and familial associations. Whereas the first *The Fast and the Furious* film only features Asian American villains, Han is a refreshing character giving prominence to the Asian American-inspired culture of sport compact cars – something that was not recognized by the first two films.[21]

Justin Lin's work builds on that of Rob Cohen and John Singleton, who directed the first two films in the series. Although Lin has resisted being pigeonholed as "only" an Asian American filmmaker, he often uses Asian American themes, characters, and actors in his films.[22] The feel of *Tokyo Drift* clearly benefits from Lin's experience in the Asian American independent film scene. In the director commentary to the film, he gives many insights into his directorial choices, which indicate a nuanced view of Tokyo and of drifting subculture. Lin strays away from stereotypical Orientalist depictions of the city as mysterious, foreign, full of geishas, and crowded; instead, it appears as ultramodern, clean, and hip. When Sean first arrives in Tokyo, Lin comments: "And this is the Tokyo that I see, you know. That, if you ever go to Tokyo, this is what you'd see too. And it's funny, you see Hollywood films and it's usually geishas and gongs and buddhas and temples and stuff like that. But it's not. It's actually ultramodern. A very postmodern city."

Sean interacts with Tokyo not as a foreign space, but as a different city, as if he were visiting a large US city for the first time. Lin's strategic choice to represent Tokyo as a postmodern city and to get beyond tired exotic representations of it parallels choices he makes about the representation of drifting. In addition to the respect he has for the subculture, he is also keenly aware of character stereotypes and tropes and makes casting decisions based on them. In the documentary *The Slanted Screen* (2006), Lin talks about his experience with the character Han when dealing with the studio. He says he purposely wrote in the character of Han. However, the studio wanted the character to be African American, and Lin had to fight both for the inclusion of Han and for the part to be played by an Asian American. The casting of DK involved a global search, and Brian Tee was ultimately given the role. Historically, Tee has been typecast as an evil Asian villain and has had small bit parts on television. Thus, Lin reframed Tee as a complex main character.

Finally, Lin wanted to represent a global cast, and Neela's character helped do that. Where the white male lead usually ends up with the Asian female, this is not the case in *Tokyo Drift*. Lin makes a note of this trope, indicating that most would assume Neela to be a "hot Japanese girl." But Neela is racially ambiguous; her biographical background and her racial heritage are left open to interpretation.[23] Thus, *Tokyo*

Drift directly opposes the typical "white male–Asian female" relationship of the past and even pokes fun at it. In one scene, Sean is talking to Neela outside a pachinko bar, DK's abode in Tokyo. Neela moves to leave just as Han comes out of DK's place. Han recognizes that Sean can get into trouble with DK by talking to Neela. As Sean gets into the car, Han states slyly, "Why can't you go find a nice Japanese girl like the rest of the white guys around here?" This line indicates that Han is quite aware of the fetish that white men stereotypically have for Asian and Asian American women. However, it also indicates Lin's awareness of this issue and his attempt to challenge this dominant racial representation. In the director commentary to *Tokyo Drift*, Lin states that this question of Han's is his favorite line, and that "if you're Asian American you'll know exactly what I'm talking about and if it's not, you're pretty quick, you probably don't even remember it." Thus, this line becomes an inside joke for those who understand the problematic nature of historical interracial relationships between Asian and Asian American women and white men on film.

Despite the praise the movie has received, it is not without its problems. Brian Tee, a native of Los Angeles, plays a Japanese villain, which one could read as an instance of ethnic yellowfacing. There is a reification of gender roles, especially at the beginning, when Sean and Clay, played by Zachary Bryan, race to win a woman who announces that the "Winner gets me." Even though the film is set in Tokyo, the main story revolves around a white character. However, Lin states that it is a "summer popcorn film" within a franchise. Thus, the amount that he was able to push the envelope was limited, even though he was able to make it in a (what Ebert describes as) "surprisingly fresh and intriguing" fashion.

Conclusion

In this chapter, we have discussed a variety of Asian American independent media, from the role of Asian Americans in ska–punk rock to television sitcoms and stand-up comedy and finally to mainstream movies with an independent flair. By no means is this chapter meant to survey an exhaustive list of Asian American independent media. Rather, these examples provide a sample of a variety of Asian American independent media texts and of some of the ways in which they interact with mainstream and dominant media. These cases suggest some of the tensions and issues that arise when representing Asians and Asian Americans within and between mainstream and subcultural contexts and what that oscillation between the two entails in benefits and compromises.

We sought to explicate the role of a variety of types of Asian American independent media and their effects on, against, or even within the dominant media landscape. Using Hall's audience model and applying it to texts, we see an opposition, a challenge, and sometimes a reification of dominant Asian American representations through media performances, productions, and actions. Additionally, applying Hall's model to the auteurs themselves, we see a similar set of negotiations. In looking at Mike Park, Margaret Cho, and Justin Lin, we see an important move to establish Asian American media independence. The strength of this independence is embodied in self-aware producers working within the interstices of the independent and the mainstream and challenging traditional representations.

CHAPTER

09 Asian American New Media Practices

IN the previous chapter, we discussed Asian American participation in traditional media, such as film, television, music, and visual and performance art. However, Asian Americans have also utilized new media, particularly the Internet, in resisting dominant media representations, accessing the vernacular aspect of media representation and participation, and redefining Asian American identity. Indeed, the Internet has served as a useful site and space for Asian American independent media. In this chapter, we discuss ways Asian Americans have used new media for communicating ideas and reaching audiences. Through the examples we study, it becomes evident that new media offer possibilities for activism, for the critique of dominant media, and for the creation of a vernacular, independent media art.

However, while they do offer new possibilities for independence and activism, new media are not inherently democratic, activist, oppositional, or beyond capitalist influences. We recognize that the Internet and new media are constantly changing technologies that are often in tension with the concept of freedom. That is, with the commercialization of the Web, its "Big Brother" aspect, and the digital divide, new media are by no means free. The amount of information one can glean from the Internet, the prominence of online shopping, the cost of technology, the prevalence of white supremacists and anti-queer websites and organizations, and the lack of an educational infrastructure to teach people how to use the technology optimally all complicate the notion of freedom and democracy in cyberspace. Despite the hopes of Douglas Kellner (1995, 324), new media do not guarantee a "cyberspace democracy." This is to say that, despite our arguments about the vernacular and activist activities by Asian Americans in new media, we recognize that freedom on the Internet is not assured, but is, rather, something that is a constant and continuing struggle.

Thus, in this chapter, we show how Asian Americans advantageously use new media to form identities and representations not typically seen in the dominant media. However, two basic questions drive our analysis here: What kind of activism is possible on the Internet? And, is that activism for the individual or the collective good? We look at a variety of Internet artifacts, from the webcomics of Lela Lee, to the daily blogs of AngryAsianMan and KimChiMamas, to video participatory actions of everyday Asian Americans, and finally to the use of *YouTube* for the Jim Webb senatorial campaign in Virginia. We use these examples as case studies to illustrate examples of how new media play a role in constructing Asian American identities and in supporting Asian American activism and resistance by way of independent media production.

Lela Lee's Angry Internet

We begin by examining Lela Lee's online comic strip "Angry Little Girls."[1] To gain a full understanding of Lee's project and the role of the Internet, we explain why she made the comic strip, explain its history to this point, and finally discuss its future. Lee started "Angry Little Asian Girl" (ALAG) in response to the animated shorts she saw at Spike and Mike's Twisted Animation Festival. After leaving the festival, and infuriated by the "offensive male chauvinistic behavior" she witnessed, she created an ALAG animated short using a simple video camera (Choi, 2001, 10). While the short was a creative art piece that expressed her anger, she was also ashamed of her anger and hid the video for four years before showing it to friends and eventually screening it at the 1997 American Cinematheque film festival to rave reviews (Hua, 2001).

Lee also initially made about 300 T-shirts with the "Angry Little Asian Girl" cartoon character and quickly sold them all; demand was so high for the T-shirts that she started to receive phone calls after midnight (IndieRag, 2001). Based on the success of her film short at the American Cinematheque film festival and the T-shirts sales, she started the website www.angrylittleasiangirls.com, which she used to post an ALAG webcomic strip and to sell T-shirts, coffee mugs, bags, a DVD, wallets, and make-up cases. Additionally, her products became available through select retailers, such as Zumiez, which is a skate, surf, snowboard, and youth culture apparel, music, and equipment store in malls throughout the United States.[2]

The website was highly successful, receiving about 800,000 hits per month and up to a million during the holiday season. MTV showed some interest in producing something related to ALAG but, according to Lee, determined that there was "no market for Asians" (IndieRag, 2001). Lee subsequently expanded "Angry Little Asian Girls" by adding non-Asian characters and focused the themes of the cartoons, not just

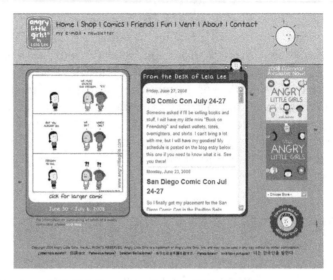

Figure 9.1   *Angry Little Girls!* homepage (accessed July 3, 2008)

on race but on emotions. She also retitled the website *Angry Little Girls!*
(ALG).

Although we discuss new media in general in this chapter, we recognize the complexity of "new media" and understand that webcomics differ greatly from blogs and *YouTube* videos, for example. Each
technology within the new medium of the Internet comes with its own
opportunities, limitations, and constraints. Webcomics build off the
print genre of comics[3] and generally do not depart from the format of
printed comics; rather, they use the Internet as a repository of information, translating the traditional print comic strip into a digital
format. Nevertheless, webcomics employ a "DIY" ethic, making the
Internet a place where one can display or show off one's comics when
print distribution is difficult or not possible.

Lee's ALG webcomic remains true to the traditional aesthetics of
comics more generally. When one enters the website (see figure 9.1),
the comic strip or comic panel occupies the left one-third of the
website. The center is taken up by a blog titled "From the Desk of Lela
Lee." Along the right side of the website are collections of Lee's comics
that are available for purchase. Appearing on top of the webpage are
the graphic hyperlinks to other sections of the website – "home,"
"shop," "comics," "friends," "fun," "vent" – which are the discussion
board, e-cards, friends, spotlights, and contact information. On the top
left of the screen is a small logo of "Angry Little Girls" Overall, the
website is basic in its design and easy to navigate.

Despite the normalcy of her website and webcomic format, the crux
of ALAG's initial popularity is the voicing of Asian American women's
opinions, opposition, and resistance. The premise, title, and main

characters, first Sue in ALAG and later Kim in ALG, are anything but the dominant media's stereotypical depiction of submissive Asian women. Rather, these characters speak their minds, sometimes blurting out their thoughts without filters. As the *Washington Post* described the lead character, the "girl's a human explosive" (Noguchi, 2001). Drawing on stereotypical Asian American experiences as a child, Lee reenacts what a child wishes she could have said in response to her overbearing mom, her own self-doubts, and ignorant teachers and schoolmates.

For example, in the first animated short, Sue encounters a teacher who compliments her excellent English and asks, "Where did you learn to speak so well?"[4] Instead of accepting the off-hand compliment with a polite "Thank you," Sue retorts powerfully, without mincing words, "I was born here, you stupid dipshit! Don't you know anything about immigration? Read some real history, you stupid ignoramus!!!" The teacher replies, "Oh my, what an angry little Oriental girl." Relentless, Sue replies, "I'm an angry Asian girl, you stupidhead!!!" The animated short ends with Sue returning home, only to be greeted by parents disappointed with her classroom behavior. Still, Sue just yells back, "Ah, fuck off!!!" Lee builds upon her own experiences but also taps into collective Asian American experiences and represents the way things *might have been* had she had the ability and wherewithal to respond with her true feelings.

Lee puts forth a new conceptual map of Asian American experiences. Typically, dominant media show the teacher's conceptual map. The dominant conceptual map entails an assumption that Asians are forever foreigners, not having a sufficient grasp of the English language. However, Lee's conceptual map asserts the right of Asian Americans to be in the United States and be citizens of it, and overturns the assumption that they are inherently foreigners and submissive. "Sue's" angry retort resists and reconfigures dominant conceptual maps of Asian Americans.

However, Lee's webcomic is not beyond criticism or without its problems. First, it reifies some stereotypical representations of Asians and Asian Americans, particularly one of overbearing and uncaring mothers. For example, two comic strips from the earlier version of the website,[5] under the title "Angry Little Asian Girl," feature Sue's interaction with her mother. In the one titled "Motherly Love," Sue says to her mom, "Mother, I have no friends. What should I do?" Her mother replies "You ugly. That why you have no friend." Sue then shakes her fist in anger. This representation might reaffirm an experience some Asian Americans might have with overbearing parents. However, this comic strip may also communicate, through the mother's broken English, that Asian mothers are also bad mothers and, because so few

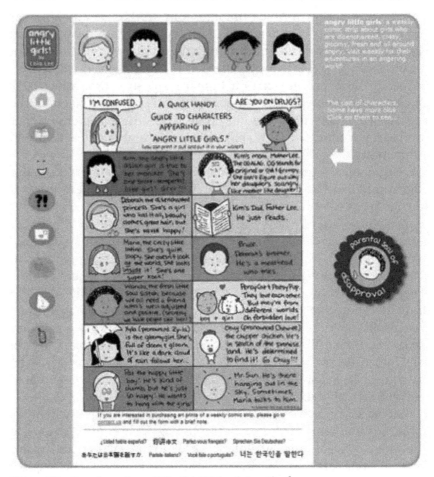

Figure 9.2   Page from *Angry Little Girls!* "Friends" section[6]

representations of Asian American mothers exist, that this is a common and possibly universal Asian American experience. In another comic strip, titled "Nobody," Sue reflects on what her mother says, recalling that, "If she's telling me to be somebody, then that means my mother thinks I'm a nobody." Once again, the comic constructs an oppositional Asian American female representation while simultaneously reifying stereotypes of overbearing Asian mothers.

Not only does Lee's webcomic occasionally simplify some Asian American parental representations, ALG also problematically and possibly unintentionally stereotypes other marginalized groups in the supporting cast. While Sue and Kim explicitly *challenge* stereotypes, the other characters arguably build upon them. "Wanda," the African American female, is described as the "fresh little soul sistah," whereas "Maria" is described as the "crazy little Latina."

Here, ALG utilizes the stereotype of African American women being soulful, fresh, up-to-date, and hip, whereas the Latina is constructed as crazy, out of control, and emotional. "Deborah" is a comic character with a Jewish surname and is described as the "disenchanted princess," which provoked some ire from "Virginia" in a chatroom discussion on the online *Washington Post* (2001), who commented that he/she was "rather offended by the character of Deborah" and asked Lee "Why it is bad for other people to make assumptions about Asians, but OK for you to make references to "Jewish Princesses?" Lee states that the focus is actually on the adjective "disenchanted," and pays little attention to the concern about a "Jewish princess." She admits that she is no activist but rather an artist who speaks for herself. Still, her art and webcomic inhabit culturally contested grounds, even as she makes important headway on the Internet for Asian Americans.

Ultimately, ALG has a fair amount of supporters, from everyday people and critics alike, along with a number of detractors. In the end, it is the humor – the ironic juxtaposition of adult understandings of race and gender, fiery temper, and articulate rebuttals with "Hello Kitty"-like cuteness – that gains and holds fans. Perhaps it is also an overturning of the longstanding stereotype of Asian Americans as quiet, demure, and unwilling to protest or break social convention in order not to offend that gathers attention. "She gets to say on the spot what too many have felt and thought in silence, and that, according to both Ms. Lee and her fans, is the core of her appeal" ("Hand Grenade," 2001). The webcomic also shares some of the relentless anger of the earlier comic strips. However, Lee does acknowledge that the strip has changed because of her personal maturity and the widespread audience. When questioned about the main character calling a teacher "stupidhead" and the possibility of educating instead of insulting, Lee replied, "Now that I've aged, I see what you're saying and firmly agree. Also because I have an audience (which I never thought about when I first created the video) I do have to be careful of what I say. I've changed ALAG and the strip a lot. I want it to be a positive read." Thus, the turn from ALAG to ALG marks a decided shift from an Asian American-driven and inspired webcomic to a universal "underdog" one. In connecting Asian American experiences of childhood to those of a wider non-Asian audience, Lee states that "the stereotype is something we all experience, but we never put words to it. We talk in the privacy of our friends and in hindsight think, 'I wish I could have said this.' But this comic strip character says right at the moment what she is feeling. And that's what people enjoy" (Choi, 2001). Although dominant representations do not position Asians and Asian Americans as marginalized or as "the underdog," Lee's webcomics of ALAG highlight her own experiences and those of other Asian Americans and other women.

Despite her success as an independent webcomic artist, Lela Lee's comic has not been syndicated. The cost of production prevents her from publishing it in print herself, but the low cost of the Internet allows it to be distributed widely. However, despite having 800,000 hits on her website per month, she states, "I would still continue doing it (ALG) on my website and continue doing it on the level that I am doing it where I am doing it all myself. But I'm thinking it has a potential to reach a mainstream audience. I really think it has the potential to be in the newspaper" (Janice Chan, 2003). Thus, Lee suggests she uses new media because she does not have access to traditional media. However, the question is whether her success would continue, shrink, or expand were her cartoon to be distributed via a traditional medium. While entering the mainstream might offer her a larger audience, what audience would she reach? She would gain more status, more recognition, possibly more credibility, and perhaps more money, but would her independent comic then become a watered-down mainstream product? Would the characteristics of the characters, the jarring humor, the expletives and cursing, and the resistant feminist and anti-racist representations that she has been able to cultivate in the new media context succeed as well in the dominant mainstream media?

The Asian American Blogosphere

Lee utilized the Internet to carve out a space for ALAG and ALG and thus inserted herself into the media sphere. In this section, we look at the Asian American presence in the blogosphere by considering the AngryAsianMan and KimChiMamas blogs. Weblogs, better known as blogs, are personal journals on public websites. Depending on technology and skill, one can change who can view, what they can view, who can comment, and the amount of interaction possible. Blogs also allow for hyperlinking, which is the ability to connect to other websites by selecting a highlighted word. Authors can also embed other media on blogs, such as digital video or music.

We recognize there are numerous Asian American-focused blogs we can study that attend to a variety of issues, both political and non-political. These might include Hyphen.blog, the Asian Americanists, Racialicious, and Asian-Nation.com, to name a few.[7] The May 2007 issue of *KoreAm* highlights some Korean American blogs that are not specifically politicized, such as thedeliciouslife.blogspot.com and metrodad (metrodad.typepad.com). Within this context, we choose to examine AngryAsianMan and KimChiMamas in more detail for specific reasons. First, blogs often become additions to current projects and websites. Thus, a filmmaker or journalist may have a blog as a side project or in addition to their primary form of media production. For example, the Asian American print magazine *Hyphen* has a website and a blog. AngryAsianMan and KimChiMamas, however, operate primarily within the blogosphere. They are known because of their blogs and not because of other, if any, media work. Second, both exhibit the capabilities and potentials of blogs in an Asian American independent media space, while moving from static weblogs with comment restrictions (AngryAsianMan) to multiple voices under a single moniker (KimChiMamas). Our goal is to explore the potential of these blogs to construct a different type of Asian American independent media made possible by new technologies and spaces.

Half Blog, Half Man, All Angry[8]

Despite his title, AngryAsianMan states that he "is not as angry as you think." However, anger at racism and anti-Asian American sentiments are central to the blog. Started in February of 2001 by Philip Yu, AngryAsianMan.com serves as a site to "rant about issues surrounding Asian American politics, identity, and representation in the media and pop culture" (Pak, 2007). But what started as a personal space for ranting about Asian American issues quickly attracted a larger audience on the Internet, garnering roughly 200,000 hits a month. The blog provides announcements about the Asian American community, satirical musings about daily life, occasional biting comments about Asian Americans in the media, and anti-Asian sentiments in public life. Although the various topics of the postings are not unique within the blogosphere, AngryAsianMan, in addition to having a catchy title, is a useful example of how blogs and the blogosphere allow for an Asian American voice and opposition, and serves as a central site for information and to discuss many different topics.

AngryAsianMan.com is still written and maintained by Philip Yu. To help maintain his singular voice, he does not allow for public comments from the readers, nor does he provide a space for readers to comment publicly on his own postings or other comments. Yet, at the same time, Yu is performing or enacting a character of "AngryAsianMan," whose catchphrase is *"that's racist."* This character is a satirical take on a caricatured stereotype of an overzealous Asian American, or "yellow power" activist, who sees racism everywhere while additionally pointing out (what Yu sees as) obvious instances of racism against Asians and Asian Americans. The character is constructed as Yu's response to what he imagines to be misguided Asian pride and power. Yet his facetious approach to this pride is rooted in the presence of actual racism directed toward Asians and Asian

Americans. Thus AngryAsianMan is a comic exaggeration that attends to and highlights anti-Asian sentiments in popular culture.

Although one can contact him through email, in essence Yu's blog is more of a traditional journal in which the audience is now privy to read. However, Yu's new media soapbox does allow for cross-referencing and hyperlinking to other blogs and sites, enabling readers to check another blog quickly for further commentary or to double-check the event that is being criticized by AngryAsianMan. For example, in the posting of August 22, 2007, the blog covers roughly four different topics, titled "the international gesture for 'chink,'" "lees unite!," "alive not dead," and "yet another stupid t-shirt design." In the "yet another stupid t-shirt design" posting, AngryAsianMan rants about racism and T-shirts, particularly a T-shirt titled "Flied Rice" that has an image on the front of a fly on a bowl of rice with a graphic of a Chinese restaurant menu in the lower right corner. In his rant, AngryAsianMan refers to Abercrombie and Fitch's T-shirt debacle, hyperlinks to another "tired joke" regarding Asian Americans on T-shirts and to the actual "Flied Rice" shirt itself, and finally to the Racialicious blog, which gives a more thorough breakdown of the T-shirt's racist imagery, in addition to allowing for comments from readers. Despite the singular voice and lack of audience participation in AngryAsianMan.com, the blog does *encourage* interaction with other texts, providing opportunities to tap into other blogs, media artifacts, and sources to increase information and understanding of Asian American issues in general. Thus, the blog provides a means for audiences to engage with mainstream information and gain access to a thoughtful, educated perspective.

Whereas AngryAsianMan is a singular voice with no comment streams, in looking at KimChiMamas we see another manifestation of blogs that incorporate other novel features of new media – participatory interaction via comment streams that allow for multiple voices within a single blog.

One Blog, Many Voices

Founded in April of 2006, KimChiMamas is a blog that addresses Korean and mixed-race Korean female parents. Initially started by Stefania Pomponi and six other mothers, it is a collaborative blog by fourteen women, each of whom also has her own separate blog. According to *KoreAm*, KimChiMamas is a "collective voice to moms balancing culture, identity, and race" (Pak, 2007). The blog challenges the stereotype of fiery and opiniated Korean mothers but, while superficially reifying the stereotype, actually complicates it by providing a multiplicity of voices. This complicates the dominant representation of Asian American parents, particularly the stereotype of bad mothers as being overprotective. Butler acknowledges complicating Asian American representation, stating "Asians are multi-dimensional. We're funny. We're irreverent. And we're just like everyone else!" (ibid.). Perhaps as a counter to the "angry" aesthetic of ALG and AngryAsianMan, KimChiMamas is concerned with parental experiences. However, Asian American parents are not, in fact, "just like everyone else," and the blog serves as a space to attend to the issues of difference, the difficulties, and the joys of being Asian American parents, and engages in explicit resistance to dominant one-dimensional portrayals of Asians and Asian Americans in the media. The KimChiMamas collective allows for Asian American parents to look at a variety of topics and to follow individual KimChiMama blogger personalities, perhaps viewing them as role models as parents. On the sidebar of the website are hyperlinks to each of the contributors' individual websites. Thus, readers may view any or all of the personal blog postings in addition to the collective blog.

In addition, the blog allows for a vernacular discourse among Asian American parents, which occurs in the comment streams of topics posted by the KimChiMamas. For example, they have "Open Thread Thursdays," where they simply ask, "What's on your mind today?" In this posting, readers of the blog are encouraged to post whatever topic is on their mind and converse among themselves. For example, on August 23, 2007, readers posted topics and commented on the backlash against China, xenophobia, and media coverage. Other topics include real-life experiences with the stereotype of cost-conscious Korean mothers, Asian parents' obsessions with brand names, and the possible tendency of Asian men and children becoming metrosexuals. The August 16, 2007, posting dealt with hair perms. Regardless of the topic, the presence of "Open Thread Thursdays" allows for audiences to communicate with others from whom they might be geographically isolated or about topics to which they may have little exposure.

More traditional media give less opportunity for the audience to oppose, negotiate, affect, or alter representations quickly and directly. However, blogs provide a mechanism for a multiplicity of voices and for the discussion of a wide variety of Asian American experiences from both producers and audiences. As a result, Asian American media representation can be negotiated or resisted in the same space and at a much faster rate, as we have seen in media protests in the previous chapter. Asian Americans' use of new media has allowed for an expanded register of representation and a constant renegotiation of the tension of what is considered a proper portrayal of Asian Americans in the media. This negotiation can include activism around political issues, as well as cultural representations and stereotypes and individual everyday experiences. We now discuss a *YouTube* video and a controversy that emerged during the senatorial campaign in Virginia between the Democratic challenger Jim Webb and the incumbent senator, George Allen.

"Macaca-Gate" and "The Daniel Dae Kim/Real Virginians for Jim Webb" Video

YouTube is a user-driven site that allows consumers access to a variety of videos: it is basically a free online videostore that welcomes donations to its stock. Users can upload videos and text onto the *YouTube* server by using a free profile. If the person who posted a particular video permits it, viewers can post text responses (which appear below the video). Among the long list of options *YouTube* offers, viewers can share, embed, mark as "favorite," rate, and upload the videos from webcams, cameras, or other digital technologies. Thus, the three primary benefits of *YouTube* are the easy access to distribution by the poster of a video, the wide Internet audience, and the ability of audiences and posters to communicate and of audiences to communicate with each other.

Posted on November 2, 2006, five days before the elections, the "Daniel Dae Kim/Real Virginians for Jim Webb" *YouTube* video was seen by more than 2,000 viewers within the first twenty-four hours of its posting. It featured actor Daniel Dae Kim, from the popular television series *Lost*, and was produced, directed, and uploaded by Eric Byler, a mixed-race Asian American independent director famous for critically acclaimed indie and mainstream crossover movies such as *Charlotte Sometimes* (2002) and *Americanese* (2006).[9] The video supported the "Real Virginians for Jim Webb" campaign, a grassroots organization started by Eric Byler and Annabel Park specifically aimed to counter the troubling remarks made about Asian Americans by the Republican incumbent George Allen. In a speech given during his tour of South Virginia, Allen had referred to an Indian American volunteer for Webb's campaign who was filming Allen's stump speech as "macaca."

As stated by Kim, the narrator, the purpose of the video is to mobilize Asian Americans to take part in the November 7 elections and to cast their votes for Jim Webb. As of August 27, 2007, it had received 19,287 hits and fifty-seven comments. Thus, we see how the discourse of the *YouTube* video frames a particular Asian American identity, while the comment stream illustrates how this representation is supported and affirmed or resisted and contested. Here, we employ a discourse analysis methodology to analyze the comments posted in response to the video. In doing so, we suggest that, no matter what media object or text is being analyzed, the method used should be relevant to the case and appropriate for the analysis being conducted. A reading of the *YouTube* discourse about the Daniel Dae Kim video allows us to see how at least some audience members are responding to a call for Asian American political participation.

Many of the comments posted were supportive of Kim's message and the *YouTube* video more generally. One comment supported Kim's construction of an Asian American political community and the message of the video while praising his participation in it, stating "I am glad that the Asian American community has people like Daniel Dae Kim urging members to vote. APIA vote. It's about time we are heard." *YouTube* viewer shiwi discusses a history of Asian American political apathy and commends both the Asian American community and Kim for his advocacy. Such comments support Asian American media activism and involvement in the political process. In addition, despite accessing a troubling representation of historical Asian American political inactivity, the representation of Asian Americans as politically active explicitly resists the dominant media representation, which often views Asian Americans as a model minority that does not protest or voice their political distaste for the status quo.

However, not all viewers wholeheartedly supported the call for political activism. Some viewers' posts, in fact, avoided the topics and, as a result, implicitly contested a call for Asian American activism by side-stepping the conversation and changing topics, focusing instead on media representation. To recognize avoidance strategies, we need to see the messages in context. Figure 9.3 is an example of such a conversation in the comment stream.

In this section of the comment stream, there are four instances of avoidance. Avoidance strategies seek to avoid or otherwise divert attention away from the conversation taking place in the comment stream and/or rhetorical goals of the video. By breaking from the thread, changing the subject, or using non-sequiturs, these comments side-step the video's message; in effect, avoidance strategies support dominant discourses about Asian Americans by diverting attention away from conversational lines that reaffirm Asian American political identity.[10] Nisleib's "Wow, Kim rocks!" is a comment about the actor and not about the content of the video's message. ThisGuysTrouble also avoids meaningful discussion and rather makes fun of Allen, albeit by using irony and hyperbole. The previous two avoidance strategies draw upon the *YouTube* text, one commenting on Kim's personality, the other parodying the "macaca" incident. However, the two other comments that use avoidance as a strategy draw upon outside information that is not relevant to the video. The first, natemorris20's "Uthers,"

almlin (6 months ago)[11]
Asian-Americans are no longer the "silent minority". They are now willing to make their voices heard in American politics. Great stuff. George Allen sucks.

nisleib (6 months ago)
Wow, Kim rocks!

shiwi (6 months ago)
I am glad that the Asian American community has people like Daniel Dae Kim urging members to vote. APIA vote. It's about time we are heard.

jilliebeans (6 months ago)
Cheers to you tube for making the silent minority heard! Now we just need to rid of the other 75% retarded Asian videos on this site and keep ones like these.

ThisGuysTrouble (6 months ago)
As an immigrant from the Isle of Macaca, I found nothing wrong with Allen's comments. I don't see Bastardians or Moronians making any fuss, it is simply a reference to their origin of birth. I have even heard some people say that there is no place called the Isle of Macaca. That is absolutely ridiculous. It is just south of Mapeepee.

> **yelli2** (6 months ago)
> Thanks for making me laugh with your comment . . . was having kind of a bad day! :)

natemorris20 (6 months ago)
UTHERS!!

morsosky (6 months ago)
heard george allen molested a girl too

weezcake (6 months ago)
I better see Webb win in Virginia on the 7th. If not, then I will have lost all faith in our country -_-

Kwekwe (6 months ago)
What a hypocrite? He was so angry with his wife yet he can speak English better than she does!!! Was he an "Other" all along?

Figure 9.3   Comment stream as it appears on the screen; yelli2's comment is indented, meaning that he/she was responding to ThisGuysTrouble.

references Daniel Dae Kim's character in the popular television show *Lost*; the attack marks Kim as an "Uther" or "Other" – names given to the villains on the show.[12] And it conflates Kim the actor with Kim's character from the television show. This type of discourse continues with Kwekwe's comment. Both postings focus on Kim's career and connect it to his personal and political message in an attempt to discredit his message.

Despite the fact that some postings reify dominant media by attempting to disrupt or rebut discussions, the new media space of *YouTube* responses also allows for continued dialogue. Consequently, some participants may defend and reaffirm the importance of media representation and of a proactive political presence for Asian Americans in media. Figure 9.4 is an example of such exchanges between the audience and director and producer Eric Byler.

Kealan8010's comment, with its vitriolic tone,[13] can be understood to be intentionally escalating the discussion. However, the director and producer of the video, named EricByler52, joins the comment stream and defends both the message and Asian American identity. Byler speaks on "behalf of our community, not to condescend, or to censor, but to bring to light," and defends Asian Americans, especially those involved with the Jim Webb campaign, from accusations of ethnic enclaving, isolation, and superiority by foregrounding Asian American political identity and democratic processes of civility.

As the "macaca incident" demonstrates, *YouTube* allows the public to view, respond to, and critique instances when Asian Americans may be humiliated in dominant media. However, as the Daniel Dae Kim video demonstrates, it also allows individuals to post videos to the Internet in order to gain wide distribution quickly, creatively, and inexpensively.[14] The technology even allows for dialogue surrounding the video and invites viewers to comment or produce their own videos. Indeed, *YouTube* offers a valuable potential space for an Asian American independent media production and discussion.

"Person of the Year: You!"[15] – Asian Americans in New Media

The case studies here help us answer a central question of this chapter: How much can Asian Americans utilize the Internet, and how powerful can the Asian American presence on the Internet be when it comes to challenging or reinforcing dominant media representations? Furthermore, can we consider the Internet an independent medium for Asian Americans?

While the majority of research points to the resistant potential of the Internet, which is certainly the case in such new media texts as ALAG and ALG and AngryAsianMan, the Internet is not inherently

kealan8010 (3 months ago)
look maybe it's time asian american's should refer to themselves as just americans and stop looking down on other americans

> **EricByler52** (2 months ago)
> actually i don't think daniel and i were looking down on george allen, or on anyone for that matter when we made this video. when someone makes a racist comment or uses hate speech, we speak for ourselves and on behalf of our community, not to condescend, or to censor, but rather to bring such comments into the light so that they may be accepted or rejected. we don't look down on those who condone the use of prejudice as a political platform. we simply disagree.

> **ares74** (2 months ago)
> Kealan – and I mean no hostility with this comment – but one could deem your comment to be very thoughtless or very ignorant. Certainly you solely wouldn't be to blame, but please realize that for many, a broader, more intensive understanding of the issue is needed in order to make a worthwhile assessment, instead of a relatively empty one, as you have made. You can reflect on this quote: "Better to remain silent and be thought a fool than to speak out and remove all doubt." – Abraham Lincoln

> **kealan8010** (2 months ago)
> it seems like your comment was full of hot air and no substance. What's your point? it seems like your deep winded comment came down to a few insults and baseless accusations coated in something someone intelligent would say,

> **CRAPPYNEIGHBOR** (2 weeks ago)
> kealan8010 maybe it's time you make a friend. looking at your channel I see that 100% of your comments are in response to your offensive comments, so why don't you just get your act together and pretend to have a better personality? no one will ever like you if you have a nasty personality so please just try and fix it. I really want to help you, we all do. take care, buddy.

> **kealan8010** (2 weeks ago)
> hahahah take your self rightious bullshit elsewhere. This ain't Barney and friends, this is YouTube buddy.

Figure 9.4

ares74 (2 months ago)
So, let's start over (on openly friendly terms!) Overall, I see you misinterpreted my comment. The very base of what I was and am trying to say is this: One needs to truly understand the complexity and deep-rootedness of the struggles of Asian-Americans – moreso than to the naked eye – before making relatively simple assumptions. Please understand that this goes not mainly towards you, but to society in general! Take care.

Figure 9.4   Comment stream for Defending

resistant. Rather, the Internet has the *potential* for actors to cultivate and use this space to construct and/or promote resistant ideas, such as on the blogs of KimChiMamas or, in some instances, on *YouTube* and in *YouTube* comment streams. Nakamura complicates the racialized assumption of Asian Americans as the "wired minority" who use the Internet primarily for consumptive purposes by arguing that it offers unique access to media that has not existed with television, film, and radio.[16] In this chapter, we have seen how individual Asian Americans inhabit the new media space and put forth different representations while contesting and sometimes reinforcing new and old media representations. New media have proven fruitful for Asian Americans, since access to traditional media venues often prove to be too difficult, too costly, and too restrictive for their voice to be heard.

Still, there is only so much that "you" can do as an individual in both new and traditional media. The new media examples we discussed in this chapter, for the most part, are not part of, nor do they aim to be, a collective effort to challenge or resist dominant media and dominant media representation; rather they document a variety of individual actions that utilize the productive potential of the Internet. Lela Lee used it to overcome the obstacle of her comic not being syndicated. AngryAsianMan and KimChiMamas utilized the blog format to make their voices and opinions available and accessible. Eric Byler and Daniel Dae Kim collaborated on a *YouTube* video to communicate an Asian American political identity and stance to Asian American audiences and others within and outside Virginia. However, these examples illustrate both the potential and the limitations of individual new media work. Individual activism has only a limited potential impact on institutions that create dominant representations of Asian Americans. Yet, the campaign for Webb and other collective efforts suggest the possibility of conjoining individual with group activism for a more long-term outcome.

CHAPTER
10
Mobilizing Organizations

IN latter chapters, we have examined protests by Asian Americans of mimicking and mocking media representations, such as Rosie O'Donnell's "ching chong" speech and JV and Elvis's prank phone call to a local Chinese restaurant. We have also examined Asian American efforts to gain media independence, ranging from the stand-up comedy performance of Margaret Cho, to work by Justin Lin to bring Asian American themes into a mainstream Hollywood film franchise, to Lela Lee and Eric Byler creatively using the Internet in an activist way.

These critiques are reactive, however, beginning only in response to a lack of images and representation or to racial humiliation in mainstream media. Explicit protests and resistance bring awareness and attention to media transgressions – and this is important – but they do not significantly shift the terrain of dominant media representation, especially over time and across space. Something or someone offends, spurring people to react collectively in what Espiritu (1992) calls "reactive solidarity." Kurashige challenges the longevity of "reactive solidarity," arguing that it does not address the "underlying social, political, and economic roots of racist violence," since the solidarity is temporary (2000, 164). As the event fades, so does the coalition that arose in response, and the underlying social problems then persist.

Moving into the mainstream by itself is not sufficient either, since gaining access to more established distribution channels or gaining sales in dominant commercial outlets may come with a compromise of an oppositional ethos and attitude, whether in the work or in the media-maker's distancing from Asian American experiences. The phenomenon of selling out, a term often used in the music industry, is a possibility, in which an artist or artists compromise their integrity and ethos in an effort to sell more and/or become more popular and profitable in a mainstream market. In thinking about implicit yellowface, gaining certain stereotyped acting roles in the mainstream media meant playing parts that ridiculed one's ethnic racial identity. In a humorous conversation between themselves for the *Tavis Smiley Show* on NPR, actors Kal Penn and John Cho discuss their experiences in the mainstream Hollywood industry in which they were often asked to perform stereotyped versions of Asians in order to be cast in roles. Filmmakers, too, might be asked by the mainstream studios to change Asian or Asian American characters to make the film more marketable, which was the case in *The Fast and the Furious: Tokyo Drift*. Fortunately, Lin won the fight to keep the Asian American character "Han," but such battles are not always won. Moving into the mainstream may have advantages in reaching larger audiences and markets, but often comes at a price.

In chapters 8 and 9, we discussed examples of independent media and media activism on the Internet, individuals occupying a niche space, as in new media, or creating a media text, such as music or movies, in order to serve a self-representational need. There, we studied examples of complex and three-dimensional Asian American representations on the movie screen, television, music audio players, and computers in the United States. Nevertheless, these new media examples tend to be the result of individual, not collective, actions and interests. Thus the new media practices we discussed depend upon individual action and focus primarily on micro-level change, not institutional change. Even when groups of individuals work collaboratively, such as in the case of Eric Byler's video or the KimChiMamas, as with reactive solidarity protests, these efforts very seldom bring about longstanding institutional change. If only a few individuals and films voice opposition loudly enough to be heard, while most remain on the margins, hidden away from the public eye, and being heard and seen by only a small group of people, the institutions that maintain dominant mainstream media systems have little reason to change. Thus, creating an independent space for self-representation does not change dominant institutions significantly; if it does, it does so indirectly.

This chapter moves from the individual to collective and institutional actions and responses by Asian Americans to the dominant mainstream media. Whether through reactive criticism and protest, media independence, independent production, new media, or institutional media organizations, Asian Americans are involved in both responding to dominant representations and institutions and working to provide an alternative to the dominant media. This chapter pays attention to sustained organizational responses to media domination, mimicry, mockery, invisibility, and intentional or unintentional exclusion as a means of enacting structural change aimed at inscribing Asian American media production and issues into the cultural fabric of the United States. In the move from individual actions to organizations and collective action, we do not argue that these are mutually exclusive. Indeed, individual actions contribute to organizations and collective actions, and organizations provide individuals with a space for collective action. Rather, we draw a distinction between the individual and the institutional in order to conceptualize and theorize the impact of organizational and institutional activism and change.

In this chapter, we look at independent film festivals, such as the San Francisco International Asian American Film Festival (SFIAAFF), as spaces of Asian American independent media distribution, exhibition, and convocation. We argue that institutions like the SFIAAFF are inherently oppositional, yet also reify a public display of Otherness. Then we discuss Asian American media activist organizations, such as the Center for Asian American Media (CAAM)[1] and the Media Action Network for Asian Americans (MANAA), as supporters of Asian American film and sustained and constant watchdogs of Asian American dominant media representations, respectively. Overall, we argue that Asian American media activism can take the form of either sustained or reactive actions, and that the combination of these strategies and the consequences of their actions can lead to long-term change in media representations at both superficial and structural levels.

Independent Film Festivals and Asian America

Since the Sundance film festival gained in popularity in the 1990s, the terrain for independent films has changed. Indeed, mainstream media and studios now regularly tap into the independent film market, in part because independent films, often made on shoestring budgets, have the potential for high profit margins if they are successful. Examples such as *Sex, Lies, and Videotape* (1989) and *The Blair Witch Project* (1999) demonstrate the potential profitability of independent films for major mainstream studios. When studios acquire rights to distribute independent films, inevitably the filmmakers are compensated, and they in turn can pay off debts (as in the case of filmmaker Kevin Smith) or possibly develop the financial backing with major studios to produce yet more films.[2] Indeed, indie films picked up by studios have become a lucrative business for both the studios and the filmmakers, who gain popularity, large audiences, and mainstream distribution. Film festivals help solve what an article in *Film Quarterly* calls a "problem of distribution" of independent film in the United States (Clarke et al., 1960, 19). Thus, the film festival has the ability to help market indie films and help indie filmmakers gain important exposure, and to make it possible for unknown directors to gain at least an initial entrée, if not a foothold, in the filmmaking industry.

Most generally, a film festival is a screening of a collection of films, often presented within a theater or a set of theaters organized around a particular theme or concept. For example, the Bicycling Film Festival centers around films that feature bicycles or bicycle culture, whereas Ebert's Overlooked Film Festival features first-run films Roger Ebert deems have been "overlooked" by mainstream audiences and critics. Most (although not all) of the time film festivals also feature panel presentations, workshops, and opportunities to speak with actors, producers, directors, and others involved in the film industry and film-making process. Importantly, some also include the potential for business deals, with distributors seeking to pick up films they think can reach broader audiences. The events are often subsidized by corporations,[3] even as the events are usually organized by those interested in creating and promoting the festival itself. If film festivals bring in money, often, parent organizations may distribute the bulk of that money in the form of grants to those wanting to make new films; thus, film festivals tend to be non-profit or low-profit enterprises. Nigel Watson (n.d.) suggests the most popular film festivals, such as that at Cannes, are a "combination of showbiz, culture, art, and film finance." However, organizing film festivals requires work and foresight: securing space and rights to films if necessary, bringing in filmmakers and others who work on films, raising money, marketing, and employing staff. Thus, festivals also have material effects involving tangible goods and physical space. When they take place, they bring varying combinations of showbiz, culture, art, glamour, media, and film finance to the setting. In doing so, they inscribe themselves within the cultural fabric of the community and location for that time; they bring something that was not there previously.

Although Sundance has become synonymous with independent film, we look to Asian American independent film festivals, examining them as organizational efforts in contrast to individual acts.[4] We start with film festivals, specifically, because of their involvement within the media landscape and their role in assisting the production and distribution of Asian American independent media. Because of their long histories we focus on the SFIAAFF, the Los Angeles Asian Pacific Film Festival (LAAPFF) produced by Visual Communications, and Asian CineVision's Asian American International Film Festival (AAIFF). Indeed, while we recognize that smaller Asian American film festivals exist, such as the Foundation for Asian American Independent Media in Chicago or the Northwest Asian American Film Festival, we discuss these three as the largest and oldest Asian American film festivals. We do this in order to understand how independent film festivals become important fixtures within the media landscape and the media industry, both independent and mainstream,[5] and these case studies illustrate the vital role of film festivals in institutional and organizational efforts to cultivate an Asian American media presence.

A Brief History of Asian American Film Festivals

The three major film festivals, the Center for Asian American Media's SFIAAFF, Asian CineVision's AAIFF, and the Visual Communications's LAAPFF, all have both historical similarities and differences. Of the three, Visual Communications (VC) was the first bona fide Asian American media organization. Started in 1970 and based in Los Angeles, it went through "every imaginable artistic and administrative challenge" in becoming established within the Asian Pacific American community. Its mission is to "promote intercultural understanding through the creation, production, presentation, preservation and support of media works by and about Asian Pacific Americans," and it was created with the recognition of the impact of the media and arts for community building, organizing, and empowerment. The VC programs include media education, media laboratories, access to and training in the use of digital equipment, historical preservation, and visual archiving.[6] Even though the primary activities of VC are media education and media production, it also sponsors a film festival, begun in 1983, which promotes independent Asian American film along with Asian international film.

Just as VC started by addressing issues of Asian American representation in and production of media, Asian CineVision (ACV) was also founded in order to address problems "in both representation in the media and access to the means of media production and distribution."[7] Started in 1976 in New York, and building on the momentum of the social activist movements of the 1960s and 1970s, ACV sought to improve social and cultural awareness for both Asian American and non-Asian American audiences. In doing so, its mission led to a multimodal effort addressing both Asian American representation and Asian American production in the media. Like VC, ACV provides media literacy training workshops, a print and media archive, and the *Cinevue Journal*. The film festival encourages Asian American production of films. Originally, ACV intended to produce Chinese-language television, but it quickly embraced a panethnic and expanding Asian American identity, organizing its first Asian American film festival in 1978.

The AAIFF in New York was the first major festival to display Asian American independent media and is dedicated to "screening works by media artists of Asian descent."[8] It has continued to premiere works of well-known Asian American filmmakers such as Wayne

Wang, Mira Nair, and Ang Lee. ACV also sponsors a touring festival. Started in 1982, the AAIFF National Festival Tour features rentals of their film library and provides a selection of newer movies that can be adapted to the individual budgets and tastes of those who wish to rent their films. Thus, the tour provides what ACV describes as the "seed-stock" for Asian American film festivals in big cities and in smaller locales.

The Center for Asian American Media (CAAM) originally hosted the AAIFF National Festival Tour from 1982 to 1984 before in 1986 starting their own film festival, SFIAAFF. SFIAAFF is closely linked to CAAM, which was established in 1980 in the spirit of 1970s activism. Originally, CAAM's mission was to "counteract negative images and stereotypes of Asian Americans in mainstream media by providing Asian American programming for broadcast on public television." Thus, its first efforts were in public television. However, CAAM sponsored the Bay Area AAIFF, which was linked to the ACV national touring festival. The year 1986 marked CAAM's first festival, known as the New Chinese Film Series. Then, in 1990, the first full-time film festival director, Bob Uyeki, secured the AMC Kabuki theaters in San Francisco's Japantown for an annual festival. Two years later the AAIFF marked another turn toward stability through its first continuous eight-day festival, instead of weekly Wednesday showings. In 1994, after an explosive showing of eighty films the previous year, the festival changed its name to the current SFIAAFF. The early 1990s also marked a shift in Asian American films at the AAIFF. Films now explored underrepresented Asian American communities, such as Hapa, South Asian, and queer groupings, moving beyond featuring only works about East Asians, Japanese American World War II incarceration, and other staples of early Asian American independent film. From the mid-1990s to the present, films at the SFIAAFF have been expanded to incorporate diasporic Asian and Asian American themes, as well as experimental films and videos, music videos, and film and video shorts.

These film festivals, in conjunction with their sponsoring organizations, are important to the development of an institutional resistance to dominant media representations. VC's presence in Los Angeles, SFIAAFF's in San Francisco, and AAIFF's in New York not only argue for but establish a long-lasting Asian American presence in cinema, analogous to the somewhat parallel case of the establishment of Asian American studies programs in colleges and universities. In each case, they represent a way in which Asian American independent media are screened and distributed within the public sphere and carve out a safe space for developing, producing, and exhibiting Asian American film. Just as important, these film festivals, through their longstanding presence in the community, communicate the importance of Asian American independent media and Asian American media presence and representation. By exploring their multiple functions, we can see how Asian American film festivals become oppositional through their presence, their cultivation, and the collaborative possibilities they provide.

VC's presence in Los Angeles, the undeniable center of mainstream US film and television, underscores an important oppositional and rhetorical point. It can be interpreted as an oppositional symbol of the need for Asian American media production and representation. In addition, it provides Asian American independent actors, producers, directors, and casting agents an opportunity to interact with dominant media players. Vice versa, it allows the mainstream to see Asian American independent media, as well as audience reactions to such media. The VC film festival invites a response from the dominant media and argues, symbolically, that Asian Americans are creators, producers, and consumers of media. VC also demonstrates that Asian American media production is not entirely separate from the dominant media but, by connecting independent filmmakers with mainstream filmmakers, is in a dialogical relationship with them.

ACV's National Festival Tour and rental library allow for multiple film festivals in different locations that extend beyond the geographical regions of the three major festivals. In this way, ACV occupies the role of distributor of Asian American independent films that may not be available at major mainstream festivals or movie studios and networks. CAAM also occupies this function as an educational institution that allows others the opportunity to view and purchase Asian American independent media that have been overlooked by the mainstream, while simultaneously providing independent filmmakers with an audience and, in some instances, a paycheck. Additionally, ACV's touring festival provides the resources, expertise, and literature for small student groups to bring Asian American independent cinema to their universities or communities. This is critical to an Asian American independent media movement because it provides access to new films, organized thematically, and easily attainable for those who decide that an Asian American film festival is what is needed in their community, universities, or cities.

Finally, the SFIAAFF demonstrates the collaborative efforts of Asian American independent media organizations, working both independently and in the public broadcasting sphere. Its relationship with CAAM provides an alternative space for distribution in the dominant mediascape. CAAM's role as the sponsoring organization provides an avenue for distribution of educational and independent works. Even though the CAAM Public Television and Distribution departments are separate from the SFIAAFF, having one's film screened at the festival "puts your work on the radar" of the other departments and can benefit the burgeoning filmmaker with future distribution of her film.[9]

We have looked at the three major Asian American film festivals and have noticed that they are not separate entities but are linked to Asian American media advocacy organizations. That is, the festivals are not just organized for the sake of Asian American filmmakers viewing other Asian American independent films but also are connected to a larger political mission of supporting organizations. Furthermore, VC, ACV, and CAAM evolved out of grassroots effort.

These three festivals all started around the same time as Sundance (founded in 1981), although Sundance's popularity comes from its backing and attendance by the Hollywood elite. Even after Sundance started, however, it seldom picked up Asian or Asian American films. Its function, then, is that it *helps* Asian American films and filmmakers by adding to the ethos of Asian American films, solidifying their legitimacy, alongside the work of the more independent Asian American film festivals.[10] Still, Sundance's rise to preeminence in the independent film world provides another space for Asian American film to be exhibited and may allow for an easier bridging to a mainstream audience, if that is the goal of a particular filmmaker. However, Asian American film festivals still provide a space for burgeoning Asian American filmmakers and films. The film festivals include the individual's need for exhibition under a larger organizational and institutional goal. They are able to secure more resources and to pass on the knowledge needed for a long-term media movement.

Films on Television: CAAM, PBS, and Interorganizational Relations

The Center for Asian American Media (CAAM), formerly known as the National Asian American Telecommunications Association (NAATA), was established in 1980 as part of the Minority Consortia, which aimed to place minority films on "public television and to create more funding opportunities for minority filmmakers" (Okada, 2005, 41). NAATA's role was to "acquire, package, and distribute independent Asian American films" (ibid.), but that original mission grew to include an educational and distributional purpose. CAAM's overall mission, therefore, is to fund, produce, distribute, and exhibit media that convey the diversity of the Asian American experience to the largest possible audience. To accomplish this, it has a variety of departments. CAAM has two funding initiatives in its Media Fund Department: the

"Open Call for Production Funds" and the "Open Door Completion Funds," both of which provide competitive awards ranging from $20,000 to $50,000.[11] Its widely known film festival, the SFIAAFF, exhibits roughly 130 works of Asian and Asian American filmmakers or Asian and Asian American themed films per year and is one of the largest Asian American film festivals, encompassing San Jose, Berkeley, and San Francisco, and its Educational Distribution Department contains a catalog that "includes more than 250 titles, constituting the country's largest collection of Asian American films and videos for educational distribution."[12] They hold such seminal documentaries as *Slaying the Dragon* (1988) and *A.K.A. Don Bonus* (1995), new documentaries such as *The Slanted Screen* (2006), and the PBS series of *Searching for Asian America* (2003). In addition, CAAM also has a relationship with PBS, a relationship that we will look into as a part of institutional transformation.

Okada's study of NAATA's relationship with PBS reveals the benefits and problems of organizational relationships for Asian American independent media. Her article outlines the impact of the Media Fund in controlling what is "Asian American film and video," stating that "NAATA has become the gatekeeper of Asian American film and video in recent years" (2005, 41). According to Okada, NAATA's relationship with PBS can restrict what national audiences end up perceiving as Asian American independent media and the Asian American experience. However, as she also admits, PBS and its documentary show *POV* is often the largest venue for Asian American independent film to be shown to a national audience, especially since it has aired such famous Asian American documentaries as *Who Killed Vincent Chin?*, *Kelly Loves Tony* (1998), *A.K.A. Don Bonus*, and *Sa-i-gu: From Korean Women's Perspectives* (1993).[13] Okada argues that *POV*'s acceptance of Asian American films put forth by CAAM falls into two categories: "the social-political documentary and the historical trauma film" (ibid., 45). As a result, she suggests that the arrangement between CAAM and PBS does not offer full access to the diverse experiences of Asian Americans, and that the film festival serves as the counterpublic and counterdiscourse to PBS as a singular public sphere. The film festival allows for response, dialogues, and community review, and is a collective social space for observation and exchange of ideas.

Okada's argument about the restrictions and limitations of CAAM's arrangement with PBS for the independent filmmaker are valid if we think of PBS as being able to control and limit the exchange of ideas for Asian Americans. However, if we conceive of PBS not just as a televisual public sphere, but also as being within the larger context of the mainstream media, we can consider a different reading of Asian American independent media and experience. In this framework, PBS operates as a marginalized and non-profit making endeavor within the dominant media. Thus, in this light, PBS's relationship with Asian American film and experience is complex and nuanced. Even if readers agree with Okada's crittique of PBS, CAAM's relationship with PBS nevertheless helps diversity media options, especially when understood within the context of the lack of representation, the ridiculed representations, and the regulated roles that Asian Americans inhabit in the dominant media. Even though the national screening of Asian American independent work on television is circumscribed by PBS, as a whole it is nevertheless diversified and expanded through the interaction and relationship between PBS and CAAM. CAAM therefore does not instigate a revolution within dominant media portrayals of Asians and Asian Americans, but it does introduce a change and a different representation.

MANAA's Organizational Critique of Stereotypes

The Media Action Network for Asian Americans (MANAA), formed in 1992, is an organization that monitors media, advocating "balanced, sensitive and positive portrayals of Asian Americans."[14] Meeting monthly in Burbank's Chinatown, members of MANAA initially came together to address the negative stereotypes that permeated the dominant media and to advocate and press for more respectful, complex, and balanced portrayals of Asian Americans. Guy Aoki, a member of the board of directors (as of Febuary 3, 2008), has previously spoken for MANAA on Adam Corolla's show about Rosie O'Donnell's "ching chong" speech. The organization has a lengthy list of goals and objectives that can be viewed under education, monitoring, advocating, organizing, and protesting for the benefit of positive Asian American media depiction. It also operates a 24-hour hotline on which individuals can report "incidents worthy of criticism or praise."[15] MANAA's particular importance in the Asian American media movement lies in its involvement with the Multi-Ethnic Media Coalition and Asian Pacific American Media Coalition, both of which meet with the top four television networks (ABC, NBC, CBS, and Fox) on issues of diversity in programming. Thus, in addition to lending support to local reactive solidarity groups, it sometimes has the power and ability to cause change in dominant mainstream media production.

MANAA's history outlines some of its influence. In July 1993, it negotiated with 20th Century Fox about the film *Rising Sun* (1993) and launched a nationwide campaign when the negotiation efforts failed. They were also able to pressure Joel Schumacher to release a public service announcement in reference to the movie *Falling Down* (1993) on account of its racially divisive message and its stereotypical treatment of Korean grocers as economic predators. MANAA has met with the president of Tristar Pictures, the executive vice-president and head of casting at CBS Television, and the editor-in-chief of *Details* magazine over several problematic media representations.[16] Thus, it seems that the organization has established itself as a prominent voice regarding Asian American media representation and has enough clout to bring concerns to at least some of those in control of the dominant media and thus to bring about positive change.

MANAA also provides resources for individuals, such as an online discussion group, a video guide, a variety of college organizations in California, media contacts, and a stereotype buster.[17] The video guide seeks to "spread awareness of video titles that resist the stereotyping of Asians" and lists movies that thoughtfully represent Asian Americans and/or feature Asian American pioneering actors. The media contact list gives television shows, newspapers, and other media along with information such as addresses, phone numbers, and emails, thus encouraging online visitors to engage actively in protest be personally contacting those in the media. The stereotype buster is an open memo to Hollywood that addresses the problems with Asian American representations on television and how to address them. Its header, "A Memo from MANAA to Hollywood: Asian Stereotypes," invites a different reading of the resources provided by MANAA for individuals. All three of these resources can all be seen as texts both for individual activists and for the industry and dominant media. The video guide provides individuals with examples of good films and indirectly tells dominant media the benefits of complex Asian American media representation: it reads, "These are good representations and we will reward future films by advocating for them on this list." Whereas media contacts might be useful for individual activists to voice their concerns to the dominant media, they also inform the dominant media that individuals *do* have the ability to contact them and are not out of sight, out of mind. The stereotype buster document is the most extensive and most complex of the resources MANAA provides; thus, we will spend some time discussing this document in more detail.

The stereotype buster employs the stylistic genre of an open memo to Hollywood and is titled "Restrictive Portrayals of Asians in the Media and How to Balance them." It begins with an introductory paragraph situating the role of the dominant media in defining the Asian image to the world and highlighting that this "has been shaped by people with little understanding of Asian people themselves – and with little foresight into how such images would impact the Asian American community." The memo points out how dominant media are currently portraying Asians and Asian Americans as "antithetical to American or

Western culture" and as having no "loyalty to the United States." The document creatively redefines stereotypes as a recurring clichéd stock of images amidst "the paucity of compensating images." In doing so, it frames the discussion of Asian American media representation in terms of what is damaging to Asians and Asian Americans, and non-Asians and non-Asian Americans alike. In a deft preemptive rebuttal, MANAA does not frame the document as a list of "do nots" and restrictions upon artistic license but rather as a challenge to create and think in new directions outside the Hollywood mainstays of clichéd stereotypes:

> This list is not intended as a bunch of "thou shalt nots" designed to inhibit the creative imagination. To the contrary, it is designed to encourage Hollywood's creative minds to think in new directions – to help our storytellers create more interesting roles for actors by avoiding old, stale images. It proposes to open up powerful and profitable story ideas previously overlooked.[18]

The memo then proceeds to list sixteen problematic depictions of Asians, each with a detailed explanation for why it is problematic, and ending with a "stereotype-buster," a simple strategy, to overcome the depiction. In terms of content, the list addresses much of what we cover in the first half of this book: the portrayals of Asians and Asian Americans as forever foreigners and yellow peril, of women as Lotus Blossoms or Dragon Ladies, of the model minority myth, and of Orientalism, without explicitly naming these stereotypes as such. Thus, its language makes it very easy to understand.

In addition, the format of the document lends itself to a certain reading. There is a lengthy amount of text devoted to the depictions and why they are problematic. However, the answer is simple enough to fit on one line. For example, one problem listed is "Asian cultures are inherently predatory." This is followed by a description of how Asian cultures, historically, have been viewed as takers without giving back and how this affects the process of their becoming citizens. Two media examples, *Falling Down* and *Rising Sun*, are given. Then, the answer and stereotype buster is simple: to show "Asians as positive contributors to American society." This format highlights the ease of changing or solving the problem of restrictive Asian portrayals. The problem – usually a stereotype – is historicized and widespread; however, the solution is simple – a one-line answer that counters the stereotype. The problem is that this is not yet being done. But the memo instructs Asians and Asian Americans that the dominant media can easily change such representations, and that it is up to Asians and Asian Americans to hold the dominant media accountable.

Despite MANAA's good work, its ability to meet and advise puts the organization in a very difficult situation. It has the ability to enact change, but under the guise of being a representative voice for Asian

Americans. It may therefore voice an opinion, or not voice one at all, thus allowing for racist portrayals or actions to go uncritiqued or even implicitly or explicitly supported. For example, it did not find Eddie Murphy's "yellowface" in *Norbit* to be offensive, despite its use of stereotype (Aoki, 2007). In this situation, MANAA's comments might serve as a justification for such media representations. In addition, MANAA is located in California, which may make it difficult for those outside of the state to participate in the organization's on-location activism. If local chapters were to develop, it might give MANAA more flexibility to attend to both local and national instances of media bias.

Just Me or Justice?: From the Individual to the Institutional

As we have seen, Asian American media independence requires individual acts as well as efforts on an organizational and institutional level. That said, it is important to acknowledge that the process by which organizations impact social change might be slower than vocal acts of reactive solidarity in response to given events as they materialize. It is one thing to send an email, or even hundreds of individual emails, to Michelle Malkin's website saying how preposterous her argument justifying the incarceration of Japanese Americans during World War II actually is. It is yet a different matter and purpose to establish a counterwebsite, or even an organization, to fight and correct innumerable historical inaccuracies about Asian Americans. However, having only individual acts as the way to create change, for example AngryAsianMan, may not allow individuals to communicate either directly or indirectly with institutions and organizations that produce representations of Asians and Asian Americans for the widest audiences. An organization or institution may gain or otherwise acquire the power to apply constant pressure for change and can become involved in the dominant media in order to create change from within with varying degrees of success. Thus, organizational bodies such as CAAM, AAJC (Asian American Justice Center), or MANAA collectively hold more clout and power than individuals, as they are able to pool resources, argue for space through a collective voice based on numerical representation, and attend to both institutional and individual levels. These organizations are pressuring mainstream media outlets to move beyond ridicule and stereotypes to produce representations that are respectful and intelligent.[19] Independent film festivals provide a space for respectful portrayals but in a small niche setting. Thus, organizations such as CAAM sometimes make it possible for Asian and Asian American media projects to gain national distribution.

Despite the prevalence of Asian American film festivals, there have not been many new activist media organizations emerging since the 1970s and 1980s. MANAA was set up in 1992, while ImaginAsian Entertainment and AZN Television were established in 2004 and 2005 respectively. ImaginAsian Entertainment is a multimedia company that focuses on Asian and Asian American inspired programming. It has five different media outlets, working across television, radio, a community based e-zine, theater, and cinema. AZN Television started as a "network for Asian America." In both cases, these outlets seek to provide a space for Asian and Asian American television programming. The former also opened a multimedia center on December 7, 2007, in downtown Los Angeles, called the ImaginAsian Center, dedicated to "first-run Asian and Asian American films."[20] However, after struggling to gain adequate distribution and advertising sales, AZN Television ceased broadcasting as of April 19, 2008. L. S. Kim (2005) comments that the "need for ethnic-specific networks and programming is acute," especially when affirming the place of Asians in America. New media outlets, networks, and organizations provide a sustained pressure on dominant media to expand and hopefully reconfigure their conceptual maps of Asians and Asian Americans. However, dominant media are not easily changed. Old historical representations do not easily fade away. New media outlets and networks, such as ImaginAsian, have the potential to create a space for self-portrayals of Asian Americans; whether or not they are independent of the dominant ideology or whether they reify Asian American stereotypes remains to be seen, but at least some spaces and opportunities are now established.

CHAPTER
11

Conclusion: Many Languages, One Voice

In the spring of 2002, the retail store Abercrombie and Fitch (A&F) released a line of Asian-themed T-shirts employing historically troubling mock Asian speech, Orientalized lettering, and squinty-eyed and buck-toothed Asian men in their designs. The Chinese Development Center in San Francisco noticed the shirts and notified the Asian American Students Association at Stanford University. Word quickly spread about A&F's T-shirts, with messages spreading across e-mail networks and posted on listservs, spurring student protests in places such as San Francisco, central Indiana, and Boston. Eventually, A&F pulled the T-shirt line from the shelves, and their public relations spokeperson, Hampton Carney, commented, "It has never been our intention to offend anyone."[1]

A&F continued business as usual, apparently forgetting both the imagery they had produced and propagated on their T-shirts and their encounter with Asian American activists who critiqued them. Despite some disappointment with the nature of the apology, Asian American activism subsided upon A&F's withdrawal of the shirts. However, Blacklava, a company that sells (among other items) Asian American themed apparel, created T-shirts that directly referenced A&F's mockery of Asian Americans, satirically challenging its propensity for tasteless humor by ripping off the name of the company and emblazoning the shirts with "Artful Bigotry and Kitsch." These T-shirts continue to be available for purchase.[2]

This example of A&F and Asian American activist responses to one of their products encapsulates many key points we make in this book.[3] A&F, a mainstream retail company circulates Orientalist representations of Asian Americans on T-shirts, reinforcing stereotypes for the sake of profit and defending their actions as "humor." A reactive solidarity emerges, and Asian American activists quickly mount a campaign to critique the T-shirts. A&F issues a non-apology, production of the offensive T-shirts ceases, and protest subsides. An already existing Asian American owned company that sells Asian American-themed products creates a counter-shirt specific to the A&F spectacle and, through sales, recirculates the memory of both the racist T-shirt and a critique of A&F.

As this example demonstrates, except for pulling the shirts, and perhaps for the fact that A&F might not make the same mistake in the future, little space existed for more complex educational work. Were it not for Blacklava, a critique of A&F's discourse might not have continued beyond the event and the initial response. Still, without even more institutional work, and without academic and public criticism challenging such representations (for example, in books such as this), and without programs and departments of Asian American studies and critical communication and media studies, the ability to understand such events in their historical, political, and cultural complexity would likely not be possible.

Certainly, critical reflection on historical media representations is needed, as we have sought to suggest, especially in the first section of this book. However, vigilant efforts to analyze, critique, and publicly comment upon media events as they occur also continue to be needed today. For instance, just as we were completing this book, yet another instance of anti-Asian and anti-Asian American discourse erupted. This reminds us, and hopefully our readers, too, of the continuing importance of conducting critical media analysis of representations of Asian Americans. On February 18, 2008, student opinion columnist Max Karson published a piece titled "If it's War the Asians Want . . . it's War They'll Get" in *The Campus Press*, the web-based student newspaper sponsored by the University of Colorado at Boulder's School of Journalism and Mass Communication.[4]

Karson begins the piece, supposedly a satirical take on racism at the University of Colorado, expressing sympathy for the plight of "Asian" students (the article sees Asians and Asian Americans as the same) and rationalizing his own past unpleasant encounters with Asians by saying to himself, "Asians are not evil cyborgs. They're human, just like you." However, after looking into an Asian's eyes, Karson changes his mind and realizes Asians simply hate whites. He then dedicates the rest of his article to delivering an anti-Asian rant, constructing Asians as yellow peril and arguing for a race war against them. He says, "And when he looked into my eyes, it wasn't just irritation and disgust that I saw – it was hate. Pure hate."

Karson's hyperbolic plan for a race war against Asians requires their capture, torture, and systematic assimilation. In part, his justification for such a war is that Asians are robotic, lack human emotions, and demonstrate the ability to do calculus problems in their head like computers. He wants whites on campus to locate such Asians, targeting math and engineering buildings to find them, and then, with extra large butterfly nets, to catch them. Once they are caught, Karson advocates dragging Asians to his apartment, "hog-tying" and then torturing them. What he calls an "Asian reformation," a process of physically enforced assimilation, concludes with Asians redecorating their homes in "American style," replacing "rice cookers with George Foreman Grills," replacing "green tea mochi with fried Snickers bars," and replacing "rice rockets with Hummers. And booster seats."

Asians and Asian Americans were justifiably offended by this article and had begun, at the time of writing, to mount protests. Blogs such as AngryAsianMan and ReAppropriate quickly commented on the opinion piece and provided templates of emails to send *The Campus Press* as well as links to other websites. On February 28, 2008, Sharon S. Lee came out with an article responding to what appears now to be a trend of satirical, backlash representations against Asian Americans on college campuses. At the same time, the campus began the process of image restoration. *The Campus Press* apologized for "any ambiguity of the satire that may have been misconstrued" (Hewlings et al., 2008). Chancellor Peterson from CU Boulder also released a statement, dated February 20, posted on a university website,[5] defending the article as free speech protected by the First Amendment to the Constitution, but stating that it was "a poor attempt at social satire laden with offensive references, stereotypes, and hateful language" and was greatly "wounding and damaging to a community."

The poorly written satirical piece had already offended people across communities, because it constructs racist caricatures, reproduces yellow peril imagery, and calls for violent physical action against Asians, such as kidnapping and torture. It constructs Asians as model minorities, but ones with robotic knowledge, not unlike the construction of Asians and Asian Americans as robots we discuss in chapter 5 in such films as *Akeelah and the Bee*. The piece paints Asians as threats to whites, a yellow peril requiring a white race war to be waged.

Initially, some might think this article is just offensive. Some might say it should not be taken seriously, because it flies under the flag of "satire." Others might think it an anomaly, that articles like it will not appear again, that it is the product of a bad seed, that it is a singular mistake, or that it is simply excusable. However, as this book has suggested, such discourse is institutionally and culturally embedded within media discourses, both historically and across media formats. There is a logic to such discourse, which means similar events will continue to occur, and in order to address it critical tools are required that help to comprehend and to recognize both its historical and its institutionally embedded nature – tools that we have sought to provide throughout this book. Such discourse has institutional, political, cultural, and historical roots and emerges regularly because of continuing, unresolved tensions relating to the history of US racism and colonialism. It has been one of our goals to understand the use of media representations, including controlling images or stereotypes, as part of the larger social logic of racism and colonialism as they relate to Asians and Asian Americans today. We have shown that racist discourse such as this often appears clothed as humor, thus diverting attention away from the serious, harmful, and sometimes painful effects it has. Finally, through our analysis across time and across media, we have shown that such discourse is by no means singular or anomalous but, indeed, is par for the course. It is deeply woven into the US media, and it is our contention that it will continue long into the future. It is useful to summarize the main arguments we make in the book in this concluding chapter.

In this book we have sought to equip readers with a broad understanding of Asian Americans and the media by situating Asian American representation across broad historical and contemporary periods and across a variety of media. We address the historical and the contemporary in order to understand the way representations function in today's hyper-communicative world. As we stated in the introduction, communication today gives the illusion of closeness within the global village that McLuhan imagined. When McLuhan coined the concept of the global village, no doubt he had in mind the crossing of cultural barriers, not the reification or reconstruction of them. As we have shown throughout the book, the community imagined by dominant media has been one of the Orientalized Other, an Other that is neither an acceptable member of Western society nor even at times a member of the human race. If they were to understand the dominant media representations, audiences would realize that media view Asians and Asian Americans as Others that include exoticized women, asexual men, a yellow peril threat to the United States, a forever foreigner, and/or a model minority.

All these media representations produce a mass psychosocial effect on both Asians and Asian Americans and non-Asians and non-Asian Americans. We posit early in the book that representations of Asian Americans in the media have been both sparse and problematic, nudging dominant society toward particular controlling images. In viewing Asians and Asian Americans through the same tired stereotypes and representations across a wide variety of media, these peculiar views become part of the archive of representations available for use, as well as representations habitually used, because people are so used to seeing these particular imaginings in media. In effect, they become the staging ground for possible interaction. Why do non-Asian and non-Asian American children taunt Asians and Asian Americans by pulling their eyelids back and speaking in a ching chong accent? If all or most of what Asian and Asian American children see on television are representations of Asian and Asian American kids doing martial arts moves, do they believe that they, too, should know martial arts?

Our book seeks to make a critical intervention in at least three ways. First, our contribution is an educational one. We seek to provide information that might be useful for understanding and analyzing media representations of Asians and Asian Americans. We wish to prepare readers for future incidents of media mimicry and mockery by providing information and a theoretical framework with which to analyze, study, and gain further knowledge about Asian Americans and the media. With this book providing a context, the slant-eyed and buck-toothed caricature appearing on a T-shirt, tennis shoe, or other commodity of contemporary capitalist culture in the future will make sense. The next time the words "Go home you Chink" are spoken, knowledge will have been acquired that these images and insults are not purely individual acts of hostility but part of a larger social logic and history of derogatory representations of Asians and Asian Americans.

Second, our contribution is a political one. By writing about and critiquing representations of Asians and Asian Americans, we seek to change the status quo, to improve the cultural condition in which we all live, and to encourage others to be critical of such representations. We also encourage readers to go beyond the experience of anger and frustration when racist media representations appear; in that way, we aim to inspire readers to be proactive, to engage in media analysis, to share critiques of media with others, to take criticism to a public level, to build websites or make art, and to form institutions that challenge the sad state of media for Asian Americans.

Third, our contribution is methodological. We aim to provide an example, through this book, of a way to analyze media representations that encourages understanding of media across historical and contemporary representation; across media formats and contexts; in the context of political and cultural experiences; and across dynamic identity spaces of gender, class, race, and sexuality. The multimedia approach sheds light on the newer instances of Asian American independent media, outside the traditional film and documentary roots of Asian American self-representation. Indeed, our focus on independent media has extended into music, the Internet, and even the dominant media. Asian Americans have especially carved out a niche in the Internet, in part because of their exclusion from other media and the ease of use and accessibility of new media technology. Central to our methodology is the notion that studying independent media, activism, and organizations is as important as studying dominant representation. Thus, we offer a combined approach, analyzing both dominant and vernacular media contexts, as we think each informs the other, and that a comprehensive media analysis requires attention to both. Finally, we encourage an intersectional analysis, one that recognizes that identities are fluid and ever changing, and that keeping in mind issues of race, gender, sexuality, class, nation, and the like is necessary for complex study.

The book begins with a review of the way yellow peril, yellowface, gendered, and model minority stereotypes have been used historically in mainstream US media to construct Asians and Asian Americans as a means for advancing particular political interests. We have argued that stereotypes were produced to reimagine particular kinds of racial and colonial relationships that have been handed down for many generations. As a result of their colonial origins, stereotypes have an ambivalent quality to them: they tend to both compliment and disparage. Thus, as Kawai (2005) has shown in her research on the model minority representation, one side of the coin is the model minority stereotype that sees Asians and Asian Americans as hardworking, dedicated, educationally successful, and the like. On the other side of the coin, Asian Americans are competitive, threatening to take over, and therefore pose a threat to the West as yellow peril.

Yellow peril discourse, too, remains in vogue, extending its lengthy history from the late 1800s into contemporary times. Historically, it existed to describe Asian Americans as threats to white women and the morale of society, morphing in the 1980s into the threat of stealing US jobs. Recently, yellow peril discourse has manifested itself in threats to urban and suburban neighborhoods in forms of gangs and model minorities respectively. For instance, when the Seattle Mariners were about to be sold to an investment group that included a Japanese American related to a wealthy Japanese man who planned to contribute money to developing the team, responses conceived of the purchase as Pearl Harbor all over again, suggesting that the Japanese were taking over America with their money, and that Japanese money mixing with US money was a bad mix – what Ono (1997) calls the "sexual threat of economic miscegenation." We can also think of the recent anti-Chinese rhetoric – SARS and lead paint on toys – as part of a yellow peril discourse. Thus, yellow peril discourse has persisted as a way of characterizing Asians and Asian Americans and has been used to advance particular partisan interests.

More contemporarily, the model minority representation has come into vogue. Stories about Asian American educational success, as well as representations of Asian Americans as medical personnel, feed into a divisive rhetoric that positions Asian Americans against other racialized minorities. The production of this kind of racial exceptionalism likely is not intentional, at least not at a conscious level. Yet, as a government report on civil rights suggests, the model minority stereotype is the number one reason why Asian Americans civil rights may be inhibited (US Commission on Civil Rights, 1992, 19–20).[6] Thus, it is important to challenge that myth, just as filmmakers such as Spencer Nakasako have done with his films *Kelly Loves Tony* and *A.K.A. Don Bonus*, and to demonstrate how the "American Dream" does not allow everyone to succeed, in fact depends – by definition – on many, many people not succeeding.

Whether discussing yellowface or yellow peril, Dragon Ladies, Madame Butterflies, or Lotus Blossoms, forever foreigners or more contemporary model minorities, *Asian Americans and the Media* has sought to investigate and critique dominant, mainstream representations of Asians and Asian Americans. Thus, this book strives to highlight Asian American activism and its many challenges to the history of derogatory imagery, while simultaneously suggesting new artistic and political ways ahead.

Beginning with a discussion of Asian American panethnic protests, then moving to define Asian American independent media arts and their histories, the chapters progress to a consideration of Asian American independent media productions, Asian American inroads into new media, and finally efforts to institutionalize through the collective efforts of Asian American media activists.

The book has attempted to highlight historical ways Asian Americans have responded to derogatory representation, such as in their protests of the Broadway musical *Miss Saigon*, Rosie O'Donnell's "ching chong" incident on *The View*, and JV & Elvis's prank radio show phone call. However, the work Asian Americans have done has been not only reactive but also proactive. Thus, they have not only responded to mainstream representations, externalizations of the dominant culture, but have created their own images, helped to produce their own art forms, and operated to forge a vernacular culture with its own complex meanings, ideas, and hopefully outcomes.

The book has explored newer ways Asian Americans have been self-constructed through media – for example, Justin Lin's creative construction of an Asian American character in *The Fast and the Furious: Tokyo Drift*, which is set in Japan and is part of a film franchise known for its Orientalist imagery. His film suggests one does not have to make an "Asian American film" for an Asian American aesthetic to appear in mainstream society. And we have explored the possibilities of the use of new media, in a similar way to Lisa Nakamura, who sees the potential for Asian Americans to play a different role from traditional media forms from which they were historically excluded. The Internet allows for new modes of activism. Whether it is the ease of distribution of short political films, evident in the Eric Byler's *YouTube* video involving Daniel Dae Kim or the prevalence of Asian American activist blogs, such as AngryAsianMan, the Internet provides an opportunity for, although not a guarantee of, activism and change.

Asian Americans have the potential to offer a resistant and emergent art in media, producing an alternative vernacular culture with its own logics, points of view, rhetorical modes, and intents and not simply a counter-culture or subculture. As Espiritu's analysis (1992) of two organizations, the Asian American Health Forum (AAHF) and the Association of Asian Pacific Community Health Organizations (AAPCHO), demonstrates, we believe that there is a benefit to working at the institutional and organizational levels, in addition to the individual level, to produce social change.[7] Espiritu's example illustrates that organizational and institutional efforts help secure resources and enable a longer term movement that is not grounded in an exigence of coalition building or reactive solidarity. We do not privilege the individual over the collective or vice versa, nor do we believe that they are mutually exclusive. Instead we want to highlight the impact of both individual and collective activism. More individual activist institutional efforts such as that by Blacklava are possible and do much to continue the momentum of more episodic activist moments. And, through such novel media forms as punk music and comedy, and through more collective efforts such as the building of CAAM, ACV (Asian Cinevision), VC, and MANAA, Asian American representations and organizations help produce and distribute Asian American media in order to challenge derogatory representations in the mainstream.

The book has also offered theoretical concepts and frameworks for understanding representations of Asian Americans – for example, that of racial ambivalence, which helps explain the dual praiseful/blameful dialectic in race and gender representations of people of color and white women. It has theorized notions of yellowface logics to suggest that explicit and implicit yellowface are parts of the historical and continuing disenfrachisement and discrimination against Asians and Asian Americans. Implicit yellowface representations are part of a system in which explicit yellowface existed, both regulating and ridiculing Asians and Asian Americans through racial performance and mockery. Mimicry and mockery are racialized strategies for making fun of Asian Americans and are embedded in complex colonial relations. However, these modes of representation can be altered creatively, as in the case of Blacklava and Margaret Cho, to respond to problematic effects of representations. Vernacular communities have emerged that produce their own discourses quite apart from dominant representations, yet affected by them. These discourses tend to be proactive, versus reactive, and help construct new logics and vocabularies of meaning. No longer are positive and negative representations the only way to understand media; rather, representations can change depending on contexts and may signify something quite different from their original meanings. Representations must also be studied as part of an intersectional effort to understand their many varied effects on multiple communities. Asian American independent art work and media, in a sense, move toward independence and open up possibilities for Asian Americans as well as an alternative space of enunciation, articulation, and representation.

Overall, this book has traced a long history of multiple, complex, and interrelated Asian American media, beginning with those in which Asian Americans played very little part (or no part at all, in the case of yellowface) and moving to media that Asian Americans fund, create, distribute, and exhibit. What we hope becomes clear now is that inertia continues to prevail where troubling representations are concerned, even though there have been inroads into altering a history of images of Asians and Asian Americans within a racially contested and neocolonial context. Even though there have been changes in Asian American representations in media, from the woeful Long Duck Dong in *Sixteen Candles* (1984) to the ultracool Han in *The Fast and the Furious: Tokyo Drift* (2006), from the opportunities had by actors such as Anna May Wong and Nancy Kwan to the more complex and flexible roles played by Lucy Liu and Sandra Oh (as not all of their roles fall into the Dragon Lady or medical personnel stereotypes), there is still sluggish change in media representations and an adherence to historical ones. Television provides a great example of this: whereas Asian and Asian American actors had been typecast as cooks or other domestic laborers (e.g., Hop Sing on *Bonanza* or Fuji on *McHale's Navy*), as female objects of sexual desire or sexually impotent men, or, in the late twentieth century, as female newscasters or anchors, there now exists yet another new typecast role, that of Asians and Asian Americans as medical personnel.

Furthermore, episodic and spectacular representations of yellow peril continue to emerge all over the media landscape, often with direct negative consequences. In the 1980s, as the US auto industry began to falter and virulent anti-Japanese sentiment arose to protest the success of Japanese automakers, Vincent Chin, a Chinese American who was seen and identified as a Japanese man, was killed in Detroit. From 1999 to 2000, Wen Ho Lee, a Los Alamos nuclear scientist, was unjustly placed in solitary confinement for nine months on trumped-up charges of espionage. More recently, in the post-9/11 era, innumerable Asians and Asian Americans, particularly South Asians and South Asian Americans, and Arabs and Arab Americans, face daily acts of discrimination and hate speech. Issues of Asian American representation and Asian American labor continue to be serious factors in contemporary media. And, since the 1960s, if not since Charlie Chan, the issue of the model minority stereotype and its effect on affirmative action policies and actions, as well as public arguments about race in US universities, such as at Berkeley, is as strong as it has ever been. Change has occurred, but new challenges, new forms of anti-Asian sentiment, which build on historically and culturally embedded and institutionally sanctioned anti-Asian and anti-Asian American discourses, and rehashed and reconfigured stereotypes still permeate the mediascape.

Given all this, what will be the future for Asian American media and Asian Americans in the media? No one can know for certain, but whatever occurs will no doubt have serious implications for Asian and Asian American inclusion, citizenship, and identity, with continuing attempts to relegate Asian Americans to the status of forever foreigners. If the traditional dominant media events continue to transpire – that is, Tsunami songs, JV and Elvises, and Charlie Chans – then we should not expect much change in the larger social views of Asians and Asian Americans.

However, one might argue, or assume, that progressive change is inevitable, that it will only be a matter of time before Asian Americans make their way more fully into both independent and mainstream media culture. As we have seen, however, there is no magical progression from bad to good. Ling-chi Wang (1998) went so far as to describe the yellow peril environment that affected Wen Ho Lee at the end of the twentieth century as being the most virulent of anti-Chinese discourse since the exclusion era a century before it. Things have not gotten progressively better. Moreover, most of the positive changes that have occurred have been ones that Asian Americans have struggled to make themselves. The status quo is always already in the process of offering hope for change and in manufacturing processes of reification and containment; it is simply not easy to change government, media producers, media moguls, and media industries.

Alternatively one might argue that capitalism will ultimately prevail, that once enough lucrative Asian American productions and Asian American actors appear (such as in *Lost* and *Heroes*, and even in the film *Harold and Kumar Go to White Castle*), it will only be a brief amount of time before Asian Americans succeed. In a way, however, the idea of "eventualism," that eventually capitalism will work in favor of Asian Americans, plays into the myth of the model minority, that Asian Americans will succeed despite all obstacles, including structural racism and colonialism. Additionally, it suggests a faith in capitalism. However, capitalism is not logical; there are no guarantees that just because some shows can make money Hollywood will air them. That is, racism and traditional ways of doing things may ultimately inhibit pro-capitalist logics.

Asian Americans are affected by what we might call *inevitablizing* narratives, which assume improvements are inevitable and all we have to do is wait. As Henry Yu (2002), Hiram Perez (2005), and Cynthia Nakashima (2005), for instance, have suggested, representations of Tiger Woods as the great mixed-race hope play on historical representations of mixed-race Asian Americans as the wave of the future, harbingers of the end of racism. What is appealing about Woods is that he has broken through the color barrier, become an internationally acclaimed, top-ranked golfer in what continues to be largely a white man's sport at the professional level. He overtly challenges historical representations of mixed-race people as tragic mulattos, as having tainted and polluted blood, as a threat to the Aryan gene pool, as psychologically mixed up and confused, as an inferior byproduct of mixed-race sexual relations. Woods inspires and, by his own proud existence, flies in the face of such archaisms.

Yet, through his connection to Nike, through the marketing of his image as "Be a Tiger," and thus through his construction as a Horatio Alger figure, not unlike Oprah Winfrey[8] and Jackie Robinson, media have facilitated his commodification in and through his mixed-race Asian American heritage. If Tiger Woods has succeeded, we must surely live in a non-racist society, right? Perhaps people think that if they can imagine themselves to be like Tiger, indeed to be Tiger, there must no longer be racism, there must no longer be unequal power and economic relations, all is well in the land of Oz – hence, the land of make believe.

Clearly, the examples we provide in this book counter inevitablist arguments that assume things will eventually get better, whether because it is inevitable that capitalism will work in our favor, or because of mixed-race and powerful heroic icons. The media representations we have seen over time and even in recent days at places such as the University of Colorado, Boulder, remind us that such easy solutions are not possible, and vigilant continued efforts to analyze and critique media will be necessary for generations to come.

We have not even begun to touch upon the future of Asian American media in the transnational and global context. In her study of Viet Kieu (overseas Vietnamese) music, Valverde (2005) demonstrates how social and political pressures in both Vietnam and the United States, particularly from the Vietnamese American community, affect how Asian American music is created and disseminated. Instead of dominant media representations, nationalism and transnational politics become the terrain of contestation. As more Asian American filmmakers are making and producing films overseas for global and local audiences, Asian American independent media critics will have to consider issues of both US and global citizenship.

While *Asian Americans and the Media* is not a comprehensive compendium of all media representations of Asian Americans, its sampling gives a glimpse into the representations in media we face currently and have faced historically. We have attempted to draw attention to multiple dimensions of media, ranging from *YouTube* videos and radio skits to newspaper articles and independent films. We have also sought to provide theoretical lenses, drawing from Asian American studies, communication studies, and media studies, from which to begin to understand representations as they appear. If readers remember the theoretical ideas circulating in this book, perhaps new images will not seem so new, so neutral, and perhaps so neutralizing. We have also sought to provide historical, cultural, and political contexts, where possible, to help readers make sense of how certain representations emerged when and how they did. The history of yellow peril, yellowface, anti-miscegenation laws, restrictions of citizenship, and stereotypes have all affected Asian Americans and have primed the media environment in a way that affects the representations produced in the mainstream as well as in independent arts.

Media are incredibly powerful, and while individual direct effects are hard to prove, it is indisputable that – overall – they have had widespread, longitudinal, geographically expansive effects. It is our contention that, through activism, research, and challenging mainstream representations of Asians and Asian Americans, changes are possible: not inevitable, not assured, but possible. It is with this hesitant optimism that we imagine a changed future of media and media studies for Asian Americans.

Appendix

Transcript of the JV and Elvis prank phone call to the Chinese restaurant. The call is initiated by Jeff, from the radio show, and there are three employees who speak on the phone.

CHINESE WOMAN:	Hi, may I help you?
JEFF:	Hi, how are you, Asian lady?
CHINESE WOMAN:	Good.
JEFF:	Very good.
CHINESE WOMAN:	Uh, place order?
JEFF:	I would like some Asian food.
CHINESE WOMAN:	Asian food?
JEFF:	Hello?
CHINESE WOMAN:	Yes, what would you like?
JEFF:	I would like some Asian food, son of a bitch.
CHINESE WOMAN:	Can you hold on?
JEFF:	Hello! Hello!
CHINESE MAN #1:	Hi, may I help you?
JEFF:	I would like some Asian food.
CHINESE MAN #1:	What kind of food would you like? This is Chinese restaurant.
JEFF:	Yes, I would love to have lots of Asian food, son of a bitch.
CHINESE MAN #1:	Okay, hang on a second.
JEFF:	Hello . . .
CHINESE WOMAN:	Hello, sir.
JEFF:	Hello.
CHINESE WOMAN:	You like pick up or delivery?
JEFF:	Maybe you can speak up?
CHINESE WOMAN:	Pick up right?
JEFF:	Can you speak up right? I can barely hear your ass.
CHINESE WOMAN:	Uh, okay . . . you want for pick up or delivery?
JEFF:	Should I come to your restaurant?

CHINESE WOMAN:	Ahuh.
JEFF:	Should I come to your restaurant so I can see you naked?
CHINESE WOMAN:	Yeah, you can come or you can come here or . . . yes . . .
JEFF:	Naked . . . or maybe I can pick it up . . . that way I can see your hot Asian spicy ass.
CHINESE WOMAN:	You can order take-out order . . . you need . . .
JEFF:	Spicy ass.
CHINESE WOMAN:	Oh yes, so you can you can come in . . . pick up . . . pick up . . . or you can order delivery . . . Do you . . .
JEFF:	Ok, I would come and pick you up.
CHINESE WOMAN:	Okay what would you like?
JEFF:	Do you have an egg roll . . . for a hungry player?
CHINESE WOMAN:	Yes.
CHINESE WOMAN:	Eh . . . the egg roll has a barbecue pork and shrimp and vegetable inside.
JEFF:	I have a big bank.
CHINESE WOMAN:	. . . You hold on one sec . . .
JEFF:	Oh . . . very sneaky.

(Switch to a different Chinese male co-worker)

CHINESE MAN #2:	Hello, may I help you?
JEFF:	Yes.
CHINESE MAN #2:	Yes.
JEFF:	Hello, hello Chinese man!
CHINESE MAN #2:	Yes, what can I do for you?
JEFF:	I would like so much some Chinese food.
CHINESE MAN #2:	Yes, that why we are Chinese restaurant, that's what we sell.
JEFF:	Ha ha ha . . . I would like many egg rolls. Can you feel me?
CHINESE MAN #2:	How many egg rolls? There's two egg rolls in one order.
JEFF:	Egg rolls, yes yes!
CHINESE MAN #2:	That's two egg rolls in one order.
JEFF:	Two times one, two times two, two orders.
CHINESE MAN #2:	That's four pieces . . . Okay?
JEFF:	Chinese man.
CHINESE MAN #2:	Is this for pick up?
JEFF:	Okay!
CHINESE MAN #2:	Okay, you know where we at . . . right? We're right at Milwau . . . right across . . . (unintelligible).

JEFF:	One, two, to do.
JEFF:	Okay.
CHINESE MAN #2:	Right, right, 853.
JEFF:	Ching! Do! Okay.
CHINESE MAN #2:	Alright, anything else?
JEFF:	I would like some sweet and sour pork.
CHINESE MAN #2:	Sweet and sour pork. We put the pork separate so all you do is mix em with the sauce when you get home, that's easier.
JEFF:	Very good.
CHINESE MAN #2:	Okay.
JEFF:	Very fresh.
CHINESE MAN #2:	Yes, it keeps it fresh without getting soggy. Okay.
JEFF:	What do you mean?
CHINESE MAN #2:	They won't get soggy if you don't mix it? You keep them separate, you know?
JEFF:	Faggy?
CHINESE MAN #2:	What?
JEFF:	What do you mean?
CHINESE MAN #2:	Soggy.
JEFF:	Faggy.
CHINESE MAN #2:	That means get moist. If I keep them separate, you don't have that.
JEFF:	You . . . faggy?
CHINESE MAN #2:	Because . . . sauce, it get soggy.
JEFF:	Ha ha ha.
JEFF:	Bull (bleep).
CHINESE MAN #2:	Okay, anything else?
JEFF:	You are very nice Chinese man.
CHINESE MAN #2:	Thank you.
JEFF:	I swear to (bleeping) God. Probably can't drive for (bleep) but who cares?
CHINESE MAN #2:	Alright, anything else?
JEFF:	I need shrimp flied lice.
CHINESE MAN #2:	Okay, large order or small.
JEFF:	Very large shrimp flied lice.
CHINESE MAN #2:	Okay, you want four pieces of egg roll, one sweet and sour pork, and one shrimp fried rice.
JEFF:	And some old dung.
CHINESE MAN #2:	Dung?
JEFF:	Old dung.
CHINESE MAN #2:	What do you mean dung?
JEFF:	Some old dung.
CHINESE MAN #2:	Dung? I don't understand.

JEFF:	Are you sure? Chinese man, tell me about your tiny egg roll.
CHINESE MAN #2:	We only get one kind of egg roll . . . got shrimp, got meat, got vegetable.
JEFF:	Your tiny egg roll . . . in your pants!
CHINESE MAN #2:	You know what an egg roll is?
JEFF:	Yes, I do.
CHINESE MAN #2:	Okay, (unintelligible) it's got (unintelligible) all this stuff that's inside.
JEFF:	You are so nice. I will see you in five.
CHINESE MAN #2:	Okay, you let me know your name.
JEFF:	My name is Jeff.
CHINESE MAN #2:	Jeff okay.
JEFF:	Jeff.
CHINESE MAN #2:	Okay.
JEFF:	Maybe I will just come down to Chinatown.
CHINESE MAN #2:	Okay, okay, you know where we at right?
JEFF:	Yes.
CHINESE MAN #2:	Okay, where you coming from? You come far from?
JEFF:	Are you Chinese?
CHINESE MAN #2:	Yes.
JEFF:	Holy (bleep), me too!
CHINESE MAN #2:	Oh, is that right?
JEFF:	I am Chinese too.
CHINESE MAN #2:	Okay, where you coming from, where you at?
JEFF:	Check this out, I am so close. I train behind the Motel 6.
CHINESE MAN #2:	Oh, Motel 6, on Milwaukee Avenue.
JEFF:	Yes, I am training in kung fu.
CHINESE MAN #2:	Are you go up north then, right?
JEFF:	Yes.
CHINESE MAN #2:	You know where we at then?
JEFF:	Yes.
CHINESE MAN #2:	Okay.
JEFF:	Yes master.
CHINESE MAN #2:	It will take me about 16 min.
JEFF:	Are you a master of Kung Fool?
CHINESE MAN #2:	No.
JEFF:	I am training. In Kung Fool.
CHINESE MAN #2:	Why do you need to know Kung Fu?
JEFF:	Why not?
CHINESE MAN #2:	Right now, they got guns with them, they just shoot you.

JEFF:	Oh hell no!
CHINESE MAN #2:	(laughter) I don't want to fool around with that.
JEFF:	No guns.
CHINESE MAN #2:	Yeah, hehe.
JEFF:	No guns.
CHINESE MAN #2:	No.
JEFF:	I have very good Kung Fool skills, bitch. Anyway, I would like to eat.
CHINESE MAN #2:	Okay, you come by here . . . you gonna pick this up or you can come here to eat if you want.
JEFF:	I'll just come over and eat everything.
CHINESE MAN #2:	Come eat here. Why don't you come here then order?
JEFF:	Hell yes.
CHINESE MAN #2:	You go to the lunch then you don't have to pick up at motel.
JEFF:	Then we can spar . . . a little bit.
CHINESE MAN #2:	Okay, you eat here then. You can order when you get here.
JEFF:	My name is Jeff.
CHINESE MAN #2:	Okay Jeff. Would you come here and then you order.
JEFF:	Yes, master.
CHINESE MAN #2:	Okay, alright, okay.
JEFF:	Yes, very good.
CHINESE MAN #2:	It only takes a few minutes to prepare.
JEFF:	Very fresh.
CHINESE MAN #2:	Okay you come here to eat . . . instead of pick it up, okay.
JEFF:	Good . . .
JEFF:	Okay then.
CHINESE MAN #2:	You order when you get here.
JEFF:	Tell the hot Asian girl that answer the telephone.
CHINESE MAN #2:	Okay fine sir.
JEFF:	I would like to tap her ass.
CHINESE MAN #2:	Thank you.
JEFF:	Later.

Glossary of Key Terms

ambivalence (racial) – key to understanding the concept of stereotype, ambivalence is the contradictory representation of both praise and blame. Representations of racial minorities, women, and other marginalized groups often are ambivalent, highlighting both reverence for and hatred of the Other.

ambivalent dialectic – contrasting representations that appear to be opposite but in fact function together in problematic ways.

ASIAN – an acronym we use to suggest the racial expectation that Asians and Asian Americans, regardless of nationality or ethnicity, are all the same and have no unique, cultural characteristics (*"All Seem Identical, Alike, No different"*).

Asian American – a political rather than a racial or biological term of identification that people choose as a self-descriptor. It is descriptive of a particular epistemology that challenges racism and seeks empowerment and democratic power relations.

Asianness – characteristics and qualities associated with what is considered to be "authentically" Asian. In yellowface logics, what is considered authentically Asian is, in fact, an Orientalist projection.

auteur – the director, producer, author, or creator of a film or other artistic work, such as an essay, a book, or an article. There is often an assumption that a given artistic work is true or faithful to an artist's vision, when in fact audiences have multiple interpretations of texts, auteurs themselves may not have created exactly what they had in mind, and the production process may have required editing, cinematography, and the like. Moreover, economic constraints often significantly affect a given auteur's ability to carry out a vision of their artwork.

authenticity – an arbitrary, subjective notion of what is real or genuine. Asian Americans have been subject to standards of authenticity. Thus, for example, Margaret Cho was deemed not Asian enough, and producers sought to make her more Asian, based on their random and uninformed notion of what real Asians and Asian Americans are like.

blogosphere – the public sphere that blogs make possible. The environment and landscape of blogs and their interactions and interconnections with other blogs.

blog – shorthand for "weblog." A personal online diary and/or a space for commentary.

"ching chong" speech – a mimicking and mocking imitation of Asian languages through a repetition of the words "ching chong." Used primarily by those who speak English, this kind of racist discourse pretends, for humor's sake, to approximate what someone speaking an Asian language sounds like. *See also* mock Asian.

colonialism – the history of imperialist expansion, the slaughter of civilizations, the conquest of territory, and the establishment of infrastructures of domination and compliance. Media play a role in contemporary neocolonialism by continuing to represent the dominance of the West over the East and the North over the South. In relation to Asians and Asian Americans, colonialism works concomitantly with Orientalism; Orientalism is a manufactured notion of the East that helps to justify colonial power relations.

conceptual maps (maps of meaning, frameworks of intelligibility) – those concepts and memories of experiences unique to individuals that help dictate how dominant ideas of the world come into being. Stuart Hall suggests each person has a different conceptual map based on their own personal, subjective experiences, and it is through the sharing of symbols – communication – that the differences and similarities can be discovered, discussed, understood, and appreciated.

constitutive rhetoric – discourse (e.g., documents, statements) that call a given group into being. Maurice Charland said that constitutive rhetoric "hails" communities into existence. Rhetoric that unites people, drawing attention to their common histories, cultural beliefs, identities, and regional affiliations helps make it possible to constitute various kinds of communities (e.g., cities, states, nations, social movements, organizations).

cultural syncretism – the idea that, when people migrate from one region of the world to another, they do not just simply become part of their new environment but in fact, through a process of acculturation and identity formation, create a novel cultural identity or art form. Jazz, hip-hop, pidgin, modified cars, and the like are examples of culturally syncretic forms emerging out of unique cultural conditions.

DIY – acronym meaning "do it yourself." A DIY ethics is associated with independent arts, such as independent music and Internet-based production. It suggests not only that individuals take pride in their work but also that they have individual responsibility for what is created and produced. Often, a DIY ethic is constructed in contrast to big corporations.

discourse – knowledge that is produced and circulated about a given subject. It can be produced, organized, and circulated to serve as the basis by which subsequent ideas are formed, future knowledge is produced, and, ultimately, how people relate to other people and how societies are formed and structured. Discourse usually is studied in themes and makes sense when common, repeated terms and ideas appear. Additionally, however, discourse tends to become identifiable when power shifts or ruptures occur.

economic miscegenation – the mixing of foreign money with US money. The fear of economic miscegenation is akin to the fear of a physical invasion of foreign outsiders. Connected with yellow peril discourse, the fear of economic miscegenation implies that, unlike an actual military takeover, foreign investment in the native US economy is a takeover of the US economic system.

eventualism – the idea that eventually capitalism will work in favor of Asian Americans. This notion that problems, especially social, political, and economic ones, will work themselves out in due time plays into the myth of the model minority, that Asian Americans will succeed despite facing numerous and difficult obstacles.

exigence – according to rhetorical studies scholar Lloyd Bitzer, an "imperfection marked by urgency," or the event or occasion that compels one to speak out and produce responsive communication.

explicit yellowface – when a non-Asian or non-Asian American plays the role of an Asian or Asian American. The substitution of one (non-Asian) body for another (Asian) one. It usually involves "playing Asian" by wearing Orientalist make-up and clothing, the use of false Asian accents, and a performance of subordination.

externalizations – the public display and enactment of conceptual maps and meanings. Representations – such as in films, published articles, books, TV shows, or music – contain externalized notions of minority groups such as Asians and Asian Americans. Externalizations can take the form of language, signs, body language, images, and other forms of communication.

forever foreigner – the stereotype that Asian Americans are not native citizens of the United States and are thus "forever foreigners," no matter how long they have been in the country. Thus, the stereotype assumes that Asian Americans do not have a rightful place within U.S. culture.

gendered – the kinds of ideas and values that have been culturally and socially ascribed to bodies relating to perceived gender and sexual differences. The constructions of gendered difference, the difference between men and women, between "sissies" and "studs," between "butches" and "femmes," and between desexualization and castration and eroticization and exoticization, for instance, that exist within a social system of power differentiation.

hyper-information society – a society saturated by media and communication, where individuals are inundated with technologies that constantly change. A society in which information is constantly produced and distributed, thus affecting our relationships with ourselves, each other, and the information available to us.

hyperlinking – a web-based navigational instrument that allows a person to access another section of a document, another document, or a separate website quickly and easily.

implicit yellowface – the practice which involves Asian and Asian American actors looking, sounding, and acting according to some notion of a normativized, authentic standard of Asianness. Implicit yellowface works by assuming both an "authentic Asian look and character" that one must play and that Asians and Asian Americans are all the same and are thus interchangeable.

independent media – non-mainstream production of media, although still existing in relationship to, and often on the margins of, dominant mainstream media production. Often conceived, written, directed, produced, and funded outside the mainstream media outlets, it aspires to allow for more artistic freedom and agency than typical mainstream media and Hollywood-funded endeavors.

media activism – contestation over symbols, language, and representation in the media. The primary emphasis of media activism is to challenge the politics of representation. It sometimes takes place when activists protest against derogatory dominant representations, but also includes artists creating resistant and challenging media productions.

media construction – the way in which media such as film, television, radio, music, the Internet, newspapers, magazines, and advertising produce visual and verbal images, whose meanings, importance, and effects can then be discussed, debated, and challenged.

media discourse – discourse circulating in media, including print, TV, film, the Internet, music, theater, and advertising texts.

media independence – what independent artists strive for in order to be free from the mainstream, dominant, corporate, and sometimes capitalist influences of media production. The creation of a space where Asian American art can be produced with its own logics, interests, topics, points of discussion, parameters, rationale, and *raison d'être*.

media racial hegemony – defined for the purposes of this study as the media's role in both continuing and contesting racial and colonial power relations. The notion that a particular way of thinking about race exists within and across media and that this way of thinking helps to guide and regulate beliefs and actions of those within society, primarily in inexplicit ways.

mediascape – a media horizon. Not unlike a landscape, a mediascape is a section or area of media. Such a space may be delimited by such terms as dominant or independent, print or visual, contemporary or historical. It includes texts that make up a significant part of the broader media environment, and useful observations about media discourse.

mimicry – strategy of copying the Other that appropriates the Other, while simultaneously functioning to clarify who has power in a relationship. Images produced by the colonial regimes and colonizers that seek to "mimic" or copy the colonized and with the intention that the produced copy is real and truthful. However, the copy also marks the colonized as different and thus as inherently inferior. It is a performance that makes the "difference" of the colonized into a spectacle while highlighting their unacceptable qualities and thus reproducing the notion of their inherent inferiority.

mixed raceness – qualities or a particular quality associated with being mixed race. The particularities or particularity that stands out as a signifying feature of belonging to a mixed-race group or social category.

mock Asian – Elaine Chun defines mock Asian as a discourse and language that "marks racial otherness" and "overtly mark Asian racial 'difference'" (2004, 264).

mockery – a degrading act that distinguishes between who is in power and who has the power to name and regulate appropriate and inappropriate behavior. It aims to evoke a humorous and enjoyable disavowal of the Other. By highlighting those qualities (1) that mark the Other as inferior and/or (2) that imply the Other has no power or control over their own representation, it functions to maintain a marginalized status position of the Other.

model minority – a stereotype that depicts minorities as quiet, hardworking, law abiding, and respectful of elders. It is a divisive stereotype that pits racialized minorities against one another. The model minority alone solves social problems rather than requesting, demanding, or advocating for social change from government.

negative difference – a process by which people come to understand themselves and come to know who they *are* by whom and what they *are not*. Negative difference is the process by which identity is formed. Thus, whiteness is not so much understood as something someone is, but rather is defined by qualities that are not found in racialized others. Thus, the process of forming one's cultural identity is a process of disavowal of those marked as not like oneself.

Oriental – as an adjective, meaning the particular and subjective features or qualities associated with being Asian, as defined by those in the West and applied to those from the East. As a noun, a now archaic and derogatory term used to refer to someone who is Asian. Rugs, pottery, food, and people are often defined and/or seen as Oriental, usually by those without much knowledge either of Asians or of Asian American histories and experiences.

Orientalism – described by Edward Said, a conception of people and things in the East that is constructed by those in the West, without input from, or self-conceptions of, those in the East. The West is constructed as in power and the East as in need of the power of the West: "Europe is powerful and articulate; Asia is defeated and distant" (1978, 57) and Western knowledge is truthful and objective, whereas

Eastern knowledge is deemed mystical and mythological, hence illegimate.

panethnicity – the suppression of the existence of differences among separate ethnic groups in order to form one large ethnic group, with a broad social identity that allows for successful political actions and movements necessary to meet the needs both of the wider group and of the different individual ethnic groups involved. In the case of Asian Americans, it means putting aside the differences among South Asian Americans, Vietnamese Americans, Filipino Americans, and Chinese Americans, for example, to form one large Asian American ethnic group.

pastiche – the creation of a unique artistic form or product constructed out of bits and pieces of dominant or other culture. Vernacular culture as well as dominant culture often creates music and other kinds of discourse by borrowing from and reassembling and recombining fragments in novel ways to yield a unique, yet signifying artistic product.

"playing Asian" – the performative practice of acting like or approximating a subjective notion of what it means to be authentically Asian.

racial exceptionalism – the tendency within a context in which power exists in a hierarchy to position some members of select racialized groups as superior and, by doing this, to recognize them as worthy of inclusion within dominant culture. Thus, racial exceptionalism results from a process by which the exceptional are distinguished and differentiated from those who ordinarily are configured as inferior.

racial masquerade – a façade by which the audience knows the actor is masquerading, that he or she is not actually the race they are playing. This illusion allows the audience to play around with race – to imagine what aspects of performance align with whiteness and imagined Asianness and to draw distinctions between the two.

reactive solidarity – a group that forms, often episodically, and in an ad hoc fashion, as a result of organizing around an event deemed to be offensive or problematic to its members. In the case of Asian Americans, panethnic reactive solidarities regularly emerge in response and reaction to outbursts or occurrences of anti-Asian sentiments and actions. Often, such formations quickly come together to seize the possibilities of the moment, and then dissolve after an apology is given or some other acceptable action is taken.

reify – to convert an abstract idea into something concrete through reinforcement and reenactment.

representation – the ways in which a group of people or objects are displayed or portrayed. Historically, representation meant to stand in for, or to present again. For example, someone in Congress represents their constituents, and images that first appeared on television may reappear, or be represented, differently in different contexts. More recently, representation consists of the complex range of strategies used by the media, sometimes arbitrarily, to characterize people, events, objects, and ideas. These representations have effects, both immediate and deferred. While representations register on the senses and in the mind, the collective, and often repeated, images and narratives become part of memory, both individual and social. Representations of Asian Americans, through their repetition and hence accreted power to educate audiences, may be used across time unwittingly, since new templates may not be available to producers.

resistant/dominant/negotiated readings – a variety of interpretations of media products made by audiences. Dominant readings accept the current ideological and hegemonic status quo, often reproducing preferred readings and receiving a message in the way it was encoded (Hall, 2006, 171), whereas negotiated readings require some acceptance of the dominant message accompanied by personal resistance and modification, reflecting the reader's own political and ideological position (ibid., 172). Resistant readings, however, do not subscribe to the hegemonic codes but rather bring oppositional frames of reference and thinking when dominant media texts are being observed and consumed (ibid., 173).

stereotype – "controlling images" that, through sheer repetition and familiarity, act as easy references of identity. The stereotype functions to fix meaning, to imply that meaning exists within the object. Transforming something from the imagination into an object produces a trick of the senses, for audiences can believe the object to stand in for the real, indeed to *be* the real. Stereotypes come to define whole groups of people, even though they contain little information, are often produced by people who themselves are not members of the group to which they refer, and are not complex, sensitive, or respectful ways of understanding others. These common and widespread assumptions are based on preconceived notions from past experiences, usually within racist and colonial environments, of what those in power imagine to be true of those without power. Stereotypes often manifest in images or representations, and thus the terms stereotype, image, and representation are often used interchangeably.

structural embeddedness – the tendency for power relations to exist across myriad levels and layers of social organization. Race is said to be structurally embedded because one can see it appear in quite similar ways across quite disparate parts of society and also because it exists across historical time and often is repeated without amendment across time, and therefore tends to inform decisions and ideas over both time and space. Structural embeddedness means that, while new people are born into a society, they tend to maintain the same ideas, practices, and beliefs, despite the fact that they themselves did not invent such ideas, attitudes, or behaviors.

subculture – the "expressive forms and rituals of . . . subordinate groups" that simultaneously indicate the "presence of difference" to dominant culture, while becoming "icons" and "signs of forbidden identity, sources of value" for subordinate groups (Hebdige, 1988, 2–3).

suspension of disbelief – an audience's willingness to privilege the fake over the real for sake of play and performance. In the example of yellowface, the audience accepts for the moment that the white actor playing an Asian is really Asian in order to gain pleasure from the occasion.

vernacular discourse – ordinary, everyday discourse and representations produced by localized and, sometimes, marginalized communities. Vernacular discourse is contrasted here with dominant and mainstream discourse in order to suggest that discourse that is not widely circulated, not funded by corporations, has specific meaning for specific social groups, and thus is worthy of analysis and study.

webcomic – comics available to be read on the Internet. Some are also published in print in newspapers or collections but many are published exclusively online.

whiteness – a default racial identity, an identity that does not come from the inside so much as being what is not observed to be constitutive of the racialized Other. According to Frankenberg, whiteness is a product of *negative difference* in which the only way white people can understand themselves as white is by contrasting their experiences to those of people of color (1996, 13–14).

yellow peril – a racial stereotype, applied to both Asians and Asian Americans and used across a lengthy historical period of time, that refers to the perceived threat that Asians and/or Asian Americans will take over, invade, or otherwise negatively Asianize the US nation and its society and culture.

yellowface – a practice primarily of white actors playing Asian and Asian American characters. It originated in exclusion-era politics in part because of racism and xenophobic policies against racial miscegenation. Asians and Asian Americans were not ordinarily given jobs in Hollywood. Asian and Asian American characters were scarce but, if present, were played by white actors following yellowface conventions. The practice is a ruse that depends on the viewer's and consumer's suspension of disbelief and legitimates Asian and Asian American subordination.

yellowface logics – the logics of explicit and implicit yellowface that entail employment discrimination, anxiety about miscegenation, the necessity of misrecognition, mocking humor, visual technologies, and Orientalist cultural imaginings. These help support and maintain a condition of unequal power relations between whites and Asians and Asian Americans.

Notes

Chapter 1 Introduction

1 "We are the World" was developed and sung for "USA for Africa" to raise funds for hunger and poverty relief in Africa in 1985.

2 This event was the impetus for the collection *Screaming Monkeys: Critiques of Asian American Images* (Galang, 2003).

3 Dominant representations are not the only representations of Asians and Asian Americans, however. Another way to challenge dominant representations of Asian Americans deriving from a history of colonial power is to show what Asian Americans are doing as media self-producers and to what degree their ownership of and involvement in media production is changing. Especially in the second part of the book, our emphasis will be on Asian American activism, independent work, and institution building. For an early historical example of Japanese migrants working to build a photography collective, see Shelley Lee, " 'Good American Subjects Done through Japanese Eyes': Race, Nationality, and the Seattle Camera Club, 1924–1929," *Pacific Northwest Quarterly*, Winter 2004–5: 24–34.

4 Hall (1981). In addition we refer to Shohat and Stam (1994) and Kellner (1995).

5 See, for instance, Espiritu (1992).

6 By critical, we mean that our approach challenges the historical and continuing representations that exist within mainstream media. By cultural studies, we refer to a broad array of scholarship, ranging from the Centre for Contemporary Cultural Studies at the University of Birmingham, England, which produced important work critical of culture beginning in the 1960s, to critical theory and the Frankfurt School analysis of media, to work that grew out of the civil rights struggles and Vietnam War protest era of the 1950s to 1970s, as well as to feminist, queer, and critical race scholarship.

7 One of the problems with the way in which the contemporary Western academy functions is that, by disaggregating knowledge, by fields being responsible for their own areas of expertise (e.g., biology versus history), the study of subjects such as Asian Americans, which for the last forty years has been an academic field in its own right, is curtailed. Indeed, whole important areas, such as sexuality studies, disability studies, and immigration studies, may be underresearched because of the particular proclivities of areas of knowledge within disciplines.

8 In a post-9/11 United States, the relevance of Arab Americans to a theory of race and media is immediate. It is thus necessary to discuss the media construction of Arab Americans and Asian Americans as a threat to the US nation-state in historical and political context. See, for instance, Naber (2000).

9   One might say this book focuses as much or more on white women, white men, and gender than it does on race and women of color. In this context, scant attention is paid to Asian Americans.

10 This book has three sections, one on racial minorities in films and television, another on news coverage of racial minorities, and a third on news coverage of racial minority social movements. Asian Americans are a component of each of these sections, along with African Americans, Native Americans, and Latinos.

11 While Greco Larson's book falls into this same category, it updates earlier work.

12 Representation primarily in newspapers is considered in Dennis and Pease (1997). A bibliography of gender and race stereotypes compiled by Joan Nordquist (2001) contains helpful references to Asian Americans.

13 See also Robert Blauner's landmark book *Racial Oppression in America* (1972). In it the author argues racism at home and racism abroad are interrelated, that each are part of broader US neocolonial relations.

14 For example, Jones (1955); Wong (1978); Moy (1993); Bernstein and Studlar (1997); R. G. Lee (1999); Leong (1991).

15 See also Denzin (1999). While, overall, his work is in the same vein, Denzin focuses on the broader race rubric and specifically on film versus other media.

Chapter 2   The Persistence of Yellow Peril Discourse

1   See McGee (1975) for a discussion of the fictional construction of the term "the people" and the phenomenal impossibility of such a term having existential materiality.

2   Robert Lee suggests "The phrase 'Yellow Peril' (*die jelbe Gefahr*) was coined at the end of the [nineteenth] century by Kaiser Wilhelm of Germany to justify Germany's grab for concessions in China" (1999, 246, n. 4).

3   Okihiro suggests the Mongols were perceived as a "swarm" threatening to take over Europe (1994, 119).

4   One long thin braid worn from the center of the head down the back.

5   Brian Donovan suggests white slave crusades were, in part, rationalized by nativist white sentiments against Chinese immigrant and newly remigrated African American laborers.

6   See also Moy (1993) and http://web.mit.edu/21h.153j/www/aacinema/bib.html.

7   In 1943, in a diplomatic move with China, the US Congress did agree to allow 105 immigrants from China per year, and Chinese were also allowed to become naturalized citizens (see Chan, 1991, 122). However, that number was so limited that, in our view, it cannot be considered a rescission of the exclusion of Chinese Americans, but rather a mechanism for continuing it.

8   According to John Higham (1955), race suicide discourse was common and was characterized by the fear that white Anglo-Saxons were losing their power and that further immigration would irreversibly dilute their dominant genetic stock. In *Strangers in the Land*, Higham writes, "In 1901 Edward A. Ross used Walker's ideas in an address before the American Academy of Political Social Science to explain how unchecked Asiatic immigration might lead to the extinction of the American people. When a higher race quietly eliminates itself rather than endure the competition of a lower one, said Ross, it is committing suicide" (1955, 147). A more recent version of race suicide appears in a book by Patrick Buchanan (2002).

9 D. W. Griffith (director of *Broken Blossoms*) was a powerful and highly visible filmmaker, best known today for *Birth of a Nation* (1915), which portrayed the Ku Klux Klan in a positive light and constructed blackface images of African Americans; it also constructed African Americans as ungovernable, as unable to govern themselves, and as not sufficiently able to understand the politics of class. Both *Broken Blossoms* and *Birth of a Nation* are troubling representations of US race relations and, we would argue, should be understood in relation to each other.

10 See Marchetti's discussion of these two films in her chapter "The Rape Fantasy: *The Cheat* and *Broken Blossoms*" (1993, 10–45).

11 Of course, the story would have been much different had Yellow Man not killed himself. Whether there would have been a "lynching," a race riot, or a dramatic legal trial is all speculation. But, given the many race riots during the previous decade – for example, in Los Angeles, in Rock Springs, Wyoming, and in Tonopah, Nevada – in which whites violently took out their hostilities upon Chinese communities, Yellow Man's death would have been a likely narrative outcome.

12 Wong (1978) mentions the following films: *The Mystery of Dr Fu Manchu* (1923), *The Further Mysteries of Dr Fu Manchu* (1924) *The Mysterious Dr Fu Manchu* (1929, US), *The Return of Dr Fu Manchu* (1930), *Daughter of the Dragon* (1931), and *The Mask of Fu Manchu* (1932).

13 It is ironic that this slate of yellow peril films comes out after the migration of Chinese to the United States has been curtailed.

14 For instance, Hamamoto writes, "In the postwar era, television has been of inestimable help in making U.S. foreign policy understandable and acceptable to the American public by producing programs with high propaganda content" (1994, 100).

15 The 1924 Immigration Act and successive Alien Land Laws are exemplary of the effects of anti-Japanese sentiment. See Leonard (1990).

16 For additional visual examples of these representations, see Keen (1986).

17 Wong quotes Joe Morella, Edward Z. Epstein, and John Griggs, *The Films of World War II* (Secaucus, NJ, Citadel Press, 1973), pp. 59–60, for this characterization.

18 It was not only fiction films that portrayed yellow peril. The 1942 Academy Award for best documentary was given to Frank Capra for his series "Why We Fight: A Series of Seven Information Films," produced by the War Department. In it, Capra depicts Japanese as completely different from Americans, as a threat to US sovereignty, and as a threatening invading horde.

19 For further discussion of contemporary representations of China as yellow peril, see Ono and Jiao (forthcoming).

20 For more on this, see Lee and Zia (2001).

21 Eventually, 278 days after his incarceration, Lee was released in a deal whereby he pled guilty to one felony count of downloading nuclear weapon design information to non-secure computers, an act that was common among workers at Los Alamos, while the federal prosecution dropped the remaining fifty-eight felony counts. His punishment: 278 days in prison, which he had already served, spending that time in solitary confinement. It is important to say that in June 2006, in order to avoid a lawsuit, the federal government and the *Washington Post*, the *New York Times*, the *Los Angeles Times*, ABC News, and Associated Press agreed to pay Lee $1.6 million in damages for the libelous charges of spying and espionage they had falsely drummed up.

22 See our discussion of ASIAN in chapter 3.

Chapter 3 Media Yellowface "Logics"

1 The relationship between yellow peril and yellowface goes beyond their common relationship to Asian and Asian American history, however. Ironically, while films with yellow peril themes often included Asian and Asian American villainous characters, whites played those roles in yellowface in part to quell white audience fears about the threat of seeing real Asians and Asian Americans on screen.

2 A recent study by Krystyn Moon suggests pre-Hollywood theatrical representations of yellowface exist before 1870 and that the first impersonation of Chinese immigrants was in a skit from 1854. However, it was after 1870 that such representations increase numerically (2005, 43).

3 In his overview, Richard Jackson Harris (2004) utilizes Cedric Clark's model of ethnic minority portrayal, which suggests that there are four stages for racial minorities on television: from invisibility, to ridicule, to regulation, to respect. Cross-applying his framework to Asians and Asian Americans, yellowface would be a mode of ridicule and regulation, at the midpoint between absolute exclusion and inclusion with respect.

4 About the unequal relationship between Asian Americans and whites, Wong writes: "Institutionalized rigidity, by rule, does not allow Asians to cross into those roles that are by the industry's definition designated as *white*. At the same time, whites can move horizontally and cross into roles otherwise designated by the industry as *Asian*, while being secure in the knowledge that there is an industry guarantee that white roles will not be violated by Asians" (1978, 12). Wong does mention that Asian actors played Native Americans in such films as *The Island at the Top of the World* (1974). And, more recently, some mixed-race Asian American actors such as Keanu Reeves, Kristen Kreuk, and Dean Cain have performed roles as white people.

5 It is instructive to consider Mari Yoshihara's work *Embracing the East: White Women and American Orientalism* (2003) to think through how white women in the United States participated in the construction of Orientalism through culturally appropriative practices from the 1870s to the 1940s.

6 Mr Yunioshi as an example of yellowface is no secret and has been commented on in various other places. Yellowworld.org put it as number 3 on its top ten list of yellowface portrayals.

7 See Pham and Ono (forthcoming) for a more detailed analysis of the Abercrombie and Fitch Asian-inspired T-shirts.

8 Tchen discusses early yellowface representations in relation to early Chinese American theatre. He suggests that the Tong Hook Tong opera troupe was considered "too strange" for New York audiences but that yellowface performances by white European American performers were considered entertaining (1999, 123).

9 A full-scale survey of the use of yellowface is beyond the scope of this book. But Marchetti (1993) suggests its first appearance was in Voltaire's *Orphan in China*, which opened in 1767. Glancing briefly through Michael S. Shull and David Edward Wilt's voluminous *Hollywood War Films, 1937–1945*, it becomes clear, especially in the section of their chapter "Images Americans Loved to Hate: Germans, Japanese and Italians on Screen" focusing on the Japanese (pp. 226–33), that yellowface was a staple of the industry. Films they mention as using it are *First Yank into Tokyo* (1945), *Behind the Rising Sun* (1943), *Little Tokyo, USA* (1942), *Invisible Agent* (1942), *Blood on the Sun* (1945), *Lady from Chungking*

(1942), *The Devil with Hitler* (1942), *That Nazty Nuisance* (1943), and *Back to Bataan* (1945).

10   The film *Slaying the Dragon* (1988) gives a sense of the development of yellowface. A chronological listing of films and TV shows in which it was used includes *The Mask of Fu Manchu* (1932), *The Bitter Tea of General Yen* (1933), *The Good Earth* (1937), *Little Tokyo, USA* (1942), *The Teahouse of the August Moon* (1956), *The Conqueror* (1956), *Flower Drum Song* (1958), *Breakfast at Tiffany's* (1961), *You Only Live Twice* (1967), *Kung Fu* (1972–5), *My Geisha* (1976), *The Fiendish Plot of Dr Fu Manchu* (1980), *Remo Williams: The Adventure Begins* (1985), *Mad TV* (Ms Swan, 1997–2002).

11   In many instances of yellowface, the character is in fact of mixed race, hence suggesting that mixed-race offspring have a whiteness within them with which white actors and white audiences can empathize.

12   It is important to note that the teacher's role in the film is to teach the King's children. What she teaches them is primarily ideological. She helps them learn British manners, to speak and sing English better, and about romance, for instance. Additionally, she tutors the wives that they are not lowlier than men and teaches the King himself how to treat British guests, the superiority of monogamy over polygamy, and the pleasures of dancing. Colonial tutelage combined with romance is the central message of the film, which has no adult Asian or Asian American principals.

13   It is important to mention that Tuptim is a character who feels imprisoned in the King's palace, and Lun Tha eventually drowns. Neither is a starring role, and the couple form part of the secondary romance. The correlation between Burmese and Latina/o here also suggests further complex racialization in the film.

14   Yellowface by minorities is uncommon. In such instances as the film *Norbit* (2007), it becomes part of a larger power dynamic, as it replicates traditional strategies of whiteness to reproduce power relations within a racial hierarchy, this time among non-white groups. Here Asians and Asian Americans are excluded for the sake of humor.

15   We address in a later chapter how Justin Lin resists this pressure and logic from the Hollywood studios in making *The Fast and the Furious: Tokyo Drift* and the character of Han.

16   Because of its offensive stereotypes of obesity, mammies, and pimps, *Norbit* was on the list of the "Ten Worst Films of 2007" compiled by movie critics such as Peter Travers (from *Rolling Stone*) and Richard Roeper.

17   Available on *YouTube* as of March 1, 2008.

18   Indeed, in the short-lived television show *Firefly*, the main cast speaks both Mandarin and English. However, at times the Mandarin is so badly garbled as to be indecipherable. The attempt to portray a multinational, multicultural, and multilingual future, thus, cannot overcome the fact that the actors themselves speak Chinese neither as their first nor as their second language. It is troubling that, despite the centrality of the Chinese language, there are no Chinese or Chinese Americans in the main cast of the show.

19   Eugene Wong (1978) suggests one of the first major full-length films with a white man in yellowface was *Broken Blossoms* (1919). The Fu Manchu films were regularly played in yellowface, as was Ming the Merciless in the *Flash Gordon* movies. Protests occurred over Charlie Chan, who was played by a white actor. Later films such as *Shanghai Gesture* (1941), *Dragon Seed* (1944), *Love is a Many Splendored Thing* (1955), *China Gate* (1957), *Seven Women* (1966), *A Girl Named Tamiko* (1966), *Lost Horizon* (1973), and *One of our Dinosaurs is Missing* (1975) depicted characters in yellowface. Sabine Haenni (2002) discusses *The Deceived*

Slumming Party (1908) and *The Mission of Mr Foo* (1914) as earlier examples of films that use yellowface.

20 A romance between two Asian Americans is anomalous within Hollywood for other reasons which will be discussed later.

21 Asian Americans playing Asians has been and continues to be an unselfconscious staple of US media industries.

22 Like Ahn, Chinese American Richard Loo played ferocious Japanese characters. Shull and Wilt mention several films in which he appeared: *The Purple Heart* (1944), *Betrayal from the East* (1945), *First Yank into Tokyo* (1945), *God is my Co-Pilot* (1945), *Back to Bataan* (1945), and *China Sky* (1945). One instance in which his representation is positive is when he plays a patriotic Japanese American in *Little Tokyo, USA* (1942) (Shull and Wilt, 1996, 229).

23 The representation of mixed-race people has a long history and encompasses stereotypes of their being confused, a contamination of racial purity, and the symbolic promise of a racial utopia.

24 We undertake a more sustained analysis of *All-American Girl* in chapter 8.

25 *Ugly Betty*, a current sitcom, provides an important analogy for Latinas/os: while the show is about a Mexican American family, the actors playing the lead characters are Latina/o but not Mexican American.

26 In the fall of 2006, the University of Illinois at Urbana-Champaign experienced a spate of racialized parties, called "Tacos and Tequilas," that targeted Hispanics, where students dressed as migrant workers and pregnant women in brownface.

27 Robert Townsend's *Hollywood Shuffle* (1987) offers a powerful corollary to the role-typing facing African Americans. The film contains a humorous skit on "Black Acting School" which teaches enrollees "jive talk 101," how to "walk black," and being a "black street hood," for instance.

Chapter 4 Problematic Representations of Asian American Gender and Sexuality

1 For example, in European paintings, representations of women and men conformed to a "rigid and conflictual difference between these female subjects and their oriental male counterparts" (Kang, 2002, 74). Kang is referring in her analysis to an essay, "The Salon's Seraglio," by Rana Kabbani.

2 Again, Kang is referring to Kabbani's essay, which she quotes.

3 See, for instance, Crenshaw (1989, 1991) and Collins (1998).

4 See, for instance, Shohat (1991).

5 Kang quotes Kabbani, saying that men were represented as trading "in female bodies," hence as "cruel captors" without civilization or humanity (2002, 75).

6 This scenario, which includes the mutual and interrelated representation of men and women, is well documented as historically narrated colonial sexual relations. Many sources exist on the subject, of which we refer to just a few here: Sharpe (1993); Deming (1982); Addison (1993); Shohat (1991); and Buescher and Ono (1996).

7 The biggest criticism, particularly by Asian American men, of the film *Joy Luck Club* (1993) is its portrayal of Asian American men as savage, mean, and abusive.

8 By gendered, we mean the kinds of ideas and values that have been culturally and socially ascribed to bodies relating to perceived gender and sexual differences. The constructions of gendered difference, the difference between men and women, the difference between "sissies" and "studs," the difference

between "butches" and "femmes," and the difference between desexualization and castration and eroticization and exoticization, for instance, exist within a social system of power differentiation.

9   The classic article by Laura Mulvey (1975) was an early work that recognized that media narratives, and especially film romances, represented women and men in ways that both demonstrated and reified notions of power between the sexes. Relations of power through domination became apparent in particular on account of the punishments by male characters of female characters.

10 Patricia Hill Collins, "Mammies, Matriarchs, and Other Controlling Images," chapter 4 in *Black Feminist Thought: Knowledge, Consciousness, and the Politics of Empowerment* (Boston: Unwin Hyman, 1990), pp. 67–90; Hamamoto (1994).

11 Renee Tajima (1989) adds "China Doll, Geisha Girl, shy Polynesian beauty" to what is entailed by the Lotus Blossom.

12 Renee Tajima gives two poignant examples of such a representation, *Teahouse of the August Moon* (1956) and *The Incredible Hulk*. As she describes, in one scene of *Teahouse of the August Moon*, actor Machiko Kyo is introduced as a geisha and is giggling. In one episode of *The Incredible Hulk*, actor Irene Sun is introduced as a "mail-order bride" and is constructed both as an object and as subservient (1989, 310).

13 This construction of Asian and Asian American women as sexually available, in combination with post-war relations between the United States and formerly occupied nations, results in the emergence of a mail-order bride industry. Discourse circulating about women as potential brides further constructs them as objects for consumption by men. As Rona Tamiko Halualani (1995) suggests, the construction of Filipinas in such literature places them in a racial and gendered hierarchy in which Anglo men are positioned as dominant and Asian women as subservient.

14 This example also reiterates our point that representations of Asian men and women work in concert, not separate from each other.

15 More recently, one might point to *The Last Samurai* as a film that contains a similar construction. *The Last Samurai* (2003) appears to follow in the footsteps of the TV series *Kung Fu*, in which the male character uses martial arts to outdo the yellow horde, of course learning to do so using the very techniques of the Asian master. And he falls in love with the Japanese woman who has nursed him back to health.

16 Gedde Watanabe has played a long string of heavily accented Asian characters, despite having been born in Ogden, Utah. In an article from the June 22–8, 2001, issue of *AsianWeek*, he admitted to making up his foreign accents and said his exposure to Asian accents comes from his older Asian relatives. Another example of a desexualized foreign-exchange student is Raja (Adhir Kalyan), a Pakistani Muslim on the TV show *Aliens in America*.

17 Mixed-race actor Tia Carrera plays Minako Okeya, who is kidnapped and needs to be rescued by Kenner and Murata.

18 A key example of this reclamation of Asian masculinity on behalf of Asian American men appears in Chin (1991).

19 As of September 7, 2007, the quotation was accessible online at http://www.asianmediawatch.net/details/.

20 http://www.glaad.org/media/release_detail.php?id=3657.

21 http://www.glaad.org/publications/op-ed_detail.php?id=3666.

22 The website "Exoticize This" is no longer up. However, Mimi Thi Nguyen does have a blog at http://www.worsethanqueer.com.

23 As of February 12, 2008, Kristina Wong's "Big Bad Chinese Mama" website was located at http://www.bigbadchinesemama.com/. Nguyen's "Exoticize my Fist" was down when we checked.

24 A *nanchaku* is a weapon made from two short sticks connected by rope, chain, or some other flexible material.

25 Chan quotes a production executive, Fred Weintraub, as suggesting that a Chinese could not be a lead in a US television series (2001, 73). The notion that Asian Americans can be "workers" but not "leaders" is a common experience of "glass ceiling" power relations that limit Asian American opportunities for leadership in professional life generally.

Chapter 5 Threatening Model Minorities

1 Deborah Woo uses the term "Asian Horatio Alger" in her work as well (2000, 24).

2 January 9, 1966, pp. 20–1, 33, 36, 38, 40–1, 43.

3 December 26, 1966, pp. 73–8.

4 This stereotype has been called interchangeably the "model minority myth" and the "model minority stereotype."

5 The first Charlie Chan film emerged in the 1920s. Wong (1978) lists the following: *The House without a Key* (1926), *Behind that Curtain* (1927), *The Chinese Parrot* (1928), and *Charlie Chan Carries On* (1931).

6 He writes: "Indeed, Charlie Chan is one of the earliest representations of a model minority in American popular fiction – someone who assimilates into mainstream American culture by moving from a working-class status to a middle-class professional one. Charlie Chan symbolizes the American dream of success: a minority who is allowed to interact with a predominantly white American society, living a life of relative economic comfort, and raising a nuclear family" (Chan, 2001, 51).

7 Emil Guillermo, "C-100 Loses by Honoring Chung," April 1, 2005, http://news.asianweek.com/news/view_article.html?article_id=6931b422036d 10377691396e6a4e248f (accessed February 15, 2008).

8 It is important to say that Connie Chung did blaze a trail that was much admired in newscasting. And, by suggesting that she has created a constraining stereotype, we are by no means taking anything away from her or her impressive career. Furthermore, it is possible to argue that, without her, the desire for and existence of Asian and Asian American women news anchors would not be as prevalent as it is today. However, it is our contention that such a limitation is, in fact, consistent within the ambivalence of model minority discourse – promising liberation while simultaneously enacting constraint – and that this does much harm even as it may produce opportunities.

9 For most of the ones we list here, see the study "Setting the Stage" (Asian American Justice Center, 2006). It is also notable that South Asians and South Asian Americans are centrally typecast in this medical professional role.

10 As the film *Roots* helped African American actors such as Levar Burton, John Amos, Cicely Tyson, Maya Angelou, O. J. Simpson, and Louis Gossett Jr., the breakout hit *The Joy Luck Club* played a significant role in advancing the careers of such actors as Tamlyn Tomita, Lauren Tom, Rosalind Chao, Michael Paul Chan, and Russell Wong.

11 Despite not knowing the Chinese language well, and despite having learned mah-jong from her Jewish friends, by the end of the film June accesses her "best heart" qualities by reuniting with her long-lost sisters in China and informing them in person of their mother's death.

12 While Oh was a serious stage and screen actor before landing her role in the 2004 indie hit *Sideways* and then becoming a regular in the television show *Grey's Anatomy*, there is little mention of her early career in her biographies on the Internet. A native of Ottawa, Ontario, Oh played roles on stage as a child and began working professionally at age fifteen with a role in the CBC television film *The Diary of Evelyn Lau* (1994). She had the lead part in *Double Happiness*, played Rita Wu in the HBO comedy *Arli$$*, co-starred in the film *Last Night* (1998) and *Dancing at the Blue Iguana* (2000), and also played Sarah Chaulke in *Scrubs* (information drawn from http://www.sandraoh.com as of September 12, 2007).

13 Ming-Na Wen left the cast of *ER*, only to return in 1999. On her return, Carter initially calls her "Deb," to which she responds that her name is Jing-Mei. From that point on she is known as Jing-Mei.

14 Given neocolonial logics, which representation meets the needs of contemporary colonial relations better in the depiction of Asian American women? Should they be partners of white men, thus playing into the neocolonial rescue from oppressive male Oriental patriarchy narrative, or not be partners of white men, thus reproducing anti-miscegenation and anti-desegregation sentiments from the pre-reconstruction and Jim Crow racist era?

15 Video (2003), co-produced by NAATA and KVIE-TV, Sacramento. Producer Donald Young.

16 See, for instance, Grice (2002). See also Nakashima (1992, 2005).

17 Kawai does not take credit for having been the first to notice this ambivalence, even as her work expands significantly its theorization. She cites Gary Okihiro as linking the model minority myth and yellow peril discourse when he writes: "the concepts of the yellow peril and the model minority, although at apparent disjunction, form a seamless continuum" (1994, 141). Kawai also quotes Robert Lee, drawing a connection between the two stereotypes: "Lee (1999) pointed out that 'the model minority has two faces. The myth presents Asian Americans as silent and disciplined; this is their secret to success. At the same time, this silence and discipline is used in constructing the Asian American as a new yellow peril' (p. 190)" (2005, 115).

18 Reports of tensions between African Americans and Asian Americans were also prevalent in the media in the early 1990s and drew attention away from black–white and Asian American–white racial tensions. In media discourse about the Los Angeles rebellion, African Americans were pitted against Korean Americans, especially after the death of Latasha Harlins, who was killed by a Korean grocery store owner, Soon Ja Du, while shopping in her store. Korean Americans were constructed as a particular variant of yellow peril, coming in to exploit the African American community economically, while African Americans were represented as lazy or violent and as unsympathetic to the Korean American community. Additionally, conspicuous information was missing in such discourse, such as the structural and economic conditions of both African Americans and Asian Americans – indeed all racial minorities – in US inner cities.

19 Section 4A. Later in the article Egan suggests this might be a larger question to be posed to universities in the United States more generally when he writes: "If Berkeley is now a pure meritocracy, what does that say about the future of great American universities in the post-affirmative action age? Are we headed toward a day when all elite colleges will look something like Berkeley: relatively wealthy whites (about 60 percent of white freshmen's families make $100,000 or more) and a large Asian plurality and everyone else underrepresented? Is that the inevitable result of color-blind admissions?"

20 As of May 11, 2008, the online version of the article includes a moving image of a person's eyes – presumably of an Asian or Asian American – looking left, then right, then left, then forward. Given the context of the article, this fragmented bodily image is objectifying and disturbing.

21 There are quotations defending meritocracy as a value, the bad press Asians and Asian Americans receive because of the model minority stereotype, and the fact that they often fail to be admitted to universities at the same rate as other minorities. Yet most of this appears in the latter half of the article, and the vast majority is dedicated to emphasizing the "Asianness" of Berkeley.

22 It is important to note that Asian Americans are not the only group that has been configured as a "model minority" in discourse. Indeed, racial exceptionalism is perhaps a better term to describe the general tendency within a hierarchical racial context to position some members of select groups as outstanding, thus as worthy of inclusion within the dominant culture. As Herman Gray suggests, racial exceptionalism has been significant in the representation of blacks on television and in politics. He writes: "People such as former head of the U.S. Commission on Civil Rights Clarence Pendleton or U.S. Supreme Court Justice Clarence Thomas (and commercial television's Cliff Huxtable) were seen by conservatives as possessing the requisite moral character, individual responsibility, and personal determination to succeed in spite of residual social impediments" (1995, 18–19).

23 There is an interesting corollary to Asian and Asian American underrepresentation in the formation of colleges (Valdivia, 2005). While there are black, Latina, Native American and white American girls in the Historical Characters line of American girl dolls, an Asian American doll appears only as a sidekick to a white doll.

Chapter 6 Asian American Public Criticisms and Community Protests

1 Scott Kurashige takes Espiritu's concept of "reactive solidarity" and asks whether or not it can be sustained in long-term community efforts and not just as a reactive coalition protest (2000, 164).

2 Dorinne Kondo's book *About Face: Performing Race in Fashion and Theater* (1997) has a chapter that provides a good overview of the *Miss Saigon* protests and events, while Yoko Yoshikawa's article "The Heat is on 'Miss Saigon' Coalition" (1994) provides a first-hand account of the difficulties of communicating Asian American issues to other marginalized groups. We attribute large portions of the *Miss Saigon* account to these two articles.

3 Kawai (2005) also analyzes the film *Rising Sun*, which we discuss in chapter 5.

4 In the 1984 Vincent Chin case, the Asian American community rallied to protest the lax punishment of Ronald Ebens and Michael Nitz, one of whom was an unemployed autoworker, who beat and killed Chin after assuming he was Japanese. Of course, many other examples of Asian American activism could be discussed.

5 Although one might argue that theater is not a "medium," we argue that it is. Rather than, for example, the silver screen mediating the image, it is the presence of the stage that mediates the performance for the audience.

6 Helen Zia, an Asian American journalist, calls attention to the role of the media in the Chin case in the documentary *Who Killed Vincent Chin?*

7 See Locke (1998).

8 In our essay "'Artful Bigotry & Kitsch': A Study of Stereotype, Mimicry, and Satire in Asian American T-Shirt Rhetoric" (Pham and Ono, forthcoming), we

apply Bhabha's theory of mimicry and mockery to understand the case in 2002 of the Abercrombie and Fitch line of Asian-themed T-shirts that involved troubling racialized caricatures of Asians and Asian Americans and the Blacklava counter-rhetoric that followed. See the conclusion for more analysis of this particular case.

9 Adam Corolla told a ching chong joke on his radio show, and Shaquille O'Neal teased and taunted Yao Ming in their first NBA encounter. See Leung (2006).

10 See Serpe (2006). A clip of Rosie making the ching chong comment may be viewed on *YouTube*.

11 "OCA Demands Apology from Rosie O'Donnell and 'The View'" (2006), http://www.ocanational.org/index.php?option=com_content&task=view&id=170&Itemid=104 (accessed August 2, 2007).

12 Whether or not it is actually Rosie O'Donnell who has written and replied on the blog is unknown (although the blog is attributed to her). For the sake of consistency, we assume that she is responsible for the comments, as otherwise she would be violating the trust of the fans who believe that the website is a forum where they can communicate with her.

13 O'Donnell's apology can be viewed on Michelle Malkin's website, HotAir: http://hotair.com/archives/2006/12/14/video-rosie-apologizes-for-ching-chong/.

14 This is a direct quotation from Rosie O'Donnell's blog: http://www.rosie.com/blog/2007/02/24/beau-sia/.

15 It first aired one day after Don Imus's derogatory comments about the Rutgers women's basketball team and was rebroadcast even after the controversy regarding Imus had reached fever pitch.

16 A transcript of the prank is available in the appendix. It was taken from www.youtube.com/watch?v=ETdcYLn88So, which gave subtitles. However, the *YouTube* video has since been removed as a result of a copyright claim by the DogHouse Entertainment company.

17 See "Prank Call Radio Segment Outrages Asian Americans," *Targeted News Service*, April 25, 2007, and "Prank Call to Chinese Eatery Ignites New Shock Jock Uproar," *CBC News*, April 24, 2007.

18 "New York City Radio Hosts Suspended Indefinitely over Racially Charged Prank Call," *Associated Press Financial Wire*, April 24, 2007.

19 Despite their apology, JV and Elvis defended themselves and their actions via web campaigns for free speech.

20 Protests countering the Asian American protests can be seen on *YouTube*, although the audio is difficult to make out (http://www.youtube.com/watch?v=jaBv_aB8q70).

21 Despite Imus initially being fired, his return to radio is pending after he threatened a multimillion dollar lawsuit against CBS for breach of contract. CBS eventually settled.

22 An editorial from the *Grand Rapids Press* frames the Imus incident as an issue of power, of Imus being a bully, but ignores the racial dimension.

23 For example, in his *YouTube* piece "An Open Letter to All the Rosie O'Donnells," Beau Sia pointed out that O'Donnell was really making a "racist interpretation of a language," not putting on an accent, which is really a "vocal affectation of speech."

Chapter 7 Asian American Media Independence

1 Two books, in particular, are helpful in thinking about media independence and independent media: Abrash and Egan (1992) and Leong (1991).

2 The movies *Clerks* (1994), by Kevin Smith, and *The Blair Witch Project* are often given as popular examples of such independent productions.

3 See, for instance, the work of Lisa Nakamura and Wendy Hui Kyong Chun. As a reminder, we employ "media" as an all-encompassing term, incorporating art, the Internet, and music along with television and film; thus, we intend to address the prevalence of independent Asian American productions within a variety of media contexts.

4 Projansky and Ono (2003) discuss the role of the auteur in "making films Asian American" in relation to public discourse about the auteurs.

5 Maurice Charland, "Constitutive Rhetoric: The Case of the Peuple Quebecois," *Quarterly Journal of Speech*, 73 (1987): 133–50.

6 Hallmark (2007). The Center for Asian American Media's educational video catalog has a wide variety of independent video topics.

7 Eric Byler, "Americanese: The Movie: Mission Statement," http://www.americanesethemovie.com/directors_statement.html.

8 Participating in the mainstream or having mainstream support may have a suppressing effect, whereas participating in the independent arena allows for more artistic freedom and the propagation of multiple, often unheard, voices in an environment that is cluttered with commercial interest. One might ask, then, if there can ever truly be "independence" when the media environment exists for commercial interests. In addition, artistic freedom brings two problems: a limitation in the size of the audience and the difficulty of securing financial resources.

9 While viewing only Asian American independent media provides an insight into Asian American agency, ignoring the material and cultural relationships with the dominant media would be irresponsible and unrealistic.

10 Cloud (1992) and Sloop (1994) address the ways in which dominant discourse limits the grounds of and sets the terms for interpretation and apology.

11 Hebdige (1988, 91). See also Attali (1985).

12 See Leong (1991) for the start of Asian American independent media, which is situated in a post-civil rights movement.

13 Weinzierl and Muggleton (2003). The postmodern subcultural approach expands subculture studies and moves away from Hebdige's binaries of opposition/incorporation and affirmation/refusal (1988, 13).

14 In addition, the conception of independent media in MAPS (Media Alternative Project) focuses primarily on documentaries, with a small percentage of narrative films. The emphasis on documentaries deals with the educational aspect of using independent films for history classes, which is the reason for MAPS.

15 Feng (2002a) argues that Asian American independent films are not "inherently" autobiographical.

16 Using the framework of Third Cinema, Asian American independents do not simply attempt to oppose dominant cinema but are aware of the "historical variability of the necessary aesthetic strategies to be adopted" in their productions (Willemen, 1989, 7).

17 In what Raymond Williams (1977) calls the "inherent dominative mode," the access to power enables the definition of superior and inferior. Thus the higher (i.e., dominant) discourses exist as the cultural center, high or low art, what is valued as social or aesthetic, and in which space it belongs. Thus, Asian American arts are still marginalized in comparison with dominant conceptions of art.

18 As in the case of Justin Lin, unknown to those outside of indie communities until his directorial debut, *Better Luck Tomorrow* (2002).

19 Projansky and Ono (2003) study the filmmakers' discourse in interviews in relation to public discourses and discover that the latter construct the filmmakers Quentin Lee and Justin Lin as Asian American, queer, and national/foreign, despite their resistance to such essentialized notions of their identity.

Chapter 8 The Interface of Asian American Independent Media and the Mainstream

1 In an interview with Mike Park, Virgil Dickerson asks if there were any changes in distribution when Lumberjack bought out Mordam, AMR's original distributor. Park replies, "It seems like I get hit up on a daily basis from other distributors." Dickerson, "Interview with Mike Park on 10 Years of Asian Man Records," http://indiehq.com/2006/06/27/interview-with-mike-park-on-10-years-of-asian-man-records/.

2 "About Asian Man Records," http://www.asianmanrecords.com/about.html.

3 Moskowitz (2005) writes that punk rockers, hardcore kids, and ska kids all say that "Mike Park's the Man!"

4 Sociologists have suggested that Asian Americans have found more freedom owning their own businesses, both because of racism creating glass ceilings that inhibit advancement and because of day-to-day racist experiences in traditional careers and occupations.

5 "Asia Pacific Arts: Parking the Microphone with Mike Park," UCLA Asia Institute, http://www.asiaarts.ucla.edu/article.asp?parentid=32754.

6 Many thanks to Sarah Cho for her translations of the song titles.

7 Park, in his interview with Asia Pacific Arts, comments that not as many Asian Americans go to his show as he would like.

8 A common critique of Third Wave ska, such as Reel Big Fish, and new pop punk music, such as Blink 182, is that these lack the kind of political edge that characterized the original genres. This might be an effect of taking the relevant subcultures and commercializing them in current dominant and mainstream cultures.

9 Asen and Brouwer's collection *Counterpublics and the State* (2001) addresses the role of Nancy Fraser's counterpublics (1993), which provide alternative spaces for those alienated by the dominant public sphere. The essays address a variety of counterpublic responses to the dominant public sphere.

10 Coincidentally, Mike Park performed a song called "The Margaret Cho Show" with his former band Skankin Pickle.

11 The topics that Cho addresses in *I'm the One That I Want* are further expanded on in her book of the same title (New York: Ballantine Books, 2001).

12 Julie Hong, "Family Ties," UCLA Asia Institute, http://www.asiaarts.ucla.edu/article.asp?parentid=38716.

13 The effects that images have on Asians and Asian Americans have not been well studied. Much ethnographic and audience research is needed here.

14 A performance while on tour in her hometown of San Francisco in 1999 was released on DVD in 2000.

15 See also L. S. Kim (2004).

16 If we extrapolate further, this has the potential to have mass psychosocial effects on Asians and Asian Americans too, especially for those who are subject to the mass media.

17 A critique of the sitcom *Friends* is that people of color are noticeably absent within the cosmopolitan city of New York. In addition, *The Cosby Show* is often criticized for its lack of topics attending to racial issues within an African

American context and its portrayal of a black middle-class family that looks and feels whitewashed. See Jhally and Lewis (1992), Inniss and Feagin (1995), and Downing (1988) for more critiques of *The Cosby Show*.

18 Assuming that Asians put chopsticks in their hair is equivalent to assuming that Americans put forks in their hair and is a form of Orientalism. Moreover, the notion that an abacus is somehow a marker of Asianness suggests an image of Asia as backward, mythological, and of the past, a common way in which Asian Americans are rendered alien and not part of modern Western culture.

19 Kim tracks the representations of Asian Americans in television from the 1960s to the new millennium, from their being present as foreigners and servants in the 1960s, to their absence from television in the 1970s, their presence as foreigners in the 1980s, their appearance as model minority and token characters, progressing to the "either/or" status in the 1990s, and finally occupying roles as females, cartoons, or children in the twenty-first century.

20 Roger Ebert, "The Fast and the Furious: Tokyo Drift," http://rogerebert. suntimes.com/apps/pbcs.dll/article?AID=/20060615/REVIEWS/60606006/1023 (accessed February 27, 2008). For a video review of *Tokyo Drift* by both Ebert and Roeper, see http://bventertainment.go.com/tv/buenavista/ebertandroeper/index2.html?sec=6&subsec=Tokyo+Drift (accessed February 27, 2008).

21 In her article "Autoexoticizing: Asian American Youth and the Import Car Scene" (*Journal of Asian American Studies*, 7/1: 1–26), Soo Ah Kwon conducts a three-year ethnographic study of Asian American members of the import car scene, drawing attention to the pan-ethnic Asian identification and pride associated with it and the early oppositional Asian American youth car culture.

22 Both Quentin Lee and Justin Lin resist being called Asian American for fear of being categorized as Asian American filmmakers and not simply good filmmakers. For instance, when Projansky and Ono asked him to "discuss his dedication to addressing Asian American and queer themes," Lee replied, "I'm not dedicated. I just want to make movies whatever movies I want to make whether it is Asian American or queer or whatever. I'm dedicated to making films, because I feel passionate about making and watching films. I'm not dedicated to any genre or content" (2003, 269).

23 Valdivia (2005) addresses the politics of hybridity, using a Latina as an example of the racially ambiguous person. Coincidentally, Nathalie Kelley was born in Lima, Peru, has an Argentinian father and a French-born mother, and was raised in Australia.

Chapter 9 Asian American New Media Practices

1 Lee is not only a cartoonist but also an accomplished actor, having played small parts in television shows such as *Scrubs* and *Friends* and in independent films such as *Yellow* (1998), and *Better Luck Tomorrow* (2002). However, because of the role of new media in this project, we focus primarily on her occupation as a cartoonist and her website *Angry Little Girls*.

2 *Angry Little Girls* is licensed and managed by The Outfit, Inc., which is a collective of independent artists.

3 According to David Kunzle, a scholar of early comics in Europe, the definition of a "comic strip" includes the following: 1) it is a sequence of images, 2) there is a preference for and prevalence of image over text, 3) it is pre-

sented in a mass medium that can be reproduced, such as print, and 4) there is a topical moral narrative within the sequence (1973, 2). More recently, Scott McCloud defines comics as "juxtaposed pictorial and other images in deliberate sequence, intended to convey information and/or to produce an aesthetic response in the viewer" (1994, 9). Comics play a role within people's daily lives – reading the "funnies" often being a daily activity for newspaper readers, both adults and children. Research demonstrated that, during a newspaper strike in 1945, people missed the comics as much as, if not more than, the front-page news (Berelson, 1949). Also, the death in February 2000 of Charles Schultz, the creator of *Peanuts*, elicited extensive media coverage.

4 This short can be seen in the PBS documentary *Searching for Asian America*, by Young et al., produced by the National Asian American Telecommunications Association (San Francisco, 2003).

5 We first analyzed the website on August 1, 2007, but its format has since changed, and the archive of "Angry Little Asian Girl" comics, which is where we found the "motherly love" strip that we are about to consider, is now missing. However, this can be found in Lee's collection titled *Angry Little Girls* (2005).

6 This snapshot was taken on August 27, 2007. While the "Friends" section has since changed format, it still has the same information and descriptions about the other characters in ALG.

7 The Asian Pacific Islander American Blog Network is a testament to the diversity of recently politicized Asian American blogs. It is "an aggregated blog network that syndicates posts from insightful, politicized Asian American blogs. Our vision is to promote the development of social consciousness and APIA identity through the development of a cohesive APIA blogging community" (www.apiablogs.net).

8 Tasha G. Oren's article "Secret Asian Man" (2005) nicely addresses the expressions of anger and grievances in Asian American popular cultural representations and suggests looking at the Abercrombie and Fitch T-shirt debacle through the lens of anger in order to shed light on the role of cultural invisibility. Also, notice the commonality of "anger" in both *Angry Little Girls!* and Angry Asian Man.

9 Although it is difficult to know without tracking an IP address whether or not this is actually Eric Byler, we will assume that it is. During a workshop that he conducted for the Midwest Asian American Student Association conference of 2007, Byler commented that he makes use of social networking websites to connect with his audiences, and in personal communication he has stated that his new work is more toward the political realm and that he uses *MySpace*, *FaceBook*, and *YouTube* to communicate with his fan base. We therefore choose to imagine it is Eric Byler who is uploading the videos and responding to viewers' comments.

10 In their study of two e-forums responding to World Bank proposals, Ainsworth et al. look at online postings, analyze the nature of participatory democracy (either consultative or deliberative), and "ascertain outcomes through an examination of online data, interviews, and documentary evidence" (2005, 132). They conclude that non-participation in the forum is an act of resistance, given the context and seriousness of the issue. Although this *YouTube* dialogue does not match the seriousness of the discussion of World Bank proposals, avoidance does not uphold or defend the messages or Asian American identity affirmed by the video.

11 The "6 months ago" and other dates in parentheses next to the names refer to when the comment was first posted in relation to the day that someone is looking at it. Thus, if one were to look at these same posts as of February 2008, this would show up as "1 year ago" (the approximate date of when these posts were copied and pasted was August 2007).

12 The term "Other" is often related to Edward Said's notion of Orientalism and the "Other." We suspend the belief that calling Kim an "Other" in the setting is referencing Orientalist notions of Othering but is rather one that references his character in the show.

13 Otherwise known within online forums as "flaming."

14 However, the number of people who view a video depends on several factors, such as who is involved in it, how well made or entertaining it is, or simply how well "tagged" it is for searching.

15 This is the headline used by *Time* magazine when it revealed its Person of the Year for 2006. See Grossman (2007).

16 See Nakamura (2007) and (2002a).

Chapter 10 Mobilizing Organizations

1 The Center for Asian American Media was known from 1980 to 2005 as the National Asian American Telecommunications Association (NAATA).

2 Chin and Qualls (2001) estimate that there is a 1 percent chance that an independent film will get a big payout from a large mainstream studio. But it does happen, as in the case of Kevin Smith. When Miramax Studio bought the rights to his film *Clerks* (1994) he was able to pay off all the debts, and he went on to make some movies with Miramax as distributor.

3 We recognize that corporate sponsorship is inevitably intertwined with "independent" film festivals. For example, the Los Angeles Asian Pacific Film Festival was sponsored by Honda and Macy's, among others. The SFIAAFF 2007 festival was presented by Comcast, with a variety of other major corporations contributing. According to the SFIAAFF, the corporations benefit from access to a very specific Asian American market. Corporate sponsorships also provide the financial capital needed to organize a film festival. Thus, the film festivals might not be truly "independent." However, since public arts funding is not reliable from year to year, corporate sponsorship might well be needed for the long-term survival of film festivals.

4 That is not to say that film festivals are put on by organizations without individual effort. We simply focus on the organizational part in order to emphasize that, even as individuals come and go, the festival will remain. Typically, a festival is not defined by an individual, nor will it disappear when an individual does, in the way a blog might disappear when its primary writer withdraws.

5 It is possible that the notion of Asian American independent media and the Asian American experience could be tracked through what is shown at film festivals and what becomes privileged or labeled, shown, and hopefully distributed thereafter as "Asian American" independent cinema. However, such an undertaking is beyond the scope of this book.

6 Most of this information can be found on the Visual Communications website: http://www.vconline.org/aboutvc/index.html.

7 "Our Roots and History," http://asiancinevision.org/aboutus.html.

8 "Asian American International Film Festival Fact Sheet," http://asiancinevision.org/press/AAIFF_FACT_SHEET.html.

9 "Faq," http://festival.asianamericanmedia.org/submissions/faq/.

10 Justin Lin's *Better Luck Tomorrow* was an "official selection" at the 2002 Sundance festival. Thus, it seems that Asian American independent films are gaining greater acceptance, especially as their technical aspects are becoming more sophisticated.

11 Okada's article describes the contractual obligations that accompany the awards, such as appearing in the SFIAAFF and relinquishing broadcast rights. As she describes, issues of representational power arise in these contractual obligations.

12 "About us," http://distribution.asianamericanmedia.org/about-us/.

13 Okada highlights Amy Chen's experience with the PBS and NAATA arrangement, where in the end PBS did not pick up her documentary. Chen calls attention to another problem, the lack of broadcasting outlets for minority independent films, which Okada also addresses.

14 "Manaa History," http://www.manaa.org/about_history.html.

15 Ibid.

16 In 1994 Tristar Pictures released *It Could Happen to You*, in which Korean grocers were negatively depicted, in 1997 MANAA met with officials of CBS television to discuss the "dismal handling of Asian American regulars on their programs," and in 2004 MANAA and other Asian American organizations met with the editor-in-chief of *Details* over its "Gay or Asian" section. This information was also taken from the MANAA website.

17 All online as of February 3, 2008.

18 "Stereotype Buster," http://www.manaa.org/articles/stereoBust.htm.

19 If we frame the institutional change through Clark's and Harris's four stages of portrayal, from invisibility to ridicule to regulation to respect (see chapter 3), these organizations are pressuring mainstream media outlets to move beyond ridicule, beyond stereotypes, to regulation and minor occurrences of respect.

20 "ImaginAsian Entertainment to Launch New Asian American Film & Cultural Center in Downtown Los Angeles on December 7, 2007," ImaginAsian Entertainment press release, 2007.

Chapter 11 Conclusion

1 Associated Press, "Abercrombie & Fitch Asian T-Shirts Trigger Boycott: Shirts Depict Stereotypes of Asians," NBC, 2002, http://www.nbc4.tv/print/1406052/detail.html [accessed May 14, 2008].

2 As of February 25, 2008, these T-shirts were listed for purchase at http://blacklava.net/store/.

3 See Pham and Ono (forthcoming) for an expanded and in-depth analysis of the Abercrombie and Fitch incident and Blacklava's response.

4 As of February 25, 2008, the article could be found at: http://media.www.thecampuspress.com/media/storage/paper1098/news/2008/02/18/Opinion/If.Its.War.The.Asians.Want-3216954.shtml?refsource=collegeheadlines.

5 As of February, 25, 2008, the president's statement was available at: http://www.colorado.edu/news/r/537a10e44b68770c42ff1040aff5de90.html.

6 The report cites the model minority as one of the barriers to equal opportunity. It also cites as additional barriers the perception of Asian Americans as foreigners and as docile and uncommunicative. All three of these barriers are historically and continually represented in the media.

7 In their pressing of Congress for a collection of separate health data on individual Asian subgroups, they included the needs of smaller subgroups within

the framework of a larger, pan-Asian group, possibly knowing that many sub-groups may not individually have been able to influence change at the level of the legislature.

8   See Cloud (1996).

References

Abrash, Barbara, and Catherine Egan, eds (1992), *Mediating History: The Map Guide to Independent Video by and About African American, Asian American, Latino, and Native American People*. New York: New York University Press.

Addison, Erin (1993), "Saving Other Women from Other Men: Disney's *Aladdin*," *Camera Obscura*, 31: 5–25.

Ainsworth, Susan, Cynthia Hardy, and Bill Harley (2005), "Online Consultation: E-Democracy and E-Resistance in the Case of Development Gateway," *Management Communication Quarterly*, 19/1: 120–45.

Anderson, Benedict (1983), *Imagined Communities: Reflections on the Origin and Spread of Nationalism*. New York: Verso.

Aoki, Guy (2007), "Wknd Feedback: Asian Portrayal Was Left out of the Discussion," *Los Angeles Times*, February 22.

Asen, Robert, and Daniel C. Brouwer, eds (2001) *Counterpublics and the State*. Albany: State University of New York Press.

Asian American Justice Center (2006), "Setting the Stage," http://www.advancingequality.org/files/aajc_tv_06.pdf.

Attali, Jacques (1985) *Noise: The Political Economy of Music* (Vol. 16, Theory and History of Literature). Minneapolis: University of Minnesota Press.

August, Justin (2005) "Interviews: Mike Park," http://www.punknews.org/article/11786.

Berelson, Bernard (1949), "What 'Missing the Newspaper' Means," *Communications Research, 1948–1949*, ed. P. F. Lazarsfeld and F. N. Stanton. New York: Harper.

Bernstein, Matthew, and Gaylyn Studlar, eds (1997) *Visions of the East: Orientalism in Film*. New Brunswick, NJ: Rutgers University Press.

Bhabha, Homi K. (1994), "Of Mimicry and Man," *The Location of Culture*. London: Routledge, 85–92.

Blauner, Robert (1972), *Racial Oppression in America*. New York: Harper & Row.

Boyle, Deirdre (1992), "Critical Doubts and Differences: Independent Video and Teaching History," in Barbara Abrash and Catherine Egan, eds, *Mediating History: The Map Guide to Independent Video by and About African American, Asian American, Latino, and Native American People*. New York: New York University Press, 16.

Buchanan, Patrick (2002), *The Death of the West: How Dying Populations and Immigrant Invasions Threaten our Culture and Civilization*. New York: St Martin's Press.

Buescher, Derek, and Kent A. Ono (1996), "Civilized Colonialism: *Pocahontas* as Neocolonial Rhetoric," *Women's Studies in Communication*, 19/2: 127–53.

Campbell, Leonie (2006), "AAJC Shocked by Rosie O'Donnell's Racist References to Asians on ABC's 'The View,'" http://www.advancingequality.org/files/2006%5Fview%5Fpr%5B1%5D%2Epdf (accessed August 2, 2007).

Carlson, Erin (2006), "Rosie Says She's Sorry for Mocking Spoken Chinese on 'The View,' but One Group Isn't Satisfied," *Associated Press*, December 14.

Chan, Jachinson (2001), *Chinese American Masculinities: From Fu Manchu to Bruce Lee*. New York: Routledge.

Chan, Janice (2003), "Interview with Lela Lee," http://www.international.ucla.edu/asia/article.asp?parentid=5896 (accessed August 27, 2007).

Chan, Sucheng (1991), *Asian Americans: An Interpretive History*. Boston: Twayne.

Chin, Daryl (1992), "Intimate Histories: Asian-American Independent Film and Video," in Barbara Abrash and Catherine Egan, eds, *Mediating History: The Map Guide to Independent Video by and About African American, Asian American, Latino, and Native American People*. New York: New York University Press.

Chin, Daryl, and Larry Qualls (2001), "Open Circuits, Closed Markets: Festivals and Expositions of Film and Video," *PAJ: A Journal of Performance and Art*, 23/1: 33–47.

Chin, Frank (1991) "Come All Ye Asian American Writers of the Real and the Fake," in Jeffery Paul Chan et al., eds, *The Big Aiiieeeee!: An Anthology of Chinese-American and Japanese-American Literature*. New York: Meridian, 1–92.

Choi, Glen (2001), "Lela Lee's Comic Strips Cause a Fury," *Korea Herald*, September 7.

Choy, Philip P., Lorraine Dong, and Marlon K. Hom, eds (1994), *Coming Man: 19th Century American Perceptions of the Chinese* (Seattle: University of Washington Press.

Chuh, Kandice (2003), *Imagine Otherwise: On Asian Americanist Critique*. Durham, NC: Duke University Press.

Chun, Elaine W. (2004), "Ideologies of Legitimate Mockery: Margaret Cho's Revoicings of Mock Asian," *Pragmatics*, 14/3: 263–89.

Chung, Philip W. (2007), "The 25 Most Infamous Yellow Face Film Performances Part 1," November 28, http://asianweek.com/2007/11/28/the-25-most-infamous-yellow-face-film-performances-part-1/.

Chung, Hye Seung (2005), "Between Yellowphilia and Yellowphobia: Ethnic Stardom and the (Dis)Orientalized Romantic Couple in *Daughter of Shanghai* and *King of Chinatown*, " in Shilpa Davé, LeiLani Nishime, and Tasha Oren, eds, *East Main Street: Asian American Popular Culture*. New York: New York University Press, 154–82.

Clark, Cedric (1969) "Television and Social Controls: Some Portrayals of the Ethnic Minorities," *Television Quarterly*, 8/2: 18–22.

Clarke, Shirley, Edward Harrison, Bill Kenly, Elodie Osborn, Amos Vogel, and John Adams (1960), "The Expensive Art: A Discussion of Film Distribution and Exhibition in the US," *Film Quarterly*, 13/4: 19.

Cloud, Dana (1992), "The Limits of Interpretation: Ambivalence and the Stereotype in *Spenser: For Hire*," *Critical Studies in Mass Communication*, 9/4: 311–24.

Cloud, Dana L. (1996), "Hegemony or Concordance? The Rhetoric of Tokenism in 'Oprah' Winfrey's Rags-to-Riches Biography," *Critical Studies in Mass Communication*, 13 (1996): 115–37.

Collins, Patricia Hill (1998), "Some Group Matters: Intersectionality, Situated Standpoints, and Black Feminist Thought," *Fighting Words: Black Women and the Search for Justice*. Minneapolis: University of Minnesota Press: 201–28.

Crenshaw, Kimberle (1989), Demarginalizing the Intersection of Race and Sex: A Black Feminist Critique of Antidiscrimination Doctrine, Feminist Theory, and Antiracist Politics," *University of Chicago Legal Forum*: 139–67.

Crenshaw, Kimberle (1991), "Mapping the Margins: Intersectionality, Identity Politics, and Violence against Women of Color," *Stanford Law Review*, 43: 1241–99.

Cruz, Wil (2006), "Liu Takes a Dim View of Rosie's Remarks," *Newsday*, December 11.

Deming, Caren J. (1982), "Miscegenation in Popular Western History and Fiction," in H. W. Stauffer and S. J. Rosowski, eds, *Women and Western American Literature*. Troy, NY: Whitston, 90–9.

Dennis, Everette E., and Edward C. Pease, eds (1997), *The Media in Black and White*. New Brunswick, NJ: Transaction.

Denzin, Norman (1999), *Reading Race: The Cinema of Violent Cultural Differences, 1980–1995*. London: Sage.

Dines, Gail, and Jean M. Humez ([1994] 2003), *Gender, Race and Class in Media: A Text-Reader*. 2nd edn, Thousand Oaks, CA: Sage.

Donovan, Brian (2006), *White Slave Crusades: Race, Gender, and Anti-Vice Activism, 1887–1917*. Champaign: University of Illinois Press.

Downing, John D. H. (1988), "'The Cosby Show' and American Racial Discourse," in *Discourse and Discrimination*, ed. Geneva Smitherman-Donaldson and Teun Adrianus van Dijk. Detroit: Wayne State University Press, 46–73.

Dubrofsky, Rachel (2002), "Ally McBeal as Postfeminist Icon: The Aestheticizing and Fetishizing of the Independent Working Woman," *Communication Review*, 5: 265–84.

Egan, Timothy (2007), "Little Asia on the Hill," *New York Times*, January 7.

Espiritu, Yen Le (1992), *Asian American Panethnicity: Bridging Institutions and Identities*. Philadelphia: Temple University Press.

Feng, Peter (2000), "Recuperating Suzie Wong: A Fan's Nancy Kwan-dary," in Darrell Hamamoto and Sandra Liu, eds, *Countervisions: Asian American Film Criticism*. Philadelphia: Temple University Press, 40–56.

Feng, Peter (2002a), *Identities in Motion: Asian American Film and Video*. Durham, NC: Duke University Press.

Feng, Peter, ed. (2002b), *Screening Asian Americans*. New Brunswick, NJ: Rutgers University Press.

Frankenberg, Ruth (1996), "'When We Are Capable of Stopping, We Begin to See': Being White, Seeing Whiteness," in Becky Thompson and Sangeeta Tyagi, eds, *Names We Call Home: Autobiography on Racial Identity*. New York: Routledge, 3–17.

Fraser, Nancy (1993), "Rethinking the Public Sphere: A Contribution to the Critique of Actually Existing Democracy," in Craig Calhoun, ed., *Habermas and the Public Sphere*. Cambridge, MA: MIT Press, 109–42.

Fung, Richard (1991), "Looking for my Penis: The Eroticized Asian in Gay Video Porn," in Bad Object Choices, ed., *How Do I Look? Queer Film and Video*. Seattle: Bay Press, 145–68.

Galang, M. Evelina, ed.(2003), *Screaming Monkeys: Critiques of Asian American Images*. Minneapolis: Coffee House Press.

Gonzalez, Alberto, Marsha Houston, and Victoria Chen, eds (1994), *Our Voices: Essays in Culture, Ethnicity, and Communication*. Los Angeles: Roxbury Press.

Gray, Herman (1995), *Watching Race: Television and the Struggle for "Blackness"*. Minneapolis: University of Minnesota Press.

Greco Larson, Stephanie (2006), *Media and Minorities: The Politics of Race in News and Entertainment*. Lanham, MD: Rowman & Littlefield.

Gregg, Richard B.(1971), "The Ego-Function of the Rhetoric of Protest," *Philosophy and Rhetoric*, 4: 71–91.

Grice, Helena (2002), "Face-ing/De-face-ing Racism: Physiognomy as Ethnic Marker in Early Eurasian/Amerasian Women's Texts," in Josephine Lee, Imogene L. Lim, and Yuko Matsukawa, eds, *Re/Collecting Early Asian America: Essays in Cultural History*. Philadelphia: Temple University Press, 255–70.

Grossman, Lev (2006), "Time's Person of the Year: You," *Time*, December 13, http://www.time.com/time/magazine/article/0,9171,1569514,00.html.

Haenni, Sabine (2002), "Filming 'Chinatown': Fake Visions, Bodily Transformations," in Peter Feng, ed., *Screening Asian Americans*. New Brunswick, NJ: Rutgers University Press, 21–52.

Hall, Stuart (1981), "The Whites of their Eyes: Racist Ideologies and the Media," in George Bridges and Rosalind Brunt, eds, *Silver Linings: Some Strategies for the Eighties*. London: Lawrence & Wishart, 28–52.

Hall, Stuart (1997), "The Work of Representation," in Stuart Hall, ed., *Representation: Cultural Representations and Signifying Practices*. London: Sage, 13–64.

Hall, Stuart (2006), "Encoding/Decoding," in M. G. Durham and D. M. Kellner, eds, *Media and Cultural Studies: Keywords*. Oxford: Blackwell, 163–73.

Hallmark, Kara Kelley (2007), *Encyclopedia of Asian American Artists*. Westport, CT: Greenwood Press.

Halualani, Rona Tamiko (1995), "The Intersecting Hegemonic Discourses of an Asian Mail-Order Bride Catalogue: Pilipina 'Oriental Butterfly' Dolls for Sale," *Women's Studies in Communication*, 18/1: 45–64.

Halualani, Rona Tamiko, and Leah R. Vande Berg (1998), "'Asian or American': Meanings in, through, and around *All-American Girl*," in Leah R. Vande Berg, Lawrence A. Wenner, and Bruce E. Gronbeck, eds, *Critical Approaches to Television*. Boston: Houghton Mifflin, 214–35.

Hamamoto, Darrell Y. (1994), *Monitored Peril: Asian Americans and the Politics of TV Representation*. Minneapolis: University of Minnesota Press.

Hamamoto, Darrell, and Sandra Liu, eds (2000), *Countervisions: Asian American Film Criticism*. Philadelphia: Temple University Press.

"A Hand Grenade with Pigtails" (2001), *Japan Times*, Sept 2.

Harris, Richard Jackson (2004), *A Cognitive Psychology of Mass Communication*. Mahwah, NJ: Lawrence Erlbaum.

Haucke, Dave (2003), "Mike Park: This Punk is Going Solo Acoustic," http://www.kaffeinebuzz.com/interviews-mikepark.php.

Hebdige, Dick (1988), *Subculture: The Meaning of Style*. London: Routledge.

Hewlings, Cassie, Vanna Livaditis, Ashleigh Oldand, and Jason Bartz (2008), "Regarding the 'Asians' Satire," http://media.www.thecampuspress.com/media/storage/paper1098/news/2008/02/20/News/Letter.From.The.Editors-3223782.shtml (accessed February 21 2008).

Higham, John (1955), *Strangers in the Land: Patterns of American Nativism, 1860–1925*. New Brunswick, NJ: Rutgers University Press.

Hua, Lee Siew (2001), "Comic Strip Star Fights Stale Images of Asians," *Straits Times*, September 8, 10.

Hua, Vanessa (2006), "Asian American Advocates Decry Parody by TV's O'Donnell," *San Francisco Chronicle*, December 14, A5.

Hutchinson, Bill (2006), "Pol's 'View' of Rosie: She Offends," *Daily News*, December 11, 4.

Hwang, Suein (2005), "The New White Flight: In Silicon Valley, Two High Schools with Outstanding Academic Reputations are Losing White Students as Asian Students Move in. Why?" *Wall Street Journal*, November 19.

IndieRag (2001) "Interview with Lela Lee: Creator of Angry Little Asian Girl & Angry Little Girls," http://www.indierag.com/content/interviews/010606 lelalee.html (accessed August 27, 2007).

Inniss, Leslie B., and Joe R. Feagin (1995), "The Cosby Show: The View from the Black Middle Class," *Journal of Black Studies*, 25/6: 692–711.

Ito, Robert B. (1997), "'A Certain Slant': A Brief History of Hollywood Yellowface," http://www.brightlightsfilm.com/18/18_yellow.html.

Jenn (2006), "Rosie O'Donnell's Publicist Tells Asians to Get a Sense of Humor," http://www.reappropriate.com/?p=582 (accessed August 13, 2007).

Jhally, Sut, and Justin Lewis (1992), *Enlightened Racism: The Cosby Show, Audiences, and the Myth of American Dream*. Boulder, CO: Westview Press.

Jones, Dorothy B. (1955), *The Portrayal of China and India on the American Screen, 1896–1955*. Cambridge, MA: MIT Press.

Kabbani, Rana (1986), *Europe's Myths of Orient: Devise and Rule*. London: Macmillan.

Kang, Laura (2002), "The Desiring of Asian Female Bodies: Interracial Romance and Cinematic Subjection," in Peter Feng, ed., *Screening Asian Americans*. New Brunswick, NJ: Rutgers University Press, 71–100.

Karson, Max (2008), "If it's War the Asians Want ... it's War They'll Get," http://www.thecampuspress.com/home/index.cfm?event=displayArticle&usto ry_id=c07cea4a-0e65-4465-a9c4-17d6deb357e8 (accessed February 21 2008).

Kawai, Yuko (2005), "Stereotyping Asian Americans: The Dialectic of the Model Minority and the Yellow Peril," *Howard Journal of Communication*, 16: 109–30.

Keen, Sam (1986), *Faces of the Enemy: The Psychology of Enmity*. San Francisco: Harper & Row.

Kellner, Douglas (1995), *Media Culture: Cultural Studies, Identity and Politics between the Modern and the Postmodern*. New York: Routledge.

Kim, Elaine H. (2003), "Interstitial Subjects: Asian American Visual Art as a Site for New Cultural Conversations," in Elaine H. Kim, Margo Machida, and Sharon Mizota, eds, *Fresh Talk, Daring Gazes: Conversations of Asian American Art*. Berkeley: University of California Press, 1–50.

Kim, L. S. (2004), "Be the One that You Want: Asian Americans in Television Culture, Onscreen and Beyond," *Amerasia Journal*, January 30, 125–46.

Kim, L. S. (2005), "Azn Television: The Network for Asian America," http:// flowtv.org/?p=298.

Kim, Ryan (2002), "Yuji Ichioka . . . Asian American Studies Pioneer," *SFGate*, September 12.

Kolko, Beth E., Lisa Nakamura, and Gilbert B. Rodman (2000), *Race in Cyberspace*. New York and London: Routledge.

Kondo, Dorinne (1997), "Art, Activism, Asia, Asian Americans," *About Face: Performing Race in Fashion and Theater*. New York: Routledge, 227–60.

Kunzle, David (1973), *History of the Comic Strip*, Vol. 1: *The Early Comic Strip: Narrative Strips and Picture Stories in the European Broadsheet from c. 1450 to 1825*. Berkeley: University of California Press.

Kurashige, Scott (2000), "Pan-Ethnicity and Community Organizing: Asian Americans United's Campaign against Anti-Asian Violence," *Journal of Asian American Studies*, 3/2: 163–90.

Lam, Joseph (1999), "Embracing 'Asian American Music' as an Heuristic Device," *Journal of Asian American Studies*, 2/1: 29–60.

Lee, Lela (2005), *Angry Little Girls*. New York: Harry N. Abrams.

Lee, Rachel C. (2004), "Where's my Parade? Margaret Cho and the Asian American Body in Space," *New Drama Review*, 48/2: 108–32.

Lee, Robert G. (1999), *Orientals: Asian Americans in Popular Culture*. Philadelphia: Temple University Press.

Lee, Sharon S. (2008), "Satire as Racial Backlash against Asian Americans," *Inside Higher Education*, February 28.

Lee, Wen Ho, with Helen Zia (2001), *My Country versus Me: The First-Hand Account by the Los Alamos Scientist who was Falsely Accused of Being a Spy*. New York: Hyperion.

Leonard, Kevin Allen (1990), "'Is That What We Fought For?' Japanese Americans and Racism in California: The Impact of World War II," *Western Historical Quarterly*, 21: 463–82.

Leong, Russell, ed. (1991), *Moving the Image: Independent Asian American Media Arts*. Los Angeles: UCLA Asian American Studies Center.

Leung, Wendy (2006), "Outrage against CBS and Corolla," http://news.asianweek.com/news/view_article.html?article_id=d22f4695127f8a3f1fde4c064826be65 (accessed August 13, 2007).

Lipsitz, George (2001), *Time Passages: Collective Memory and American Popular Culture*. Minneapolis: University of Minnesota Press.

Liu, Cynthia (2000), "When Dragon Ladies Die, Do they Come Back as Butterflies? Re-imagining Anna May Wong," in Darrell Hamamoto and Sandra Liu, eds, *Countervisions: Asian American Film Criticism*. Philadelphia: Temple University Press, 23–39.

Locke, Brian (1998), "Here Comes the Judge: The Dancing Itos and the Televisual Construction of the Enemy Asian," in Sasha Torres, ed., *Living Color: Race and Television in the United States*. Durham, NC: Duke University Press, 239–53.

MacDonald, J. Frederick (1978), "The 'Foreigner' in Juvenile Series Fiction, 1900–1945," in Jack Nachbar, Deborah Weiser, and John L. Wright, eds, *The Popular Culture Reader*. Bowling Green, OH: Bowling Green University Popular Press, 151–67.

Makwakwa, Onica (2006), "Statement on Rosie O'Donnell's Racial Comments on ABC's *The View*," http://www.unityjournalists.org/news/news121106.html (accessed August 13, 2007).

Malkin, Michelle (2004), *In Defense of Internment: The Case for "Racial Profiling" in World War II and the War on Terror*. Washington, DC: Regnery.

Mannur, Anita (2005a), "Culinary Fictions: Immigrant Foodways and Race in Indian American Literature," In Kent A. Ono, ed., *Asian American Studies after Critical Mass*. Malden, MA: Blackwell, 56–70.

Mannur, Anita (2005b), "Model Minorities Can Cook: Fusion Cuisine in Asian America." In Shilpa Davé, Leilani Nishime, and Tasha G. Oren, eds, *East Main Street: Asian American Popular Culture*. New York: New York University Press, 72–94.

Marchetti, Gina (1993), *Romance and the "Yellow Peril": Race, Sex, and Discursive Strategies in Hollywood Fiction*. Berkeley: University of California Press.

McCloud, Scott (1994), *Understanding Comics: The Invisible Art*. New York: HarperPerennial.

McGee, Michael C. (1975), "In Search of 'The People': A Rhetorical Alternative," *Quarterly Journal of Speech*, 61: 235–49.

McLuhan, Marshall, and Quentin Fiore (1967), *The Medium is the Massage: An Inventory of Effects*. New York: Bantam Books.

McShane, Larry (2007), "US Radio Network Drops Shock Jocks 'JV and Elvis' over Asian Slurs," *Associated Press Worldstream*, May 13.

Moon, Krystyn R. (2005), *Yellowface: Creating the Chinese in American Popular Music and Performance, 1850s–1920s*. New Brunswick, NJ: Rutgers University Press.

Moskowitz, Danielle (2005), "Mike Park," http://d1489577.u45.websitesource.net/interview_39_mike_park.html.

Moy, James S. (1993), *Marginal Sights: Staging the Chinese in America*. Iowa City: University of Iowa Press.

Mulvey, Laura (1975), "Visual Pleasure and Narrative Cinema," *Screen*, 16/3: 6–18.

Naber, Nadine (2000), "Ambiguous Insiders: An Investigation of Arab American Invisibility," *Ethnic and Racial Studies*, 23/1: 37–61.

Nakamura, Lisa (2002a), "Alllooksame? Mediating Visual Cultures of Race on the Web," *Iowa Journal of Cultural Studies*, 73–84.

Nakamura, Lisa (2002b), *Cybertypes: Race, Ethnicity, and Identity on the Internet*. New York and London: Routledge.

Nakamura, Lisa (2007), *Digitizing Race: Visual Cultures of the Internet*. Minneapolis: University of Minnesota Press.

Nakashima, Cynthia L. (1992), "An Invisible Monster: The Creation and Denial of Mixed-Race People in America," in Maria P. P. Root, ed., *Racially Mixed People in America*. Newbury Park, CA: Sage, 162–80.

Nakashima, Cynthia L. (2005), "Asian American Studies through (Somewhat) Asian Eyes: Integrating 'Mixed Race' into the Asian American Discourse," in Kent A. Ono, ed., *Asian American Studies after Critical Mass*. Malden, MA: Blackwell, 111–20.

Nakayama, Thomas K. (1994), "Show/Down Time: 'Race,' Gender, Sexuality, and Popular Culture," *Critical Studies in Mass Communication*, 11: 162–79.

Nakayama, Thomas K. (1988), "'Model Minority' and the Media: Discourse on Asian America," *Journal of Communication Inquiry*, 12/1: 65–73.

Nguyen, Mimi (2007), "Bruce Lee I Love You: Discourses of Race and Masculinity in the Queer Superstardom of JJ Chinois," in Mimi Thi Nguyen and Thuy Linh Nguyen Tu, eds, *Alien Encounters: Popular Culture in Asian America*. Durham, NC: Duke University Press, 271–304.

Nishime, LeiLani (2005), "14 Guilty Pleasures: Keanu Reeves, Superman, and Racial Outing," in Shilpa Davé, LeiLani Nishime, and Tasha Oren, eds, *East Main Street: Asian American Popular Culture*. New York: New York University Press, 272–91.

Noguchi, Irene (2001), "'Asian Girl': Comic Strip of a Different Stripe," *Washington Post*, August 27, C01.

Nordquist Joan (2001), *Gender and Racial Images/Stereotypes in the Mass Media: A Bibliography*, Santa Cruz: Reference and Research Services.

Okada, Jun (2005), "The PBS and NAATA Connection: Comparing the Public Spheres of Asian American Film and Video," *Velvet Light Trap*, 55/Spring: 39–51.

Okihiro, Gary Y. (1994), *Margins and Mainstreams: Asians in American History and Culture*. Seattle: University of Washington Press.

Ono, Kent A. (1997), "'America's' Apple Pie: Baseball, Japan-Bashing, and the Sexual Threat of Economic Miscegenation," in Aaron Baker and Todd Boyd, eds, *Out of Bounds: Sports, Media, and the Politics of Identity*. Bloomington: Indiana University Press, 81–101.

Ono, Kent A. (2002), "Guilt without Evidence: Informal Citizenship and the Limits of Rationality in the Case of Wen Ho Lee," in G. Thomas Goodnight, ed., *Proceedings of the Twelfth NCA/AFA Conference on Argumentation*. Annandale, VA: National Communication Association, 76–88.

Ono, Kent A. (2005), "From Nationalism to Migrancy: The Politics of Asian American Transnationalism," *Communication Law Review*, 5/1, 1–17.

Ono, Kent A., and Joy Yang Jiao (forthcoming), "China in the U.S. Imaginary: Tibet, the Olympics, and the 2008 Earthquake," *Communication and Critical Cultural Studies*.

Ono, Kent A., and John M. Sloop (1995), "The Critique of Vernacular Discourse," *Communication Monographs*, 62: 19–46.

Oren, Tasha G. (2005), "Secret Asian Man: Angry Asians and the Politics of Cultural Visibility," in Shilpa Davé, LeiLani Nishime, and Tasha Oren, eds, *East Main Street: Asian American Popular Culture*. New York: New York University Press, 337–59.

Osajima, Keith (1998), "Asian Americans as the Model Minority: An Analysis of the Popular Press Image in the 1960s and 1980s," in Gary Okihiro et al., eds, *Reflections on Shattered Windows: Promises and Prospects for Asian American Studies*. Pullman: Washington State University Press, 165–74.

Pak, Ellyn (2007), "My Life is an Open Blog," *KoreAm*, 41.

Perez, Hiram (2005), "How to Rehabilitate a Mulatto: The Iconography of Tiger Woods," in Shilpa Davé, LeiLani Nishime, and Tasha Oren, eds, *East Main Street: Asian American Popular Culture*. New York: New York University Press, 222–45.

Pham, Vincent, and Kent A. Ono (forthcoming), "'Artful Bigotry & Kitsch': A Study of Stereotype, Mimicry, and Satire in Asian American T-Shirt Rhetoric," *Asian American Rhetorics*. Salt Lake City: University of Utah Press.

Porter, Michael J. (1998), "The Structure of Television Narratives," in Leah R. Vande Berg, Lawrence A. Wenner, and Bruce E. Gronbeck, eds, *Critical Approaches to Television*. Boston: Houghton Mifflin, 140–57.

Prashad, Vijay (2003), "Bruce Lee and the Anti-imperialism of Kung Fu: A Polycultural Adventure," *Positions: East Asia Cultures Critique*, 11/1: 51–90.

Projansky, Sarah, and Kent A. Ono (2003), "Making Films Asian American: *Shopping for Fangs* and the Discursive Auteur," in David A. Gerstner and Janet Staiger, eds, *Authorship and Film*. New York: Routledge, 263–80.

Said, Edward W. (1978), *Orientalism: Western Conceptions of the Orient*. London: Pantheon Books.

Serpe, Gina (2006), "Rosie *Really* Sorry for 'Ching-Chong' Crack," http://www.eonline.com/news/article/index.jsp?uuid=b33c7760-8170-4fca-83b3-ecf82ebb11d0 (accessed August 1, 2007).

Sharpe, Jenny (1993), *Allegories of Empire: The Figure of Woman in the Colonial Text*. Minneapolis: University of Minnesota Press.

Shim, Doobo (1998), "From Yellow Peril through Model Minority to Renewed Yellow Peril," *Journal of Communication Inquiry*, 22/4.

Shiu, Anthony Sze-Fai (2006), "What Yellowface Hides: Video Games, Whiteness, and the American Racial Order," *Journal of Popular Culture*, 39/1: 109–25.

Shohat, Ella (1991), "Gender and Culture of Empire: Toward a Feminist Ethnography of the Cinema," *Quarterly Review of Film and Video*, 13/1–3: 45–84.

Shohat, Ella, and Robert Stam (1994), *Unthinking Eurocentrism: Multiculturalism and the Media*. New York: Routledge.

Shull, Michael S., and David Edward Wilt (1996), *Hollywood War Films, 1937–1945: An Exhaustive Filmography of American Feature-Length Motion Pictures Relating to World War II*. Jefferson, NC: McFarland.

Sia, Beau (2007), "An Open Letter to All the Rosie O'Donnells," http://www.youtube.com/watch?v=VJCkHu3trKc (accessed August 13, 2007).

Sloop, John M. (1994), "Apology Made to Whomever Pleases: Cultural Discipline and the Grounds of Interpretation," *Communication Quarterly*, 42/4: 345–62.

Stallybrass, Peter, and Allon White (1986), *The Politics and Poetics of Transgression*. Ithaca, NY: Cornell University Press.

Tajima, Renee E. (1989), "Lotus Blossoms Don't Bleed: Images of Asian Women," in Asian Women United of California, ed., *Making Waves: An Anthology of Writings by and about Asian American Women*. Boston: Beacon Press: 308–17.

Tchen, John Kuo Wei (1999), *New York before Chinatown: Orientalism and the Shaping of American Culture 1776–1882*. Baltimore: Johns Hopkins University Press.

Tu, Thuy Linh Nguyen (2003), "Good Politics, Great Porn: Untangling Race, Sex, and Technology in Asian American Cultural Productions," in Rachel C. Lee and Sau-ling Cynthia Wong, eds, *Asian American.Net: Ethnicity, Nationalism, and Cyberspace*. New York: Routledge, 267–80.

Twain, Mark (1923), "Welcome Home: Address at the Dinner in his Honor at the Lotos Club, November 10, 1900," in *The Complete Works of Mark Twain: Mark Twain's Speeches*. New York: Harper.

US Commission on Civil Rights (1992), *Civil Rights Issues Facing Asian Americans in the 1990s*. Washington, DC: United States Commission on Civil Rights

Valdivia, Angharad, ed. (1995), *Feminism, Multiculturalism, and the Media: Global Diversities*. Thousand Oaks, CA: Sage.

Valdivia, Angharad (2005), "Geographies of Latinidad: Constructing Identity in the Face of Radical Hybridity," in W. Critchlow, G. Dimitriadis, N. Dolby, and C. McCarthy, eds, *Race, Identity, and Representation in Education*. New York: Routledge.

Valverde, Kieu Linh Caroline (2005), "Making Transnational Vietnamese Music: Sounds of Home and Resistance," in Shilpa Davé, LeiLani Nishime, and Tasha G. Oren, eds, *East Main Street: Asian American Popular Culture*. New York: New York University Press, 32–54.

Wang, Ling-chi (1998), "Race, Class, Citizenship, and Extraterritoriality: Asian Americans and the 1996 Campaign Finance Scandal," *Amerasia Journal*, 24/1: 1.

Wang, Oliver (2001), "Between the Notes: Finding Asian America in Popular Music," *American Music*, 19/4: 442.

Washington Post (2001), "Angry Little Asian Girl with Lela Lee," http://www.discuss.washingtonpost.com/wp-srv/zforum/01/comic_lee0831.htm (accessed August 27, 2007).

Watson, Nigel (n.d.), "The Sense and Sensationalism of Film Festivals," http://www.talkingpix.co.uk/ArticleFilmFestivalSensations.html.

Weinzierl, Rupert, and David Muggleton (2003), "What is 'Post-Subcultural Studies' Anyway?," in Rupert Weinzierl and David Muggleton, eds, *The Post-Subcultures Reader*. New York: Berg, 3–26.

Willemen, Paul (1989), "The Third Cinema Question: Notes and Reflections," in Jim Pines and Paul Willemen, eds, *Questions of Third Cinema*. London: British Film Institute, 1–29.

Williams, Raymond (1977), *Marxism and Literature*. Oxford: Oxford University Press.

Wilson, Clint C., II, and Felix Gutierrez (1985), *Minorities and the Media: Diversity and the End of Mass Communication*. Beverly Hills, CA: Sage.

Wilson, Clint C., II, and Felix Gutierrez (1995), *Race, Multiculturalism, and the Media: From Mass to Class Communication*. Thousand Oaks, CA: Sage.

Wilson, Clint C., II, Felix Gutierrez, and Lena Chao (2003), *Racism, Sexism, and the Media: The Rise of Class Communication in Multicultural America*. Thousand Oaks, CA: Sage.

Wong, Eugene Franklin (1978), *On Visual Media Racism: Asians in the American Motion Pictures*. New York: Arno Press.

Woo Deborah (2000), "Inventing and Reinventing 'Model Minorities,'" in *Glass Ceilings and Asian Americans: The New Face of Workplace Barriers*. Walnut Creek, CA: AltaMira Press, 23–41.

Wu, Esther (2006), "O'Donnell's Mockery of Chinese is No Joke," http://www.dallasnews.com/sharedcontent/dws/dn/localnews/columnists/ewu/stories/DN-wucolumn_14met.ART0.North.Edition1.3ebcca7.html (accessed August 2, 2007).

Yoshihara, Mari (2003), *Embracing the East: White Women and American Orientalism*. New York: Oxford University Press.

Yoshikawa, Yoko (1994), "The Heat is on Miss Saigon Coalition: Organizing across Race and Sexuality," in Karin Aguilar-San Juan, ed., *The State of Asian America: Activism and Resistance in the 1990s*. Boston: South End Press, 275–94.

Yu, Henry (2002), "Tiger Woods at the Center of History: Looking Back at the Twentieth Century through the Lenses of Race, Sports, and Mass Consumption," in John Bloom and Michael Nevin Willard, eds, *Sports Matters: Race, Recreation, and Culture*. New York: New York University Press.

Zia, Helen (2000), "Detroit Blues: 'Because of You Motherfuckers,'" in *Asian American Dreams: The Emergence of an American People*. New York: Farrar, Straus & Giroux, 55–81.

Index